The Success-Fearing
Personality

The Success-Fearing Personality

Theory and Research with Implications for the Social Psychology of Achievement

Donnah Canavan-Gumpert
Boston College

Katherine Garner
New York University

Peter Gumpert
University of Massachusetts

With contributions by
Nina E. Cohen and **Marice Pappo**

Lexington Books
D.C. Heath and Company
Lexington, Massachusetts
Toronto

Library of Congress Cataloging in Publication Data

Canavan-Gumpert, Donnah.
  The success-fearing personality.

  Bibliography: p.
  Includes index.
  1. Success. 2. Fear. 3. Achievement motivation. I. Garner, Katherine, joint author. II. Gumpert, Peter, joint author. III. Title.
BF637.S8C277   1978   616.8'522   76-42853
ISBN 0-669-01075-8

Published simultaneously in Canada.

Printed in the United States of America.

International Standard Book Number: 0-669-01075-8

Library of Congress Catalog Card Number: 76-42853

Dedicated to Morton Deutsch,
from whom we learned much about the value of cooperation

Contents

List of Figure and Tables

Preface

Almost seventy years ago, Sigmund Freud reported two case histories of persons who thoroughly destroyed their lives just after achieving important successes they had long hoped and worked for. Since Freud's early paper on "those wrecked by success," clinical investigators have observed that certain people are indeed afraid of their own successes and unconsciously strive to avoid or sabotage them. Our work on the fear of success was stimulated by the observations and thoughts of these clinical theorists and practitioners. In this book we present a body of systematic theory and empirical research that shows that the fear of success is a very common neurotic problem affecting men and women in all walks of life, in childhood as well as in adolescence and adulthood, and in different ways in a variety of settings and circumstances.

While we have taken a psychodynamic-personality approach to the fear of success, we recognize that to be fully useful, a theoretical perspective on the fear of success should be connected with a larger framework of ideas about the complex of factors that motivate people to succeed, accomplish, and do productive work. Accordingly, in Part III we turn our attention to an analysis of this broader issue. Unfortunately, the theory of achievement motivation that has dominated the thinking about the psychology of achievement for nearly three decades is overly narrow for our purposes. Thus, we have begun to develop a theoretical perspective of the social psychology of achievement that includes a number of factors other than personality characteristics that contribute to a person's desire to do productive work. Our ideas and findings about fear of success have connected well with this broader framework.

This book is intended for a wide variety of readers who are interested in the phenomena we have studied: academic psychologists, clinicians, teachers, counselors, parents, and, for that matter, anyone else. For our fellow researchers and colleagues in psychology we have included in Part II reasonably detailed explanations of our research procedures and various technical details in the tables of results. For those readers who have no interest in such matters, we have kept numbers out of the text as much as possible by confining them to tables and a notes section at the end of each chapter. Moreover we have tried to make our descriptions of the research we have conducted brief and readable. The results of all of our research studies can be understood without reference to the statistical tables. Part III of the book, and particularly chapter 7, contains some detailed descriptions and critiques of theoretical and research work on achievement motivation and achievement conflict in women. The technical sections of these chapters may be skipped over without impairing the reader's understanding of the thread of our argument.

As with all projects of this size, a number of people have assisted us at various stages, and we most gratefully acknowledge their assistance. Nina E.

Cohen and Marice Pappo, both listed as contributors, conducted as their doctoral dissertations the first seminal pieces of research in the line of investigation we report herein. Yohel Camayd, Marjory Kessler, Karen Kurlander, Richard Werther, and Nellie Vanzetti served as experimenters in the various other studies reported in the book. Kathy Ault, Sandra Headen, Eliza Hewat, Socorro Llubien, and Deborah Rubin served in various ways as observers, interviewers, and schedulers in those studies. Lois Biener, David Danforth, Kay Deaux, Morton Deutsch, Giselle Harrington, Murray Horwitz, Alexandra K. Rolde, M. Beverly Rosenberg, Joseph Speisman, Morris I. Stein, and Kathleen White gave helpful comments on earlier drafts of sections of the manuscript. Murray Horwitz deserves special acknowledgement and thanks for his constructive suggestions, incisive criticism, and support throughout the writing of the book.

Richard Koppenaal and William Strockbine facilitated the collection of the field data reported in chapter 6. We wish to acknowledge also the superintendents, principals, teachers, parents, and children who made possible our studies with elementary school children.

Various grants for the typing of the manuscript came from the graduate schools, respectively, of Boston College, Boston University, and New York University. We wish to express our gratitude to these institutions for their aid.

Marilyn Fartely patiently, expertly, and cheerfully typed and retyped the manuscript. We are grateful for her excellent work.

Finally, we feel a particular debt of gratitude to Mike McCarroll at Lexington Books, Donald White at Boston College, and Peter Szego in New York, whose support and encouragement saw us through this project.

For those readers who may have an interest in these matters, we note that the three authors of this book participated equally in its conception and execution. The order of authorship is alphabetical, and no seniority is implied.

**Part I:
Historical and
Contemporary Theoretical
Perspectives**

Introduction to Part I

In the first section of this book we introduce and present a historical account of the notion that some people suffer from a fear of success. We begin chapter 1 by suggesting why such an idea seems foreign to most of us and why it has been so slow to be accepted by the American public. Next, we illustrate the fear of success by presenting a few descriptions of success-fearers reported by Freud and some more prosaic and commonplace observations and examples of our own. Following these illustrations we discuss in detail the explanations offered by several well-known clinical theorists and their followers to account for the development of fear of success in their patients. While these clinical points of view emphasize somewhat different aspects in early childhood development, they are quite similar to one another in a number of respects, and their points of convergence are used by us to develop a more complete description of the fear of success as a psychodynamic problem. In the final section of chapter 1, we turn to the clinical authors to formulate our own conception of fear of success and outline some of the basic theoretical and methodological commitments that have guided the research program reported in Part II of this book.

1

Who Fears Success, Why, and When?

Our search for the answer to the question posed in the title of this chapter is the subject matter of this book. While the fact that some persons in our success-oriented society are fearful of success, become anxious when personal success is near at hand, and do something to avoid or sabotage actually obtaining success may seem paradoxical, it is indeed true. And it is true for a sizable number of people who may appear to their friends and acquaintances to be quite normal and ordinary in other respects: school children, high school and college students, and adults—men and women alike—in all walks of life. Our search for an understanding of why some people develop problems of fearing success has led us to the rich and fascinating writings of some of the foremost clinical psychologists of this century. The works of Sigmund Freud, Harry Stack Sullivan, and Karen Horney among others have all contributed clues that help solve the puzzle concerning the origins and maintenance of the personality characteristic called fear of success. Our theoretical perspective and the research presented in Part II suggest that contrary to what we might initially expect, persons who fear success do not avoid success-oriented activities entirely, nor do they always sabotage their potential successes to the same degree. The conditions under which success-fearers become particularly anxious in the face of success and the consequences for the way they think about their performances, feel about their performances, and actually perform are discussed throughout this and the following chapters.

Fear of Success and the American Success Ethos

In the United States, striving for success is an almost universal way of life. As a people, we discuss success (and failure) constantly. Successful people are admired, envied, emulated, and extolled as models of virtue. Parents begin to worry about the potential for success of their children almost as soon as the children are born. Male graduates of Ivy League colleges used to be said to reserve places at their alma maters for their infant sons. Parents are concerned if their children have not begun to crawl at (or before) the age when crawling usually begins. They go on anxiously to compare the size of their infants' vocabularies with the vocabularies of other children of the same age. By the time the children are in school, they are themselves imbued with the success ethic and begin to do their own worrying about success.

5

Our bookstores are filled with self-improvement books that purport to enhance our chances for interpersonal success (winning friends, influencing people, being beautiful), commercial success (obtaining and using power, successfully selling oneself and products of all descriptions), academic success, and success in courtship, marriage, and sex. For those whose problems with success are beyond self-help books, elaborate and expensive courses offer the key to a more success-filled life. Clearly, a well-understood belief among Americans is that success is the product of a combination of virtues—ability, hard work, perserverance, and perhaps a bit of luck—and that to be successful is to be virtuous almost by definition.

Psychologists and other social scientists have added their voices to the chorus. A considerable number of psychologists concern themselves with investigating achievement motivation (see chapter 7), which has been assumed by many to be a sine qua non for success. Some of these investigators have gone so far as to suggest that other nations' failure to develop more quickly along industrial lines can be traced to an insufficiency of achievement motivation among their citizens, and training courses have been developed to increase the level of achievement motivation among business executives and other managerial personnel. Sociologists and political scientists have studied the social antecedents and correlates of aspirations to upward social mobility.

Rather obviously, we Americans tend to assume that success is an almost universally desired commodity and thus, most of us cannot easily conceive of otherwise normal people as being *fearful* of success. An anecdote will help to illustrate what we mean. During the autumn of 1971, when we were just beginning the research reported in this book, one of our colleagues approached a wise and eminent professor of psychology at Columbia University for advice regarding the analysis of data collected to develop a questionnaire to measure the fear of success. The advice, as always, was given generously and without comment. At the end of the conference, however, the professor could not refrain from expressing his puzzlement. "You're not," he asked, "seriously suggesting that people actually have a fear of *success* are you?" When our colleague replied that she was indeed serious, the professor insisted that whereas some or even many people might well be fearful of failure, this notion about fear of success was destined to come to no good. "Surely," he said, "you don't expect this kind of scale to predict much behavior!" As the reader will soon see, the skeptical psychologist proved to be quite wrong.

Although the idea that some people fear or avoid success has not until very recently entered into the popular literature,[1] the fear of success has been identified as a neurotic problem by psychotherapists since Sigmund Freud first wrote about it. Freud, writing in 1915 about people "wrecked by success" [31], told stories of two typical persons who had apparently fallen ill "precisely because a deeply-rooted and long-cherished wish [had] come to fulfillment." The first example Freud recounted concerned the case of a zestful young woman who ran away from home and began to live with an artist whom she met on her adventures. They lived together for many years quite happily, but were apparently unable to marry because the young man's family protested the liaison. Eventually, however, the artist was able to persuade his family to recognize the woman, and he was prepared to marry her. At that critical point, when her wish to be the legitimate wife of her companion seemed about to be fulfilled, the woman is reported to have gone to pieces. She neglected the house, believed herself persecuted by her lover's relatives, became very jealous, hindered the artist's work and social life, and "soon fell into incurable mental illness" [31, p. 325].

Freud described a second example of a man who also became ill when he was about to achieve the goal he had long sought:

On another occasion I observed a most respectable man who, himself a professor at a university, had for many years cherished the natural wish to succeed the master who had initiated him into the life of learning. When this elder man retired, and the other's colleagues intimated that it was he whom they desired as successor, he began to hesitate, depreciated his own merits, declared himself unworthy to fill the position designed for him, and fell into a state of melancholy which unfitted him for all activity for some years after.

Different as these two cases are, they yet coincide on this one point—that illness followed close upon the wish-fulfillment, and annihilated all enjoyment of it [31, p. 325].

Other clinical writers have followed Freud's lead and have published descriptions and analyses of people whose neurotic problems appear to worsen at the moment that success seems imminent. Karen Horney has theorized explicitly and extensively about the fear of success [46], and reports of persons who fear success by other clinicians have also appeared [86,102,115]. Clinicians, then, do not appear as surprised as nonclinicians to find persons who fear success. The fear-of-success case studies published in psychiatric and psycho-analytic journals do, however, tempt the reader to believe that this neurotic problem is very rare—that is, restricted to a small subgroup of very odd people. Our research indicates, quite to the contrary, that nothing could be further from the truth.

When we began our research on the fear of success, we did what most psychologists do in the early stages of thinking about a problem: We looked close to home for evidence of the fear of success—at ourselves, our friends, our colleagues, and our students. Some examples of the rather commonplace, prosaic actions we saw will help to illustrate the success-fearing person.

One common problem we began to attribute to the fear of success was "dissertationitis" in all its manifold forms. One student who was writing his Ph.D. dissertation carried the manuscript everywhere with him because he was afraid it would be stolen or consumed in a fire in his absence. This student inadvertently left the almost-completed manuscript somewhere on two separate occasions: once in a fast-food restaurant near campus and once in a taxicab. Fortunately, it was recovered both times. We knew a number of other graduate students who made excellent progress through their graduate programs and who had developed all the skills necessary to do a dissertation easily, but who became effectively immobilized at one or another stage of this final step in their graduate school careers. We knew several graduate students who repeatedly found ways to sabotage their graduate school careers when the idea that they could finish successfully began to be clear. Still another very frustrating doctoral student seemed completely unable to bring *any* important project to completion without making numerous vital errors in its execution. The examples to be found among graduate students are discouragingly numerous.

Examples are not confined, however, to graduate students, who are often thought to be a bit peculiar anyway; undergraduates, who do not have the same reputation for eccentricity, also engage in success-avoidant behaviors. Everyone who has been to college is familiar with students who approach the final examination for a course with an excellent chance of maintaining a grade of "A" in the course and somehow "clutch" on the final. The pattern is not at all unusual. The student manages to put off studying for the exam until the night before, stays up all night cramming, and succeeds only in undermining his alertness during the exam. Or the student falls asleep in the early morning hours, forgets to set or doesn't hear the alarm, and sleeps through the exam. We have all seen instances of undergraduate students who are doing well in a course and who do not finish the course because they are unable to complete a term paper. Slightly less common, fortunately, is the student who decides to change his or her major one or a few courses short of completing it or who decides to withdraw from school or transfer to another school during the final year.

School is not, of course, the only environment in which successes are averted, sabotaged, or not enjoyed by success-fearing persons. There are successes to be avoided in interpersonal relations, in work contexts, in thera- peutic contexts, and even in games. Everyone is acquainted with people who play a game (such as Ping Pong, squash, golf, chess, and so forth) brilliantly in the early stages, but who somehow contrive to lose near the end, even if they are at that point far ahead of their competitors. Such persons, we suggest, may also be suffering from the fear of success.

If the fear of success is not the exclusive malady of a few bizarre people—if it is not rare, but common—then what is it, and how can we identify it? After all, the examples we have just cited could all be explained in other ways. Why do we account for them by suggesting these people fear success? How do these people come to fear success in the first place? We turn now to an in-depth examination of clinical approaches to the fear of success—that is, what it is and how it develops. Based on common elements in the writings of Freud, Horney, and Sullivan, we shall arrive at a fuller description of the fear-of-success phenomenon.

Clinical Perspectives

Clinicians make many assumptions about human dynamics, and the descriptions of the origins of fear of success that follow will be clearer if several of these are kept in mind. First, clinical theorists consider childhood to be a time of life during which children feel or can be made to feel totally and intensely dependent on their caretakers. This dependency, based realistically on survival needs, also extends to needs for affection and approval, which are seen as mediators of the needs for survival. Children are thus considered to be profoundly influenced by the feelings and actions of their parents or caretakers. A second important assumption is that a large part of adult behavior, particularly irrational and dysfunctional behavior, receives its impetus from unconscious motivation—that is, certain intense and very threatening childhood experiences (thoughts, desires, and feelings) are forced out of conscious awareness and reside in the unconscious mind where they still exert influence on behavior, but in ways that are not recognizable to the conscious mind.

Several clinical writers have done scholarly analyses of the problem of human destructiveness. Beginning with Freud's analysis of *thanatos*, or the death instinct, the topic of destructiveness toward the self and toward others has been scrutinized by Reik in *Masochism in Modern Man* [94], by Fromm in *The Heart of Man* [33] and *The Anatomy of Human Destructiveness* [34], and by Warner in *Self-Realization and Self-Defeat* [116]. The related question of the forces that threaten and oppose constructive self-realization have been the focus of other prominent works, notably Fromm's *Escape from Freedom* [32] and May's *The Courage to Create* [78]. Relatively few clinical writers have directly addressed the more specific topic of fear of success. Similarly, our conversations with practicing clinicians reveal that while they are aware of the problem of fear of success in many of their patients, they tend not to single it out from the complex of other self-defeating symptoms patients bring to psychotherapy. Although in this book we are focusing on this problem as manifested in large numbers of people, a clinician focuses on an individual person, tries to understand the unique ways in which he or she developed as he or she did, and thus considers the characteristic of fear of success as being only a part of that development. From the clinician's point of view, then, that so few of them have chosen to write about this particular aspect of their patients' personalities is not surprising.

Sigmund Freud

Historically, Freud was the first to record his observations of "those wrecked by success." In his only reference to the fear of success, "Some Character-Types Met with in Psycho-Analytic Work," he described the "surprising, indeed bewildering . . . discovery, that people occasionally fall ill precisely because a deeply-rooted and cherished wish has come to fulfillment. It seems as though they could not endure their bliss . . . " [31, p. 324] . In the case histories Freud cited and in his extended character analyses of Shakespeare's Lady Macbeth and Ibsen's Rebecca (Gamvik) West, the person's grave illness almost immediately follows the knowledge that a major wish fulfillment is actually at hand and thus destroys all enjoyment of the success. In fact this neurotic reaction frequently prevents the person from taking the final step in realizing the success, such as in Freud's examples of actually getting married or actually taking the important position. Freud explained that most illnesses or neuroses arise when people meet with frustration and obstacles to fulfilling their forbidden (and therefore hidden) wishes and impulses.

On the face of it, then, the statement that the fulfillment of the desire rather than its frustration induces illness may seem contradictory. Freud solves this apparent paradox by distinguishing between internal and external frustrations. External frustrations arise from circumstances outside the person, and internal frustrations arise from the pressures of conscience within the person. External frustration may arouse anger, unhappiness, and yearning, but it does not cause neurosis. Rather the cause of neurosis is the conflict within a person between the urge to satisfy strong desires and needs and the internal prohibitions (conscience) against fulfilling those desires. If for instance, a person dreams of marrying a certain attractive woman who is married to another, then he is frustrated from an external source. If and when she becomes free and marriageable, the external frustration is removed and he should be satisfied or pleased with the possibility that his wish can now be satisfied. Suppose, however, that the woman the person yearns for is not married, but is his mother or his sister. In that case, the frustration of his wish fulfillment derives from internal sources that are based on strong social proscriptions and his ideals for his own character. If his incestuous desire is very strong, then the internal forces of conscience will be mobilized, which results in great inner conflict and perhaps neurosis.

Now let us consider a slightly more complicated instance. Suppose that the married woman the person desires is in reality neither mother nor sister but has been unconsciously equated with, say, the mother, perhaps because she has some characteristics that remind the person of his mother. Here we have a special instance in which the apparent external frustration—the unavailability of the desired woman—serves the same function as the internal prohibition against incestuous desires for the mother. Since the equation of the unavailable woman with the mother is unconscious, the unconscious wish for the mother can be allowed a certain amount of innocent expression since the real woman is unavailable and the fulfillment of the wish appears impossible or extremely remote. The point here is that the external frustration is sufficient to keep the event from happening, and as a consequence, the internal prohibitions are less strongly activated—that is, the wish for the mother finds a certain amount of indirect expression in the wish for her symbolic representative. If the married woman is suddenly widowed and becomes available, however, this delicate balance is upset, particularly if the man feels that he was in some way responsible for her availability to him, such as by wishing her husband were dead. At this point the external frustration, which had been doing the work of the internal prohibition, has disappeared; from the outside, success appears imminent. The internal unconscious prohibition is now activated and takes a serious toll. Not only must the man stop himself from marrying this woman, but he probably must try to stop himself from having the feelings of attraction that were present when their fulfillment had seemed impossible. Thus the success of the long-cherished wish throws the person directly into the kind of internal conflict that causes neurosis; the person may withdraw from this severe unconscious conflict, for example, by becoming ill.

In Freudian theory, the Oedipus conflict is central to an understanding of the enigmatic observation that some people fear success.[2] In the Oedipus complex the child has strong self-generated incestuous and exclusivity desires for the parent of the opposite sex. Seeing the same-sex parent as an obstacle and an adversary motivates the child to have jealous, competitive, and hostile feelings toward this parental rival. Perceiving that the same-sex parent is very powerful, the child fears serious harm if he were to act on the impulse to vanquish the rival and gain an exclusive relationship with the other parent. In addition to such fears of parental retaliation, the thought of eliminating the like-sex parent must raise in the child feelings of dependency and insecurity at the prospect of losing that parent's support and care. Most often the conflict between the wishful impulse itself and the fears associated with acting on the impulse is resolved; the fear becomes internalized as a prohibition in the child's conscience, which threatens guilt if the impulses are acted upon. The child then suppresses into the unconscious the hostile and sexual impulses and replaces them with a desire to be like the same-sex parent.

In some instances, however, the Oedipal conflict is less well resolved and continues to be expressed in indirect ways, such as in conflicts over substitute goals—other successes or competitive victories. As long as these substitute goals remain distant and improbable of realization, their contemplation partially satisfies the desire to fulfill the hidden impulses and the need to prohibit them. Presumably, the person does not clearly and consciously recognize the connection between the symbolic goal and the original forbidden Oedipal desires. Our best reading of Freud indicates that as long as there is not appreciable success, the person in the conflict can work toward the goal fervently and relatively unambivalently. If and when the success becomes probable, however, the guilt and anxiety associated with the old conflict come to the fore and replace the reality frustration (nonsuccess) with even more frustrating internal prohibitions.

A Contemporary Version of the Freudian Point of View

Psychoanalytic theory has grown considerably since Freud presented its framework. Not only the famous neo-Freudian theorists (such as Jung, Adler, Horney, and Fromm) but also the less well-known psychoanalytic practitioners have contributed much to the development and elaboration of the theory. In this section, we present a brief, modern-day psychoanalytic analysis of the fear-of-success phenomenon. Our analysis is based primarily on Freud's Oedipal framework, but it also includes important events in the pre-Oedipal period in the child's development. Since parts of the analysis draw on the writings of Ovesey [86], Shuster [102], and Warner [115,116], this section represents what is essentially an amalgam of current psychoanalytic thinking on the subject.

Prior to the Oedipal stage, fear of success can be engendered in children by negative parental responses to the child's expressions of self-assertiveness and to his strivings toward achievement and independence. The focus here is on that stage of development in which the child sees himself, and is seen, as becoming increasingly separate from and independent of the parent(s). For individuation and separation to occur successfully, the child must experience security and support for his increasing self-expression and mastery. Some parents, however, react to the child's natural moves toward independence as though the child were abandoning or competing with them. Thus, they experience feelings of insecurity and rejection, and/or hostility, and a competitive struggle for control and supremacy. Anxiety, anger, interference, disapproval, overcontrol, and rejection are some of the many ways in which the parent(s) can communicate their negative reactions to the child's burgeoning efforts at attaining mastery and independence. The child who is feeling insecure about his new attempts at independence is particularly vulnerable to the negative and disapproving parental reactions. The child, experiencing these negative reactions, comes to feel insecure and to experience anxiety rather than pleasure in his normal growth processes.[3]

The child may strive toward mastery and independence, but his self-assertion and success are likely to become unconsciously confused with his aggressive and competitive impulses and thus to become associated with guilt and anxiety. Because he comes to expect or fear abandonment, loss of love, or fantasied retaliation for his successful accomplishments, which are equated with destruction, qualified success may come to have tranquilizing effects. Since the young child is unable to make fine distinctions among the parent's negative reactions, his ambivalence and fear of accomplishment are likely to be generalized to most endeavors rather than limited to specific arenas of activity.

Up to this point in the description of the kinds of parent-child interaction that give rise to fear of success, we have stressed the negative or independence-inhibiting part of the interaction. In fact, the interpersonal communications that take place between parent(s) and potentially success-fearing offspring are more complex. Presumably, the parents also have and express conscious wishes that their children should grow and mature and become independent. In addition both parents and children are subject to strong cultural pressures and demands for achievement.

The child, in the face of these inconsistent admonitions, is likely to be somewhat confused and in fact ambivalent; his natural needs for growth and mastery interlock with the cultural and social requirements that lead him to venture out, yet his attempts produce a certain amount of anxiety and insecurity, particularly as success and recognition near. There are a number of strategies or psychological defenses that help people with fear of success to reduce the uncomfortable feelings of anxiety associated with undertaking tasks associated with independence and competence. One strategy involves shifting attention and concern to peripheral aspects of the tasks and, where relevant, to the external requirements for doing them. A related strategy involves acquiring a self-disparaging view of oneself as an inadequate performer. Both of these strategies serve to keep the performer, and even observers, deflected from the competence- and independence-producing aspects of the task being undertaken. The anxiety and insecurity initially produced by negative parental reactions to the child's success eventually become internalized and operate independently as the "dictates of conscience." Thus, the complete early syndrome is carried to adulthood, to be generalized and repeated.[4]

Further, the ramifications of the parental injunction to inhibit success striving are suggested to be felt most keenly when the parent and child are the same sex. The negotiation of the Oedipal phase for all children requires that genital longing for the opposite sex parent be given up in favor of a same-sex identification. In this process the hostile and destructive feelings felt for the same-sex parental rival who is seen as responsible for the deprivation are repressed. The child is forced to acknowledge that this parent has won out over him. By identification with that person, however, he is reassured that some day he, too, will be a big adult and accorded the same chance to select a mate.

For the success-fearing person this process becomes contaminated. If such a person's same-sex parent repeatedly communicates his concern that the child is attempting to outdo and oust him, the child's normal rivalrous feelings are heightened. Fantasized Oedipal victory is lent a greater sense of reality, and the child in this situation must intensify his efforts to keep self and others from knowledge of his destructive intentions. Open recognition of interest in success for these persons carries with it the potential risk of retaliation by the parental competitor.[5] Awareness of success in any arena will be anxiety provoking in view of its unconscious equation with aggressive and exhibitionistic needs. But the defeat of a same-sex competitor will be particularly threatening. To be pitted against a like-sex opponent is to revive the Oedipal drama in the unconscious, with its associated murderous impulses and its attendant guilt and fear. Success is symbolically equated with fantasied murder and childhood sexual potency.

Many post-Freudian writers including Deutsch [22], Horney [46], Ovesey [86], and Warner [115,116] postulate that intense sibling rivalry is another cause of fear of success. If a child believes that his parents accord greater love and esteem to a brother or sister, then the child is likely to feel intense envy and competition toward the preferred sibling. This intense rivalry leads to strong impulses to vanquish the preferred sibling and to usurp the more favorable position with the parents. As in the Oedipal conflict, fear of punishment and retaliation from the sibling and from the parents become internalized in conscience and lead to feelings of guilt and to an inhibition of competition with the sibling.

Karen Horney

Karen Horney [45,46] argues that in addition to the early childhood influences postulated by other Freudian thinkers, cultural influences also play a major role in the generation of fear of success. She postulates that three cultural factors form a social context that is fertile for the development of neurotic fears of competition and rivalry. First, ours is a society dominated by a competitive individualistic spirit. Competition is a driving force in both our economic activities (getting and keeping jobs) and in our interpersonal activities—in the family, between siblings, in school, and in social relations (keeping up with the Joneses). Second, we tend to attribute an unrealistically positive set of characteristics (competence, courage, and enterprise) to people who succeed and a similarly exaggerated set of negative attributes (worthlessness, incompetence, and laziness) to those who fail. No account seems to be taken in the culture either of the fact that possibilities for success are limited or that other factors such as unscrupulousness or luck may play a role in becoming successful. As a result, the successful, though admired, are also envied, and the failures are regarded with contempt, which of course lowers their self-esteem and makes them envious and potentially untrustworthy. A third cultural factor—the social and moral admonition that we should be modest, unselfish and even self-sacrificing—helps to close a kind of vicious circle. Thus, the expression of spirited competition and the need to establish positive self-regard through successful achievement are directly opposed both by society's demand that we should be modest and by our fear of others' destructive envy of our prospective successes.

Horney speculates that unfavorable early childhood environments, particularly those in which the dominant theme is rivalry and competition between the strong and the weak (in actuality or in imagination), generate strong feelings of insecurity, hostility, and anxiety in children. These feelings of insecurity and anxiety, particularly in our cultural context, lead simultaneously to an intense desire to be first in any competition and also to a boundless craving for affection and admiration and a desire to be loved. These desires may seem difficult to fulfill simultaneously, but they are in reality not incompatible. A more careful inspection of the process through which success-fearing neurotics attempt to meet these goals reveals that to them the goals are subjectively and perhaps objectively incompatible. Their rivalries, as will be remembered, are fired with hostility and feelings of insecurity. Thus, conscious or unconscious hostility toward their opponents plays a crucial role in their strivings to upset these opponents and to take over the much-envied position of Number One. Shortly after embarking on the road to a competitive goal, however, they find themselves caught—indeed frequently immobilized—between the fear of failure and the fear of success, the Scylla and Charybdis of the neurotic competitor's world. If they fail, they will be subject to further feelings of insecurity and anxiety as well as humiliation. They will expect that others will regard them with contempt, and they will regard these others with intensified hostility and envy. If they succeed, on the other hand, then they anticipate that they will become the *object* of the hostility and envy of others, which are the very feelings they have for the successful.

In the final analysis, success is perceived by the success-fearing neurotic to bring not love and admiration but an endless parade of hostile challengers for the successful position. There are two related characteristics of the goal of the rivalry that should be made clear. First, the goal is usually subjectively defined as an exceedingly and unrealistically lofty one—to be not just good but the best, to be Number One. Second, the person assumes that in achievement or success-oriented strivings, a victory by one spells the defeat of all other contenders—that is, the envy and hostility motivating the undertaking have resulted in the destruction of others, thereby incurring their wrath and retaliation rather than winning their love and admiration. If we assume that the initial sense of hostility and insecurity is strong and motivating, then a kind of repetitive, vicious cycle is set in motion in which the hostility and envy lead to rivalrous striving, which in turn leads to a fear of retaliation and rejection, and which finally returns to the uncomfortable feelings of hostility, envy, and insecurity.

According to Horney, neuroses concerning competition may take on one of two dominant themes: a fear of failure or a fear of success. Persons with neurotic conflicts about competition may or may not be consciously aware of fearing humiliation and the consequent feelings of hostility and envy, which are failure's rewards, or consciously aware of fearing retaliation, envy, and rejection, which result from success. Whether or not the person is conscious of the basic elements of these fears and the anxiety these fears generate, they are nonetheless the essence of the neurosis. If fear of failure predominates, then the most likely consequences are recoil from competition and withdrawal from risks and efforts that might be viewed as pathetic attempts at self-betterment. Persons for whom the fear of failure dominates will consider diverting themselves in innocuous and solitary activities as being safer and may in fact give the appearance of indolence and laziness. The safer course is not to do the things they want to do, to remain modest and inconspicuous, and above all to avoid competition. Needless to say, the result of these attempts to avoid failure may lead to great personal impoverishment and warping of potentialities.

For persons for whom the fear of success is the dominant prong of the conflict over rivalry, there are somewhat different manifestations and consequences. Unlike the failure-fearers, the success-fearers stay in the competitive arena. Their efforts are characterized by ambivalence and vacillation, however. Their behavior is driven by a frantically grandiose and compulsive ambition to be first in the race and at the same time by an equally great compulsion to check themselves as soon as they get well started or make any significant progress. The observable result is a set of checkered and unpredictable performances varying from excellent to terrible and even including periods of performance interference that look like immobilization.

The neurotic success fearers employ several strategies that enable them momentarily to satisfy their lofty ambitions and needs to check themselves. When they are progressing well, they are likely to belittle themselves and thus to create in their imaginations a great chasm between themselves and their competitors. Holding a low opinion of themselves and their abilities, they can allay anxiety about succeeding while still progressing. They reject favorable information as flattery or being chance produced and are likely to attribute their progress to luck, to other people, or to virtually any factor that will allow them to maintain the perception that they are nowhere near a success. On the other hand, when disturbances in progress or self-denigrating attitudes become too overwhelmingly painful, success-fearers have a tendency to use fantasy as a remedy. They substitute grand ambition and ideas about themselves for attainable goals.

Generally, because of their unrealistically positive and negative views of themselves and because of the unevenness in their actual striving for success, such persons do less well on the average than would be predicted from a realistic assessment of their potential. Success-fearing persons tend to recoil from a success when it seems imminent, and if they do have a success, they tend not to enjoy it and in fact not to feel it as their own experience.

Harry Stack Sullivan

Careful reading of the works of Harry Stack Sullivan reveals no direct reference to the phenomenon of fear of success. However, several notions that are basic to his theory of personality are illuminating when applied to an analysis of the fear of success.

Sullivan's theory of personality [106], more than any other, postulates that relations with significant others are the primary determinants of the self-concept and thus of personality. He sees the influence of biological needs for growth, mastery, and even a true self as weak and tenuous and easily overshadowed by demands and information that come to the child from his interaction with significant others, particularly the mothering one, in Sullivan's phrase. While the mothering one is frequently the child's biological mother, the role may be filled by anyone who has primary care-taking responsibilities for the child.

Because of the child's enormous dependency on the ministrations of the mothering one, the child develops a great need to have her approval and to avoid her disapproval. More specifically, Sullivan postulates that the child attends to the emotional states and reactions of the mothering one with great intensity by using a kind of emotional radar to detect verbal and nonverbal cues of emotional state. If the mothering one's state is positive, then the child feels secure and, by implication, accepted and in contact with the mothering one; his self-concept is positive—that of a good child. If the child detects a negative state, particularly anxiety in the mothering one, then he feels insecure, not accepted, and out of contact with the mothering one. This insecurity leads the child to try to restore a positive state, usually by changing his behavior. We should mention parenthetically that in Sullivan's view the tragedy of childhood is that the child believes himself and his behavior to be a cause of all the mother's negative states. He sees himself as a "bad" child and as causing her anxiety or withdrawal and seeks to modify himself or his behavior in order to change her state and thus restore himself to a state of security and to the feeling of being a good child. Only when the mother's state is positive does the child feel the security necessary to direct his attention elsewhere, to play, to develop competence, and so forth. If for some reason (e.g., fear of the child's independence, competition with the child), the mother is made anxious by the child's successes, then the child begins to associate negative reactions with his successes and to avoid, disguise, or sabotage them in order to avoid the feelings of insecurity and of being a bad child that the mother's anxiety or anger evoke.

In summary then, the child's most dominant motive or need is to feel secure. The child has an uncanny ability to sense the mother's emotional state. A positive state in the mother leads the child to feel secure and to feel free to attend to other activities. Because the child sees himself as causing the mother's state and because he acquires his self-concept from the reactions of significant others to him, a positive state in the mother also leads to a positive self-concept in the child. If the emotional state of the mother is negative and particularly if she is anxious, the child feels banished from contact with his source of security and is terrorized. He feels that he is a bad child for having caused this state in the all-important mother and invests all of his energy in trying to change himself and his behavior in the hope of changing the mother's state and therefore his own.

Abraham Maslow

Abraham Maslow [75,76] was a social psychologist whose major theoretical concerns were directed to the task of describing self-actualized individuals—

that is, a very small group of people who exemplified the development of the highest and healthiest potential inherent in humankind. Perhaps surprisingly, therefore, he is listed along with Freud, Horney, and Sullivan—psychoanalysts who dealt with human psychopathology—as one of the people who has noticed and analyzed the phenomenon of fear of success.

In the course of his studies, Maslow observed in both self-actualized and normal people an impulse to growth, or a desire to develop themselves to their full potential. In asking the question of what might block this growth and what makes the growth so slow, he identified a psychological defense that enables people to evade growth. He described this defense as a fear of greatness, or an ambivalence toward the highest and grandest achievements in ourselves and in others. The "Jonah Complex" is the name he gave to this phenomenon that bears striking similarity to the neurotic fear of success described by Freud and Horney. Low levels of aspiration, voluntary self-crippling, pseudo-stupidity, and mock humility are examples of the consequences of the fear of greatness inherent in the Jonah Complex. Although Maslow postulated that the Jonah Complex is most severe in neurotics, less so in normals, and least present in the self-actualized, he nevertheless believed that some amount of the fear of greatness was a part of socialized human nature. In particular, he cited three usual human reactions to greatness or perfection. First he speculated that in the face of great men and women and great accomplishments, we always feel inferior, inadequate, and often even jealous and envious. Our implicit assumption is that these people intended that we should compare ourselves to them—to compete, compare, and suffer humiliation in the comparison. He reasoned, as did Horney, that we would thus expect others to react as negatively to our accomplishments as we do to theirs. A second reaction refers to a frequent human response to intense and ecstatic feeling, to passion. Maslow postulated that in the most extreme state of positive affect people withdraw or run away saying things like "I can't stand it," "it's too much," or "I could die." He interpreted these responses as indicating that as people, we have a universal weakness that prevents us from enduring delirious happiness for very long, as though we are afraid of losing control or being shattered. Finally, he speculated that some people cannot manage the graceful integration between humility and pride that is required for creative work. If a person's urges to greatness and creativity are motivated by pride untempered with humility and amusement, then he or she may well become fearful of his or her own arrogance, or grandiosity, and as a result may recoil from the motive to create in order to avoid the fear generated by this untempered "sinful pride" [76, p. 38].

Common Elements in the Clinical Positions

In the foregoing discussion of the early work on fear of success, there are many points on which the various theorists are in agreement; there are also several points of difference among their positions. The purpose of this section will be to highlight these agreements and disagreements. A major difference among the theorists lies in whether they see fear of success as originating primarily in the child or primarily in real events in the external social world which then affect the child. Since these differences are likely to be in relative emphasis, the question is really one of how active or passive the child is seen to be in the creation of his fear of success. The Freudian position clearly sees the child as very active in the generation of fear of success. The Oedipal complex is considered to be a product of the child's imagination based on his fantasies about what would happen if he acted upon his forbidden impulses to murder one parent and thus win the exclusive attention of the other. The anticipated fear of retaliation is a projection of the child's own destructive feelings onto the same-sex parent.

Karen Horney's position is in some respects similar to Freud's in seeing the child as active in creating the fear of success. Again, the defense mechanism of projection plays a major role. The child feels envious, hostile, and competitive toward his adversary and anticipates via projection that the adversary (if vanquished) would retaliate with the same degree of hostile feeling that the envious child has. In addition to the active role, however, Horney also suggested that in some instances people do meet with real retaliatory competition as a consequence of their successes.

The child is most passive in the reconstructed Sullivanian position. Here the child is postulated to learn to fear success only in response to the mothering one's negative reactions to success. We should add here, however, that while passive in the initiation of fear of success, the child becomes unwittingly active in the later maintenance of it, when the specific mothering one's approval is no longer realistically relevant to the adult's security needs. The fear of success, then, though realistic in its origin, is not realistic in its maintenance.

Related to the notion of whether the child is active or passive in the generation of his fear of success is the question of what constitutes a success and what the surplus meaning of a successful act is to a success-fearing person. In the Freudian version, the child's forbidden Oedipal desires are repressed. Nevertheless these desires exert an influence on behavior in a disguised or symbolic form. In this view, the feared success is the attainment of whatever goal or event has come to symbolize the successful destruction of the same-sex parent. Generally such events will take an obvious form, such as wooing a married man or woman away from his or her spouse or in becoming more attractive or competent than the same-sex parent along some important dimension. The ways of the unconscious mind are sometimes strange, however, and we should emphasize that a feared success may involve *any* goal that represents the forbidden Oedipal desires to the person.

In Horney's view, a success is easiest to understand. Those fears and accomplishments that the general culture labels as successful are the stimuli for fear of success. This view suggests that very subjectively defined and unconventional successes in which there are no competitors would not stimulate success anxiety. Neither, however, would such accomplishments promise popularity, love, and recognition.

Maslow's position is similar to Horney's, but more restricted. Maslow's "Jonah Complex" refers primarily to great intellectual and social products. Nevertheless, social validation of the importance of the task and the presence of competitors is of importance in Maslow's notion of success or greatness.

In the Sullivanian position, which comes closest to a learning theory position, the range of events that can be defined as success is broadest. Competition and consensual agreement are of no necessary predictive importance, since the competencies that are prohibited are those that have evoked anxiety and negative affect in the mothering one. The Sullivanian account of the fear of success is also dependent to some extent on the child's potential for faulty generalization. Nevertheless, these successes could range from any events that demonstrate the child's competence or independence to something as specific as success at those tasks about which the mother herself feels inadequate or insecure. In a sense, the Sullivanian position, in allowing potential interference in the child's execution of solitary competence, has the broadest range of definition of successes that can be feared.

Whatever the definition of success, an important aspect to note is that in all three positions, success is seen as destructive and as promising very negative consequences. In the Freudian and Horneyian positions, the success "destroys" someone else and invites retaliation; in the Sullivanian framework, it destroys secure relations with the mother and invites insecurity and a negative self-image.

If success (however it may be defined) is likely to bring on such negative consequences in success-fearers, we might well ask why they try to succeed at all. Indeed, the striving to succeed seems to be an integral part of the fear-of-success syndrome. Speaking of self-sabotage is not really sensible unless the person has made some progress, through striving, toward the feared goal. Freud's and Horney's points of view would seem to say that desire or wanting provides the impetus to the goal. Horney is somewhat more specific in saying that the culture holds out two incompatible goals: the desire to be loved and the goal of being successful. The Sullivanian position relies on a weak but enduring intrinsic need for growth or mastery, which though frustrated near a success is not frustrated during the early stages of its progress. In addition, the Sullivanian position postulates that the mother gives ambiguous cues. While the mother may punish or otherwise squelch the specific successes, this view postulates that she is likely to promote verbally those acts that children must learn in order to succeed in this society.

Another point of difference among the three major clinical theories concerns the way fear of success is manifested over time. The theories of Freud and Sullivan seem to describe a pattern in which the success-fearing person embarks unambivalently on his goal until he begins to near a success, at which time he engages in self-sabotage or some other defensive maneuver to prevent, deny, or deflate the success. Horney, on the other hand, describes the process as involving vacillation from its beginning to its end—that is, a process involving highly variable performances.

The last point in this section is one on which all the clinical theorists agree. People who develop fear of success occupy a low-power and probably even a low-status position in relation to the people who are important in the induction of their fear of success. Freud's child is the underdog in the struggle for the opposite-sex parent; Horney's competitor for the limelight is out of the limelight during the competition; and Sullivan's child is clearly inferior in power to the mother.

In summary, people who have high fear of success are seen by the clinical theorists as having five characteristics. First, they are highly ambivalent about success, since they have motives both to succeed and not to succeed. Second, their ambivalence about success represents a real or imagined competition or conflict of interest with powerful or important others. The success-fearers experience and see themselves consciously as wanting to succeed, yet they simultaneously and less consciously incorporate fears or inhibitions to success that represent the expected reactions of important others to their successes. Third, the ambivalence is expressed by the dual behaviors of success-oriented efforts and by success-avoidant responses (self-sabotage). Fourth, fear of success beyond adolescence is seen as an irrational and largely unconscious motive that success-fearers actively maintain because of their interpretation of their child-hood experiences. In other words, there are very few adults whose fear of success is rationally justified by any realistic negative consequences of success in their contemporary lives. And fifth, people who fear success employ a wide range of rationalizations or defense mechanisms that protect them from the anxiety instigated both by their great ambition and their tendency to defeat their successes. Among these deep-seated defense mechanisms are low self-evaluation, a tendency to externalize the motivation to succeed by seeing it as raised by external requirements rather than an internal desire, and a tendency to externalize the cause of success when it occurs by seeing it variously as due to luck, an easy task or as a result of the help of others, rather than as being consequent to one's own competence and effort.

Our Own Perspective

In the first section of this chapter we reviewed the theoretical positions of a number of major clinical writers whose work has direct or indirect implications for understanding the early childhood origins of the neurotic fear of success, and we attempted at the same time to convey at least a flavor of what the experience of being a success-fearer might be like. In this section we outline the essentials of the theoretical perspective that has both guided and evolved from our research, and we present a more explicit description of the characteristics of success-fearers. Our own perspective draws heavily on the work of the clinical writers reviewed earlier. It is closest to the ideas of Karen Horney, whose position is broad and inclusive enough to incorporate the ideas on fear of success ascribed to other neo-Freudian writers, and is consistent also with many of the ideas elaborated by followers of Sullivan. The breadth of Horney's position derives in part from her decision to deal directly and at length with the fear of success as a common neurotic manifestation of American culture and from her conviction that such common phenomena are overdetermined—that is, caused and main-tained not by one isolated event or factor, but by many.

Psychologists with an experimental orientation who undertake research on clinical phenomena face various vexing theoretical and tactical dilemmas. In our own case, an important issue was holding on to the richness and vividness of the descriptive and theoretical work on fear of success of the clinical writers. At the same time emphasis was necessary in our own thinking on independent variables that are manipulable as well as clearly observable and on dependent variables and mediating variables that are observable and measurable. For us, this emphasis meant an early stress on: (1) finding a useful definition of fear of success; (2) finding ways to measure fear of success so that we could identify persons who are presumably afflicted with it; (3) assessing correlates and consequences of fear of success and the conditions under which those consequences would be likely to occur; and (4) assessing the strength and importance of fear of success in the everyday lives of a wide variety of people.

While the clinical writers have certainly dealt with fear of success descrip-tively and in terms of its consequences, they have not dealt with issues of measurement, or questions of the importance of the phenomenon in the lives of normal, nonpatient populations.[6] On the other hand, these clinical observers and theorists have provided us with more descriptions of what causes fear of success than we were ready or able to use immediately in our research. Our theoretical position, then, was constructed to enable us to research the questions we believed we could answer and to avoid at the outset taking a position on questions we could not profitably research until later; namely, questions of causes and potential cures.

Virtually any situation in which a person can achieve something contains the potential not only for success, but also for nonsuccess or failure. Our point of view must be able to deal with this complexity; avoidance of success is seen as one characteristic or motive in a constellation of motives that guides the success-fearing person's behavior in situations in which achievement is at issue for him or her. We have assumed, then, that such a person's fear of success coexists with certain other motives and characteristics of the person that are manifested in achievement contexts. Thus we recognize explicitly that people who fear success actually have a strong (usually unconscious) *ambivalence* about success. On the one hand, they view success as imbued with a multitude of attractive positive qualities and consequences; on the other, success is tinged for them with negative potential consequences as well. In addition, they view failure quite without ambivalence as having highly negative consequences.

We see the behavior of success-fearing persons in achievement situations, then, as guided by three principal motivational tendencies. First, they have a strong motivation to achieve success that energizes and directs them to strive for achievements. They also possess, however, a primarily unconscious motivation to retreat from or avoid success. This motivation is likely to be aroused when they are close to achieving success and helps them to ward off or cope with the anxiety that imminent success engenders in them. Finally, these persons live with a strong motive to avoid failure that leads them to ensure that they remain as far from failing as their abilities allow.

Thus, our definition of success-fearing persons asserts that they have a trio of achievement-related motives: a motive to avoid failure, a motive to achieve success, and a motive to avoid success. We are in basic agreement with Horney in viewing the success-fearing person as having all three motives with a neurotic intensity that is fired largely by unconscious conflict about competition. Failure is equated with being a "loser" in an important competition and is therefore viewed with exaggerated alarm; thus the imminence of failure leads to (facilitating) anxiety and to energetic attempts to escape the failure. Success also has exaggerated importance for success-fearers, particularly since being a "winner" is the only real antidote to the humiliation of failure. At a distance, success seems to offer a solution to the painful feelings of worthlessness associated with failure and to the equally uncomfortable feelings of envy and hostility toward those who have not failed. The third motive—a motive *not* to succeed—coexists with the other two but does not come into play unless success appears to be close at hand.

In Horney's view, a person with a neurotic fear of competition [46, pp. 207-29] comes to emphasize either a fear of success or a fear of failure in the expression of his or her neurosis. The case history material she presents to illustrate the two patterns, however, frequently overlaps, and the evidence is not convincing. Our position on this point is that situational rather than personological factors largely determine which of the three motives will be dominant in the success-fearing person. Our position is perhaps best expressed in the language of Kurt Lewin, particularly in his discussion of behavior in conflict situations [62]. The responses of the person must be seen as due not only to the stable characteristics of the person but also to the characteristics of the psychological environment the person encounters at a given moment. While success-fearers have all three motives in latent form, the psychological proximity of success and/or failure regions in the life space[a] determines which motive or motives will be acti-

---

[a]Life space represents the total constellation of factors, both personal and environmental, that affects a person's thoughts, feelings, and actions at a given moment. These factors may or may not be available to the person's conscious awareness.

vated. When these persons see themselves as close to a negatively valent failure region, for example, the force exerted on them to move away from that region is stronger than when the failure region is seen as distant.

Lewin's notions about differentiation in the life space allow us to describe the person who is psychologically distant from a particular success region as viewing that region as totally positive and coordinated to his or her needs. As the person approaches the region, however, it may become differentiated in the sense that the person is increasingly "aware" (with or without consciousness of the awareness) that there are negative as well as positive consequences of entering that region. Since the rate of increase with decreasing psychological distance of the force exerted by valent regions is greater for negative than for positive valences [62,81], we are able to make the following assertions about the success-fearing person: (1) while the person is moderately distant both from success and failure, he or she will work diligently toward success; (2) as the person moves gradually closer to the success, he or she will work toward the success with increasing energy; (3) as the person begins to approach the success still more closely, he or she will become anxious and will show signs of ambivalence about success, either by changing actual behavior or by changing his or her cognitive representation of the nature of the success or his or her distance from it; (4) as the person moves away from the previously approached success region (and perhaps toward the failure region), he or she will again begin to work energetically toward the success or toward a substitute for it. Thus, if the success-fearing person sabotages a success, both his or her anxiety about success and the strength of the motive to avoid success are reduced, and the person's motive to succeed is reinstigated. If the self-sabotage leads to failure or near-failure, the person's motive to avoid failure is strongly instigated as well, and he or she will work with even greater vigor. We should note that the pattern of behavior here described is very different than the pattern of responses to success and failure encountered in persons who do not fear success. These persons are more likely to work especially hard in the presence of success and to become discouraged in the presence of apparent failure [14,28,45,59,85].

While we propose, then, a set of motives that taken together direct the behavior of success-fearing persons in achievement situations, a related set of attitudes, feelings, and behaviors can also be specified as characteristic of success-fearing persons. These characteristics are likely to arise directly from the success-fearers' unconscious conflict about competition and success and are commonly erected as defense mechanisms to help them cope with the anxiety that is aroused when they are close to success. These characteristics are more readily observable and measurable than the underlying motive structure.

Because conflicts about competition and competitive success are often focal for success-fearers, these persons are likely to demonstrate a particular preoccupation with competition and a preoccupation with evaluation. Success-fearers feel they must be constantly on the watch for situations that may contain competitive elements because such situations are the focus of their internal conflicts. At the same time, they want to be loved, admired, and respected and they lack confidence and entertain doubts about their skills and abilities; thus they are especially likely to be concerned with how others evaluate their performances. Indeed success-fearers are likely to impute competition to situations that are neutral or noncompetitive in nature, and they may feel evaluated in situations in which no evaluation is taking place.

When success-fearers are actually confronted with successful performances, or when such successes seem very likely, they often engage in a repudiation of their competence, which may be manifested in many ways. For instance, success-fearers may arbitrarily dismiss a compliment by devaluing its content or the person who gave it; they may disclaim responsibility for their successful performances by attributing good performances to factors external to themselves (such as luck) and downplaying the contribution of their own ability, effort, or motivation; or they may simply refuse to believe the evidence of their success. By derogating or denying their successes in these ways, success-fearers are psychologically divorcing themselves from the positive experience of the success in an attempt to short-circuit their anxiety.

Finally, in the event that success-fearers are forced to notice that they are close to or have unwittingly attained success, anxiety is likely to be aroused. These persons may unconsciously sabotage their current performances, perform more poorly in the future, or undermine the experience of pleasure from the success. Such self-sabotage behaviors and attenuated positive affect following success are an attempt to remove the anxiety-arousing situation altogether. They may be manifested by difficulties in concentrating, general distractability, or a feeling that one's "mind is wandering" or that it has "gone blank." As with the other characteristics, the tendency to engage in self-sabotage behavior can occur in many ways. It is a particularly important characteristic of those who fear success.

These characteristics and defense mechanisms have provided the basis for developing the various paper-and-pencil tests that we have used to identify people who fear success and that we report in the following chapters. Accepting provisionally the assumption of the clinicians that the fear of success is an unconscious neurotic problem, we chose to measure it in an indirect manner. We reasoned that if fear of success is unconscious, it would be experienced by success-fearers not as a fear of success, but rather in terms of the various defense mechanisms they might have erected to deal with it. We also assumed that people could observe and report on their self-defeating behaviors even if they were unaware of any motive to avoid succeeding. We therefore defined success-fearing persons as having the following traits:

1. A low and unstable self-esteem;
2. A preoccupation with being evaluated and with competitive implications of performance;

3. A tendency to repudiate their competence, as by citing external factors such as luck or the help of others to explain their accomplishments;
4. A tendency to become anxious in the face of impending or imminent success and to sabotage the success, usually by doing something to prevent its actual occurrence or by preventing their enjoyment of its fruits.

In our theoretical position success is broadly defined, encompassing the definitions of each of the clinical theorists described earlier. A success is any achievement in the personal, interpersonal, or academic/occupational domains which a person regards as a success. While success is thus subjectively defined by individual persons and can therefore include idiosyncratic examples, we expect that there is likely to be a large degree of consensus among people about what events constitute and portend successful attainments.

Our Perspective Regarding the Origins of Fear of Success

How, then, can we understand the development and maintenance of this set of traits in certain people? Because fear of success is multiply determined, this question must be answered on a number of different levels. The development of fear of success begins in the early childhood experiences within the family. It is given impetus by interpersonal factors in the family such as the competitiveness of parents or siblings and attempts by parent(s) to interfere in the child's movement towards independence. The existence of such contributing factors in the family serves to feed, strengthen, and make more real for the child his or her self-generated competitive fantasies.

Moreover, as Horney's contribution underscores, the understanding of a culture and its consensually shared beliefs and values is vital to a full understanding of any common neurosis. In the case of fear of success, a set of cultural beliefs and practices concerning competition, achievement, success, failure, winning, and losing helps not only to maintain the neurotic conflict about such issues once they are initiated in the family setting, but it also helps to create the family contexts within which such issues come to have overriding importance. The important concerns of a culture are usually reflected in its families and other socialization institutions. The concern—some might say obsession—of our culture with competition, then, creates a ripe breeding ground for intrapsychic conflicts about competition and success. American culture emphasizes and perpetuates in its institutions the belief that people *should* compete; that winning is good and winners have a host of highly desirable characteristics; that losing is bad and losers have many highly undesirable characteristics; and furthermore that winners are envied and may be retaliated against by losers. Most of the elements of the internal conflict of success-fearers are there. Indeed, because competition is so pervasive in American culture and most socially valued successes are gained in competitions with others, some people may come to confuse and equate any success, even the successful acquisition of competence or mastery of a skill, with competitive success. "Competition" and "success" are ideas that for success-fearers are hopelessly intertwined. The existence of a constellation of motives to achieve success, to avoid success, and to avoid failure, as exemplified in the individuals we have called success-fearers, becomes more understandable in light of the cultural context within which it is initiated and maintained.

While these ideas, culled from the theorizing of the clinicians reviewed in the first part of this chapter, provide an understanding of the origins of fear of success, they offer only partial clues about the specific nature of parent-child interactions in the families of success-fearers. The Lewinian perspective described above suggests that the socialization of success-fearing persons must strongly establish in them all three of the achievement-related motives we have discussed. The person must be taught that performing well is a very good thing, that performing poorly is very bad, and that performing well is also bad and/or dangerous to the person's welfare. Clearly these ideas can be taught in a variety of settings and in a multitude of ways.

There are two related but different lines of thinking in the clinical literature about factors that give rise to fear of success. The first line of reasoning, which focuses on a very early stage of development, sees as focal the child's separation-individuation conflicts. This view, represented primarily by Rank and Sullivan, assumes that fear of success will emerge to the extent that the developing child's efforts in the direction of achieving mastery and independence encounter negative reactions from a parent (most likely the mother). Research on the development of fear of success predicated on this perspective would presumably test the notion that the complex of conflicts represented by fear of success is associated with an *absence* of security-providing and encouraging responses surrounding the child's efforts to achieve mastery and independence— and with the *presence* of negative responses to such efforts. But what negative responses? A great many are possible, including, for example, parental anxiety, anger, criticism, dominance (overcontrol and overprotection) responses, punishment, ridicule, and parental distress (I miss you *so* much when you are away from me).

The second clinical perspective on the development of fear of success is represented by the views of Freud and Horney. This position involves the Oedipal stage of development; its more modern version assumes that fear of success is generated through competitive struggles between the child and the parents and/or between siblings. In this view, fear of success can be understood as developing from subtle or open competition between the parent and child over whether the child's desires and wishes are to be allowed expression and fulfillment or whether the parent's presumably opposing will and greater power remain in control. Thus, when the parent acts in such a way as to define conflicts between parent and child as win-lose conflicts, the child comes to feel intensely disturbed and guilty about the expression of his or her desires and about movement toward the achievement of goals. More specific to the Oedipal conflict, the battle of wills surrounds a symbolic competition between the child and the same-sex parent for the affection and exclusive possession of the other parent.

As with the conflict over separation and independence, many specific parental behaviors are potential inducers of fear of success. Among these are a tendency on the part of the parent to make explicit invidious comparisons between the child's skills and abilities and his or her own, the parent's taking over and/or interfering in the achievement-related activities initiated by the child, and some of the same parental reactions described above in connection with the separation-individuation conflict.

Our position with respect to the development of fear of success, then, must be rather vague at the outset. We have assumed that fear of success develops in early childhood as a consequence of as yet unspecified parent-child interactions. We have assumed also that the parents of success-fearers communicate to their children certain attitudes that they themselves hold with considerable intensity: to succeed is good and important, and to fail is bad. Finally, we speculate that the parents of success-fearers probably show evidence of ambivalence about their children's independence, accomplishments, or both. Whether the central instigating conflict is the conflict over the child's separation-individuation or the Oedipal conflict, the manifestations of the conflict are likely to involve competition in some form between the parent and the child over the child's achievement-related desires and performances—that is, in more general terms, competition about whether the child or the parent will be in control of the child's behaviors.

A Note about Researching Fear of Success

One of the basic assumptions of the clinical perspective we have taken is that personality dispositions, including fear of success, have their origins in (1) early parent-child interactions; (2) the child's perceptions of those early childhood experiences; and (3) the meanings the child imputes to them. Because the young child is highly dependent and vulnerable and because his capabilities for rational thinking are limited, his perceptions and interpretations of his world are often shaped by and infused with intense emotions and irrational fantasies, wishes, and fears (such as omnipotence and importance). Thus, the assumption is that certain particular behaviors and dimensions of interpersonal relations in the family come very early to have potent meanings that are highly charged with emotion for success-fearing children. More specifically, those of their behaviors that signal competence or winning will for success-fearing children come to have additional meanings: competence brings the threat of abandonment and insecurity, and success in competition indicates both a destructive action directed at a displaced winner and the possibility of jealousy-inspired retaliation from the loser(s) to the child. For the older success-fearer, then, situations like competition or opportunities for the development of independence, which on their face are not fear-producing, are instigators of the old fears and meanings learned in early childhood contexts.

A major difficulty in doing research from this clinical perspective, however, is that the intense fantasy-based interpretations of the meanings and consequences of ordinary behaviors that signal competence, success, and competition are usually unconscious and not directly observable or reportable to investigators. While psychoanalysts and other psychotherapists have ways of diagnosing and inferring these fantasies and covert beliefs in individual patients within the therapeutic process, and even have means of treating them, these procedures are generally limited to one-to-one intensive interaction over a long period of time and thus are of little help to the ordinary psychological researcher whose interest is in the phenomenon as exhibited by groups of persons rather than in the unique personality configurations of a single person. The problem of studying fear of success among many people is quite different from the problem of treating one person who may, among his or her other problems, fear success.

The approach that we have taken to this problem is to focus on the categories of behaviors and situational contexts that are presumed to have different meanings for success-fearers and those who do not fear success. As researchers we have no direct access to a person's early childhood experiences and his childhood interpretations of those events. We are, therefore, limited in our investigations to looking at people's contemporary responses to contemporary situations and stimuli whose characteristics we can observe and influence experimentally. The situations and contexts in the here and now in which we can study fear of success seem mundane in comparison to the rich and complex childhood origins that, alas, are distant, ethereal, and difficult to pinpoint exactly. Nevertheless, the fear of success is an important phenomenon because adults who manifest it are doing so in just those mundane everyday contexts we are able to look at—those that exist long after the circumstances originally responsible for the development of the fear of success no longer exist or are no longer relevant. The assumption here is that personality dispositions, although learned early and in specific contexts, generalize to other situations and people that stimulate the early-learned perceptions. Feelings of competence, independence, success, and rivalry are frequently provoked. A child who learned to fear wiggling his small toe because it meant something hostile and provoked great parental anger and fear of punishment would probably not encounter situations in later life in which he was required or motivated to wiggle his small toe, and would therefore probably not have toe-wiggling neuroses of much importance or consequence; he can stop wiggling his toes at any time without incurring cost or notoriety or interpersonal difficulty. By contrast, the child who learned early on to become anxious in performance or competitive situations or when independence and task mastery were at issue for him would have a very difficult time indeed. For such a person to participate fully in this culture and to avoid such situations would be almost impossible.

As experimental psychologists investigating this personality disposition, then, we not only use somewhat different methods of inquiry than our clinical-practitioner colleagues, but we also ask somewhat different questions. Rather than seeking to understand the unique and particular contributing circumstances of each person's life history, we focus our investigations on searching for general principles that are applicable to large numbers of people who suffer from fear-of-success problems. While we necessarily lose an understanding of the unique richness and complexity of each person's idiosyncratic experience, we gain a better understanding of how success-fearing persons are similar. The questions we design our research to answer are focused on such issues as: What are the consequences of fearing success? How are people with fear-of-success problems likely to think about and feel about their experiences in achievement situations? How are they likely to act? When, or under what conditions, are such consequences most likely to occur? Do they always happen or are some situations more likely to intensify them, or diminish them, or even alleviate them altogether? How do success-fearers respond to the different situations in which they perform? What other traits and characteristics are most likely to be associated with fear of success?

Research Techniques. In order to answer these questions we have used two different research techniques that have generally been referred to as laboratory experiments and correlational studies. Regardless of the techniques we have used in a given study, the research has always been informed by our theory. In other words, we have used the theoretical ideas discussed above to help us frame our research questions and to point us in specific directions in predicting answers to our questions. The results of the research have then enabled us to confirm or disconfirm the predictions made from the theory and have also allowed us continually to expand our theoretical understanding of fear of success.

In our search for general principles regarding the instigation and manifestation of fear of success, many success-fearing persons have served as subjects in our studies. Conducting this research first required the ability to identify relatively quickly, without the aid of intensive clinical interviews, persons who fear success. Thus, the first step in the program of research has been to develop measures that can be easily administered to large numbers of people and that will identify for us those people who fear success and those who do not. In chapter 2 and 3 we report in greater detail two such questionnaires that have been developed for use with adults: one was developed by Dr. Marice Pappo, and the other by Dr. Nina Cohen. In chapter 5 we discuss a scale we have developed to identify children who fear success. In each of those chapters we describe how we went about constructing the measures and validating them.

Armed with a suitable way of identifying success-fearing persons, we have then formulated specific questions and proceeded to gather information relevant to answering them. Our basic procedure was as follows: The fear-of-success scale was administered to relatively large groups of people. On the basis of their scores on the questionnaire, people were selected to participate in our studies. A group of people who scored high on the scale (people who fear success) were selected, and their reactions to the situations created in the studies were compared to those of another group of people who scored low on the scale (people who do not fear success). All our studies included both men and women participants in order to determine whether any important differences exist between the sexes in either the incidence of fear of success or in its manifestations. To date we have found very few.

In the laboratory experiments, a number of different experimental conditions have been created. People selected to participate are randomly assigned to participate in only one of the conditions. For example, some people may be told they succeeded at a task, while others may be told they performed only at an average level or even that they failed; or some people may succeed only after gradually improving their performances on a task, while others never improve their performances; or some people may succeed at a task when they are competing against someone of the same sex, while others succeed at the task when they are competing against someone of the opposite sex. By randomly assigning individual participants to the different experimental conditions we can be confident that when we average the data over all participants in a condition, we are detecting behaviors that are due to the condition we are trying to study and not to extraneous factors. Experimental research is useful because it allows us to study precisely the conditions we are interested in and to make inferences about cause and effect; the experimental conditions are assumed to cause the various responses we observe. We have used the experiments primarily to investigate the conditions that arouse fear-of-success responses and to find out how success-fearers respond to particular situations.

Conducting the correlational studies has been somewhat different because all of the information—both the person's responses to the fear-of-success questionnaires and the other information in which we are interested—can be collected from respondents at the same time. While this information does not enable us to make clear statements about the causal relationships between fear of success and the other responses of interest to us, it does give us a fuller understanding of a wide range of characteristics that people who fear success possess and helps us determine the ways success-fearers react in naturally occurring situations. In Part II, to which we now turn, we report a series of laboratory and correlational studies designed to investigate more specifically the issues outlined in this chapter.

Notes

1. A large research literature has been accumulating during the past few years on what has been termed the "feminine fear of success" [43,60,110,111, 122]. This line of work is, by and large, unrelated to the point of view we have taken in this book and to the research reported herein. It is discussed in chapter 7.

2. Henry Murray [84] in "American Icarus" describes a neurotic psychological complex that bears some superficial resemblance to fear of success. The Icarus complex, like fear of success, involves a major investment of attention on the glories of success as well as on the despicability of failure and obscurity. Differing from fear of success, the Icarus complex develops at a much earlier time (the urethral-phallic stage) and vitiates the emotional maturation to the stage of forming lasting attachments to people that is characteristic of the Oedipal stage of development. As a result of their lesser emotional development, people who have Icarus complexes are attracted to the idea of stellar successes but do not have the emotional ability to sustain the day-to-day drudgery necessary to accomplish a long-term success of even substellar proportions; they often compensate their realistic lack of accomplishment with grand and frequently supernatural and infantile fantasies of rising magically to positions of great importance, power, and attention. The guilt and ambivalence about success, which are fundamental to the concept of fear of success, are absent in the Icarus complex. Success-fearing persons are distraught and guilty when they succeed partly because they equate the success with something forbidden but also because they see themselves as actively causing the successes. Persons characterized by an Icarus complex, on the other hand, are neither guilty nor ambivalent about success, which they see as extraordinary good fortune that sometimes happens to people.

3. Otto Rank [91,92] was perhaps the first psychoanalyst to describe the separation-individuation process as a central conflict in human development. Beginning with the traumatic separation of the infant from its mother in the birth process, Rank sees human development as a succession of events in which the person achieves increased individuality through the painful process of separation from former states and relationships. Growth involves change and change involves separation; separation is always seen as at least partly painful. Like Freud's notion of the Oedipus conflict, Rank saw the anxiety consequent upon separation as endemic to human nature. He observed, however, that people tend to project and externalize their fear of separation; thus separation is usually experienced as caused by external events. Rank used the birth trauma as a metaphor for the earliest prototype of the separation anxiety, which is experienced in later separations. The separations people usually experience as frightening are prosaic life events (such as beginning school, or getting married) and gradual "invisible" processes like becoming a psychologically separate and

independent person. While the fear of separation and therefore the fear of change constitutes one side of the conflict which Rank called "fear of life," the person's natural growth and maturation tendencies, when stifled, produce another side of this core human dilemma, "fear of death," which represents the loss of growth and the loss of individuality and creativity that occurs when people feel in close union with others. Thus, lack of change and development and maintaining the status quo raises fear of death. The dilemma of living, then, is resolving the conflict between fear of life and fear of death, or minimizing the cost of separation while maximizing the rewards of individuation.

While Rank saw the separation-individuation process as an anxiety-arousing conflict that is basic to human nature and thus internal to the person, his position would agree with the major point of this section: if in reality the parents of young children actually withdraw security and punish independence and growth, the separation-individuation conflict becomes acutely intensified. This statement, that early interpersonal relations determine later personality development in the arenas of security and independence, is the cornerstone of Harry Stack Sullivan's writings on human personality.

4. Otto Fenichel [29], for example, is specific in making the point that depending on the particulars of the person's childhood history, several kinds of conflicts may underlie the neurotic performance inhibitions characteristic of fear of success. For instance, he distinguishes between conflicts surrounding dependence and independence, since success is often seen as the road to independence, and conflicts surrounding rebellion and obedience to authority, since becoming successful is frequently seen as a demanded duty rather than a personal pleasure.

5. The case histories cited by many clinical writers [86,102] suggest that the early lives of success-fearers are in fact populated by domineering, competitive, hostile, self-centered parents who give little support and security to their children. Warner [116] notes almost with astonishment that the cruelest parents seem to manage the strongest hold on their children thereby making the child's true separation and independence almost impossible.

6. We have not included herein a comprehensive history of the idea that some people find success uncomfortable. Interested readers are referred to the recent work of Tresemer [111] for additional information about other scholars and writers who have recognized aspects of the phenomenon.

Part II:
Empirical Investigations

Introduction to Part II

The research described in Part II was designed to provide empirical evidence that (1) varying degrees of fear of success could be identified in persons; (2) that success-fearers tend to sabotage their performances when success is close at hand; (3) that success-fearers sabotage burgeoning task mastery or personal competence even when "success" is not clearly defined; (4) that success-fearers have a motive to avoid failure, which leads to improved task performance following failure, and that the sabotage of success leads to a compensatory increment in general motivation to succeed; (5) that fear of success is evident in social as well as purely academic or vocational endeavors; (6) that the consequences of fear of success are observable in field settings; and (7) that fear of success can be measured in children as young as eight or nine years and also that children who score high on the fear-of-success questionnaire sabotage their success.

In chapter 2 we describe the dissertation study of Dr. Marice Pappo, which provided us with the first measure of fear of success. Pappo's theoretical perspective was based on the ideas of Harry Stack Sullivan, and her notions about the development of fear of success differ somewhat from our own. For Pappo, the crucial factor in the development of fear of success is an interference by the parent—usually the mother—in the child's attempts at growth or independence. Although her ideas about the origins of fear-of-success problems differ from our own, the characteristics of success-fearing persons and the predicted consequences of fear of success are very similar in the two schemes. In chapter 2 we also present another study designed to explore the consequences for success-fearing persons of gradually developing mastery of a task.

In chapter 3 we turn to the neo-Freudian perspective that guided the dissertation study of Dr. Nina Cohen. For Cohen, competition arising from the Oedipal conflict is a focal issue in the development of fear of success. She developed an alternative questionnaire to identify success-fearers and conducted an experiment to test her prediction that success-fearers are more disturbed when they are successfully competing with someone of the same sex than with someone of the opposite sex.

In chapter 4 we report an experiment designed to show that success-fearers sabotage their successful performances in situations other than truly academic ones. This study also helps us understand how success-fearers react to failure experiences. In chapter 5 we demonstrate that fear of success can be identified in children of elementary school age and show that success-fearing children react in a similar way to success as do the adolescents and college students of the previous studies. Finally, in chapter 6 we present a variety of data about how success-fearing college students think, feel, and act in everyday situations.

2 Identifying Success-Fearers and Predicting Their Behavior

In this chapter we shall describe in detail the methods we have used to construct the measures of the neurotic fear of success that are presented in this book. We shall also discuss two preliminary pieces of research designed to validate the first measure and to investigate in detail and under controlled conditions the various manifestations of fear of success.

The instrument to identify persons who fear success described in this chapter was developed and validated by Marice Pappo [87] as her doctoral dissertation. This germinal work, which long before it was completed stimulated our interest in the neurotic fear of success, forms the basis of the first part of this chapter. Dr. Pappo proceeded in the following way. Drawing upon her knowledge of clinical theory and her observations of acquaintances and clients, she constructed a list of characteristics that persons who fear success would be expected to have. The list included certain early experiences, certain ideas and feelings about oneself and other people, various activity preferences, particular emotional reactions to certain kinds of situations, and so on. Pappo then used this list to construct a large number of statements that people could either agree or disagree with. If a large number of people read the statements and either agreed or disagreed with each one, those who answered in a predetermined way could be presumed to suffer from the neurotic fear of success, since they would report having the characteristics of success-fearers described by Pappo's theory. By sheer chance alone, however, some people without a success-fearing problem might be likely to answer the questionnaire just as success-fearers would be expected to answer it. People differ in a great many respects. Just how do we know that the scale Pappo devised really picks out people who have fear-of-success problems? Furthermore, do these persons actually manifest the pattern of concerns, feelings, thoughts, and behaviors that are supposedly characteristic of success-fearers? These are the primary questions we address in this chapter.

In order to show how Dr. Pappo constructed her measure of the fear of success and how she investigated it in the laboratory, we must detail her thinking about how fear of success develops. Her ideas about the origins of fear of success are, with minor modifications, summarized in the next section.

Origins of the Fear of Success: The Role of Competence and Independence Strivings

In Pappo's thinking about why some people develop fear of success and others do not, she drew much from the work of Harry Stack Sullivan which we discussed briefly in chapter 1. Like Sullivan [106] and R.W. White [117], Pappo assumed that people are *innately* motivated to strive toward competence, growth, and mastery of their worlds and that this motivation directs them from the time they are born. Fear of success, in Pappo's view, develops when this natural motivation meets with interference from a parent or someone acting in the role of parent. The central process contributing to the development of fear of success in this perspective is the transmission of anxiety to the child by the parent (usually the mother) when the child appears to that parent to be gaining skills and independence. Because this process begins when the child is very young (before he clearly knows the difference between himself and his parents), the child experiences the parent's anxiety as his own. Needless to say, this anxiety is extremely unpleasant. Consequently, the child hits upon ways that enable him to cope with the anxiety and the situation in which it is evoked, so that he can continue to strive for competence and independence. These solutions are gradually elaborated into defense mechanisms that form the constellation of thoughts, feelings, and behaviors characterizing persons who fear success. Let us look more closely at the process we have just sketched.

A child's growth toward independence, as signalled by mastery or excellence in performance, represents an emotionally charged and threatening situation for some parents that leads them to experience anxiety. Why should this be so? Occasionally, the source of the parent's anxiety may be realistic. For example, the parent may sense real environmental dangers for the child, such as the dangers presented by sharp knives or a hot stove if the child plays in the kitchen, or later the dangers presented by automobiles if the child crosses the street. The source of the anxiety, however, need not be realistic or even fully understood by the parent, and probably most frequently the case is that it is neither understood nor realistic. For instance, the parent's difficulty with the child's progress toward independence or skill mastery could arise from neurotic sources of which the parent is not consciously aware. For example, the parent's own fear of success, the parent's fear that the child will exceed his or her own achievement level, or the parent's need to keep the child dependent could all form the basis for anxiety reactions in the parent. The parent might rationalize this neurotically based anxiety by assuming that the child is in some real danger and is in need of protection for his own well-being.

Regardless of the origin of the parent's anxiety and whether or not it is conscious, that anxiety is immediately and unavoidably communicated to the child. The child, who is totally dependent upon the parent and is acutely sensitive to the parent's positive and negative feelings, senses when the parent is upset, angry, or anxious and becomes discomfitted, insecure, and anxious himself. In an effort to overcome this distress, the child attempts to restore the secure comfortable state that existed before the onset of his parent's anxiety. The child's association between his activities and the onset of the anxiety leads him to see the anxiety-provoking activities as dangerous or forbidden.

As a result of the parent's anxious reaction to the child's performance of certain tasks, the child tries hard to distinguish between behaviors that are allowed (because they do not make the parent anxious) and behaviors that are not all right (because they do make the parent anxious). By so doing, the child can try to avoid the anxiety-provoking behaviors altogether. If for some reason, such avoidance is not possible (which is often the case), he may minimize his anxiety through the use of neurotic defense mechanisms while he continues to perform the "dangerous" behaviors. The experience of anxiety when the child nears successful completion of such a task not only interferes with his enjoyment of the task but also causes him to function less well, thereby decreasing the likelihood of success. We must remember here that the child wants to grow despite these psychological obstacles, and the inherent motivation to strive for competence remains.

Frequently, the particular areas of competence development that lead to anxiety responses on the part of the parent are especially important because they are highly valued by the culture. Consequently, the child may come to need or want to gain competence in precisely those areas despite his internalized prohibition against them. In order to do so, the child will invent substitute motivations for participating in the activity. For example, he may become intensely preoccupied with possible secondary gains such as positive evaluations from others, prestige, heightened importance of his standing among peers, or he will become preoccupied with the avoidance of possible losses. The child may convince himself that he engages in the (prohibited) activity not because he likes it or wants to, but because of externally constraining circumstances: he doesn't want to lose face, his participation will please important others, he stands to win a lot by participating or lose a lot by not participating, and so forth. These may all become a person's "reasons" for engaging in psychologically forbidden activities. For Pappo, a preoccupation with competition and a preoccupation with evaluation are defense mechanisms erected by a success-fearer to deflect his or her attention away from the focal concern of the conflict—that is, gaining mastery.

The point is that the success-fearer is able to continue doing a forbidden activity, but the intrinsic pleasure derived from competence in that area is undermined. The success-fearing child's neurotic defenses enable him to partici-pate in the most important areas of living, since they reduce the anxiety likely to be aroused by the performance of parentally disapproved tasks and activities. The reduction of anxiety allows him to participate without noticing that he is, in fact, involved in a situation that is potentially dangerous to him because of its ability to arouse anxiety. Thus, the success-fearer participates in prohibited activities by shifting his attention *away* from both the intrinsic pleasure of the task (which was originally interrupted by anxiety and thus functions to signal its approach), and from the personal significance of his success outcome, and *toward* a preoccupation with other possible gains such as winning or evaluation.

These compensatory gains might well appear to the observer as a goal orientation or positive source of motivation, since they tend to be highly valued in American society. We hasten to add that concern with winning, competition, or evaluation is not necessarily neurotic. Such motives, however, are often used in the service of neurotic defenses against the anxiety of performing an internally prohibited action. Thus, when concern about these issues is used as a substitute for pleasure in the act of becoming competent, it can be considered a neurotic defense mechanism.

When persons who fear success are confronted by external evidence that they are in fact achieving success in a prohibited area—evidence that has not been disguised successfully by their defense mechanisms—they are forced to notice that they are involved in forbidden activities. This realization arouses anxiety. The intrusion of this anxiety adversely affects their functioning and leads them not only to function less well, but also to want to avoid the activities or the success outcomes. If under such conditions the success-fearing persons' defense mechanisms were functioning effectively, they would be able to maneuver themselves away from the knowledge that they were approaching or had attained success in a prohibited area (as, for example, by repudiating or denying their competence). When such defenses do not work adequately to minimize these persons' anxiety, they may unconsciously act in such a way as to interfere with or sabotage their success. This self-sabotage presumably provides some relief from the anxiety.

The child, by internalizing what he thinks is and is not acceptable to the parent and incorporating these ideas as his own unconsciously held standards, can begin to provide himself with security devices that will steer him away from what is parentally disapproved of and consequently away from what arouses anxiety in himself. In this way, activities that the child believes are forbidden remain prohibited for the adult. The success-fearing child, then, grows into the success-fearing adult.

From this account of the development of the fear of success, Pappo inferred that success-fearing persons will have certain general characteristics: a preoccupation with evaluation and competition, a tendency to repudiate their competence, self-doubt and negative self-evaluation, and self-sabotage behavior when success is imminent.

A Measure of Fear of Success

After thinking through how fear of success might develop and the characteristics that success-fearers should theoretically be expected to have, Pappo's next step was to develop a questionnaire that could be administered to large numbers of people. It would distinguish those people who fear success from those who do not and thus enable their responses to particular situations to be studied

43

specifically and thoroughly. If the people the questionnaire identified as success-fearers actually behave as success-fearers would be predicted to behave *and* if they behave differently from people who do not fear success, then we can be confident that the questionnaire is *valid*—that is, it measures fear of success as it was intended to.

Because anxiety interference is the major dynamic in Pappo's view of the origin of fear of success, she assumed that fear of success develops only around those particular areas in which the parents communicate their anxiety to the child. Thus, the success-fearer's defense mechanisms are not thought to be general responses to potential success in any and every activity in which the person may participate, but only in specific spheres of activity. The questionnaire that Pappo developed was intended specifically to identify persons who fear success in academic situations.

In order to develop the fear-of-success questionnaire, statements were constructed specifically to elicit information about the attitudes, behaviors, and emotional reactions of persons who fear success as discussed above. In addition to the criterion that the content of the items be directly derived from the conceptual framework, two other criteria were kept in mind for the items: (1) that they elicit the person's reaction to specifically described situations and (2) that they avoid stereotypic sex-role activities such as housekeeping or football. The final version of Pappo's scale contains eighty-three self-report items in a "yes-no" format.[1] Each respondent either agrees ("yes") with an item as characteristic of his behavior or beliefs or disagrees ("no") with the item, thereby indicating that it is not characteristic of his behavior or beliefs.

On the basis of a factor analysis (a statistical technique that indicates which items cluster together in the way people answer them), six factors were identified that roughly correspond to the defining characteristics of the success-fearing person. These factors are listed below, together with sample items from each to help give a flavor for the experience of success-fearers. The answer shown in parentheses is the one that is scored as indicative of fear of success. A copy of the full scale can be found in the appendix to this volume.

Factor 1: Negative Affective Reaction to Success Cues

If someone calls attention to me when I'm doing well, I often feel awkward. (Yes)

Often times, I become self-conscious when someone who "counts" compliments me. (Yes)

Factor 2: Repudiation of Competence or Motivation

Persuasive people can influence my ideas. (Yes)

I often get very excited when I start a project, but I get bored with it quickly. (Yes)

Factor 3: Sabotage of Success

When playing competitive games, I make more mistakes near the end than at the beginning. (Yes)

As a game (card game, word game, chess, competitive sports, etc.) reaches the winning point, I start thinking about other things. (Yes)

Factor 4: Preoccupation with Evaluation and Competition

I try the hardest when my work is being evaluated. (Yes)

While I'm learning something completely new, I find praise necessary. (Yes)

Factor 5: Self-Doubt and Negative Self-Evaluation

Even though I feel I have a lot of potential, I sometimes feel like a phoney or a fraud. (Yes)

There are times when I don't think I have what it takes to be a success in the area I am interested in. (Yes)

Factor 6: Distractability and Impairment of Concentration

It is easy to become distracted while taking a test. (Yes)

Frequently at crucial points in intellectual discussions my mind goes blank. (Yes)

While the scale is not ideally balanced (so that half the items are scored as indicating fear of success if the respondent agrees and half if the respondent disagrees), many of the items in the full scale are scored as indicating fear of success if the respondent disagress with them.

The distributions of scores on this scale for samples of male and female college students were practically identical, with no significant differences between the average score for men and that for women. For Pappo's original sample of 286 respondents, the mean scale score was 37.3 with a standard deviation of 12.4. The mean score for the 115 males in this sample was 38.5 with a standard deviation of 13.3; for the 170 females, the mean score was 36.8 with a standard deviation of 11.6. This indicates that there are no important differences in the way men and women answer this questionnaire. In other words, fear of success is as likely to occur in men as it is in women. (In fact, in several moderately large samples we have tested, we have never found a significant difference between the mean scores of men and women on this scale.) The reliability of the final 83-item scale was estimated at .89 by means of Kuder-Richardson Formula 20 using the previously mentioned sample of 286 male and female college students.

Concurrent Validity

One way of establishing whether or not a personality scale is valid—measures what it is supposed to measure—is to demonstrate that it is correlated in a predictable way with some other variables or measures, such as a behavioral indicator or another paper-and-pencil personality test. The term *concurrent validity* has generally been used when measures on both sets of variables are obtained at the same point in time, or concurrently [18]. Concurrent validity was assessed for the Pappo fear-of-success scale by correlating it with scores on three other well-known personality tests that measure traits relevant to the characteristics of success-fearers.

We suggested that since success-fearers are likely to deny, downplay, or repudiate their competence, they might be expected to attribute their successes to factors external to themselves. The Internal-External Scale developed by Rotter [96] measures people's general expectations of the extent to which they control their own outcomes and their own fates. People who believe the outcomes they receive are primarily determined by their own actions and who perceive they can determine the course and nature of their lives are termed *internals*, while those who believe their lives and important outcomes are primarily determined by forces outside themselves (chance, fate, other people, and so forth) are termed *externals*. As expected, persons who fear success are somewhat more likely to score as *externals* on this scale.

Additionally, since level of self-esteem in the form of negative self-evaluation and self-doubt is a core characteristic of the fear-of-success syndrome, it was predicted that success-fearers would have more negative self-esteem as measured by the Rosenberg Self-Esteem Scale [95] than would non-success-fearers, which in fact they do.

Finally, since anxiety is presumed to interfere with the performances of success-fearers when they are nearing success, success-fearers should be more likely than non-success-fearers to score high on an anxiety measure. The Debilitating Anxiety Scale of Alpert and Haber [1] was originally developed to identify persons who are debilitated by anxiety in academic testing situations. Although this test has sometimes been construed as a measure of fear of failure, an inspection of the items reveals strong parallels with the conceptualization of fear of success. This suggests that the scale is probably tapping anxiety due to fear of failure as well as fear of success. As might be expected, then, people who fear success are also more likely to express anxiety on this scale.[2]

This information, then, lends validity to Pappo's fear-of-success scale. It does not, however, indicate anything more than that the scale is useful in predicting how people will respond to other self-report questionnaires. Demonstrating that persons who respond differently on the scale do behave in different ways when success is imminent is therefore necessary. This behavioral validation was accomplished in a laboratory experiment to which we turn in the next section.

A Validation Experiment: Do Success-Fearers Self-Sabotage?

Pappo's theory leads to the interesting prediction that men and women who fear success will sabotage their performances when they are confronted with information that success is imminent. In order to test this prediction, Pappo conducted an experiment in which college students participated; half of the participants were males, half were females, and half of each of these groups were success-fearers while half were not. The experiment was designed to compare the reactions of each of these four subgroups of people when they do very well on a task—the "success" condition—with their reactions when they do only moderately well on a task—the "average" condition. Participants completed two equivalent parts of a reading comprehension test, and their performances on each of these two parts were compared. The crucial element in this study, however, was that before they began the second part, students assigned to the *success* condition were told they had done very well on the first part, while those assigned to the *average* condition were informed they had done about average on the first part. If self-sabotage occurs, we would expect it to show up as a poorer performance on the second part of the test relative to the first part because only after receiving their feedback do subjects know how close they are to success. Because we would expect that only people who fear success will self-sabotage, and even those only when they are close to success, poorer reading scores should occur on the second part of the test only for success-fearing subjects in the *success* condition, and this result should be true for both males and females. Everyone else—including success-fearers who perform at an average level on the first part—should do as well or better on the second part. The experimental procedure is discussed more fully below for interested readers.

Experimental Procedures

College student volunteers from a state university were recruited to participate in the validation study, which was billed as a study on "Expectation Formation and Predicting Strategies." All participants had previously completed the fear-of-success scale and were selected on the basis of their scores on it. Those who obtained a score at least one standard deviation above the established mean (mean = 37; standard deviation = 12) were identified as success-fearers, while those who obtained a score at least one standard deviation below the mean were designated as non-success-fearers. The eighty-nine students who participated in this study were equally distributed among the four subgroups described earlier, and they were randomly assigned to the two experimental conditions.

Each student participated individually. The female experimenter explained that she was interested in "studying the way people develop expectations." In order to do so, each person would be required to read a series of four short passages and answer comprehension questions on each passage. Before the person answered the comprehension questions on each passage, he or she would make a prediction about how many questions of the total twenty in the entire series he or she would answer correctly. Participants were told that they would be given two series of passages; the first set of four passages was described as a practice series meant to provide them with information on which to base their predictions for the "actual" test that was to follow.

After the student completed the first set of four passages, the experimenter scored the number of comprehension questions answered correctly and gave the student the predetermined feedback about his reading comprehension performance. The experimental conditions were created by using tables of fictitious group norms. For students in the *success* condition, the experimenter said, "You've done as well or better than 90 percent of the people who have taken this test. That's a really good score." For those in the *average* condition, the experimenter said, "You've done as well or better than 75 percent of the people who have taken this test. I'd say that's about average." Participants then completed a comparable set of four additional reading comprehension passages and a final questionnaire designed to ascertain their attitudes and feelings during the experimental session. After completing the questionnaire, participants were "debriefed" and the nature of the experiment was discussed with them. (The reader is referred to Pappo [87, pp. 25-29] for a more detailed discussion of these procedures and a transcript of the experimental instructions.)

Results

The results of this experiment consistently supported the hypotheses derived from the theory and therefore give us additional confidence in the validity of the fear-of-success scale. Moreover, they indicate that success-fearers do possess the characteristics we discussed earlier. Because it was important to be sure that participants who received *success* feedback actually thought their performances were more successful than those who received *average* feedback, participants were asked on the final questionnaire to evaluate how well they had done on the first series of reading passages. Not surprisingly, students in the *success* conditions did indeed believe their performances on the first part were significantly more favorable than students in the *average* conditions.[3]

Self-Sabotage Behavior. One of the most striking ramifications of the fear of success is self-sabotage behavior. As we stated above, success-fearers who received success feedback on the first set of reading passages were expected to become anxious and consequently sabotage their performance and do less well on the second part. Subjects who do not fear success were not expected to show such performance decrements after success feedback, nor were the subjects who received average feedback expected to self-sabotage (neither the success-fearers nor the non-success-fearers).

Results were exactly in line with these predictions. Both male and female success-fearers who received *success* feedback demonstrated performance sabotage by doing less well on the second reading test. The three remaining groups—success-fearers who received average feedback, the non-success-fearers who received success feedback, and the non-success-fearers who received average feedback—actually did *better* on the second part than they had on the first part. The mean number of questions answered correctly for each of the four subgroups on both Part 1 and Part 2 are presented in table 2-1. Negative difference scores indicate a poorer performance on the second part, while positive difference scores indicate an improved performance on the second part. The answer to our question, then, is: "Yes, success fearers do self-sabotage, but only when they are very close to success."

Anxiety. Responses to several questionnaire items indicated that self-sabotage is indeed accompanied by anxiety and emotional reactions that would inhibit the

Table 2-1
Reading Scores

Group	Part I Score		Part II Score		Difference Score (Part II-Part I)
	Mean	(s.d.)	Mean	(s.d.)	
Success Condition					
Success-Fearers					
Male (*n* = 11)	14.3	(3.3)	12.8	(2.6)	−1.5
Female (*n* = 11)	13.9	(2.7)	12.7	(3.0)	−1.2
Non-Success-Fearers					
Male (*n* = 11)	13.5	(2.7)	14.8	(2.1)	+1.3
Female (*n* = 11)	13.1	(2.6)	14.1	(2.7)	+1.0
Average Condition					
Success-Fearers					
Male (*n* = 11)	12.0	(2.8)	13.3	(3.4)	+1.3
Female (*n* = 11)	14.0	(2.1)	15.3	(2.8)	+1.3
Non-Success-Fearers					
Male (*n* = 11)	12.5	(3.0)	14.1	(3.3)	+1.6
Female (*n* = 12)	13.8	(3.0)	14.9	(3.1)	+1.1

Source: This table has been adapted from data presented in Pappo [87].

Note: A repeated measures analysis of variance using test scores as the repeated factor indicated a significant fear of success category x experimental treatment x test score interaction (F = 5.831, p <.025). No significant sex differences emerged nor were there significant differences among 'he groups for Part I score.

ability of success-fearers to perform well. Success-fearers who received success feedback reported that they felt under more stress and tension by knowing their scores on Part 1 than participants in the other groups, and they also reported having had considerably more difficulty concentrating on Part 2 than persons in the other groups. Inspection of the group means presented in table 2-2 (lines A1 and A2) clearly indicates that success-fearers and non-success-fearers had strikingly different anxiety responses to success feedback, whereas little difference existed between them in their reactions to the average feedback.

Self-Doubt and Repudiation of Competence. Self-doubt and negative self-evaluation were also theorized to be important characteristics of the fear-of-success profile. Persons who feel threatened by success, then, are likely to feel unsure of themselves and to lack confidence in their intellectual abilities. Reflecting this tendency, success-fearers reported on the questionnaire that they felt significantly less sure of themselves than non-success-fearers. Their tendency towards feelings of inadequacy was also reflected in their lower estimations of how many questions they thought they could answer correctly. Recall that before subjects answered the reading comprehension questions, they predicted how many answers they would get right. Success-fearers underestimated their Part 1 score to a greater extent than non-success-fearers. In addition, on their last prediction for Part 2, success-fearers thought they would get significantly fewer questions right than did the non-success-fearers.

To further test whether success-fearers repudiate their competence, participants were asked to account for their reading scores on the first part by assigning a percentage value indicating the extent to which one or more of the following factors were responsible for the score: chance, mood, error in scoring, ability, and "other factors." As anticipated, success-fearers perceived their ability as less responsible and the other factors as more responsible for their score than the non-success-fearers. Success-fearers, then, appear to avoid taking responsibility for their own successful performances by downplaying the importance of their competence (see table 2-2, lines B1, B2, and B3).

Preoccupation with Evaluation and Competition. Success-fearing persons are also thought to be preoccupied with evaluative aspects of performance situations. Although their preoccupation with how well they are doing may be interpreted as desiring to succeed, it was suggested that this preoccupation serves as a defense mechanism that enables success-fearers to participate, at least to some extent, in prohibited activities. Consistent with this idea, success-fearing subjects reported after the experiment that they were more concerned about how many items they got right, that they felt more uncomfortable about predicting their scores, and that they felt it was more important to do well. All of these attitudes reflect a greater concern about the evaluative or judgmental aspects of the experimental situation. Not only are success-fearers concerned with evaluation, but they are also likely to be preoccupied with competition.

Table 2-2
Mean Reactions to the Performance Situation

Dimension	Success-Fearers (A)(B) Success	Success-Fearers Average	Non-Success-Fearers Success	Non-Success-Fearers Average	F_A	F_B	F_{AB}	MS_e
A. Anxiety Interference								
1. Response to feedback (higher numbers indicate under more stress and tension)[a]	37.3	25.1	21.8	24.4	8.12*	2.81	6.82*	134.1
2. Concentration on Part 2 (higher numbers indicate greater difficulty concentrating)[a]	35.4	26.3	20.4	22.0	12.21***	1.25	4.09*	137.43
B. Self-Doubt–Competence Derogation								
1. Self-assurance (higher numbers indicate less self-assurance)[a]	31.2	30.4	19.5	23.1	24.62***	0.52	1.26	82.57
2. Final prediction of Part II score (highest possible is 20)	14.0	13.4	15.2	14.9	5.13*	0.61	0.06	7.14
3. Responsibility attributable to ability (percents)	48.8%	48.1%	63.1%	64.4%	17.99***	0.91	0.67	504.07
C. Concern with Evaluation and Competition								
1. Importance of doing well (higher numbers indicate greater importance)[a]	45.0	42.9	37.9	37.2	7.56**	0.37	0.08	121.02
2. Concern about others' performances (higher numbers indicate greater concern)[a]	36.5	29.6	23.9	20.9	7.08**	1.54	0.23	262.66

Source: This table was adapted from data presented in Pappo [87]. Some of the scales have been reversed to facilitate consistent interpretation.

*$p < .05$
**$p < .01$
***$p < .001$

[a]Ratings were made on 61-point dotted rating scales.

Such a competitive orientation was revealed by the success-fearers who expressed greater concern than the non-success-fearers with how other people might have performed on this task. An interesting speculation is that such a concern may reflect a more deep-seated concern with judging whether or not the person has won or lost the fantasied competition (see table 2-2, lines C1 and C2).

Further Evidence

The results of the Pappo experiment provide clear validation of the scale she developed to measure fear of success. The self-sabotage behavior said to be a characteristic defense of success-fearers emerged as predicted—that is, when success-fearers were confronted with success. In addition, success-fearing participants showed evidence in the experiment of the constellation of thoughts, feelings, and attitudes that theoretically characterize such persons. They not only reported feeling more anxious and stressed in this situation, but also feeling less sure of themselves and their abilities, and they seemed to be more competitively oriented and more worried about how they would be evaluated.

As with all good pieces of research, Pappo's work not only sheds light on some critical questions about the existence and manifestations of fear of success, but it also raises additional questions. In order to test her theory, Pappo needed to give the fear-of-success syndrome as great an opportunity to emerge as possible; thus, her experimental procedure was carefully and meticulously constructed. She did not want success-fearers to become overly anxious at the very beginning of the experiment. Such initial anxiety could conceivably interfere with their performances on Part 1 and lessen the likelihood they would do even worse on Part 2. Therefore, Pappo camouflaged the importance of the reading comprehension skills involved in the task by her apparent emphasis on "predicting strategies and how people develop personal expectations." Only after Part 1 when subjects received feedback (which dealt only with how many reading comprehension questions they had answered correctly and not at all with how accurate their predictions had been) were they likely to realize that reading comprehension abilities and not prediction were really at stake.

We wondered how important this surprise component was in eliciting the self-sabotage response. If a necessary requirement is that a success experience be totally unexpected in order to engage success-avoiding defense mechanisms, then perhaps the performances of success-fearers are not adversely affected in everyday life situations. After all, people usually understand the implications of their performances before they begin a task, and they are not so likely to be caught off their guard as were the subjects in Pappo's experiment. Students generally understand that course examinations are designed to test their knowledge and facility with the subject matter, for instance, or that standardized tests may have important consequences for their futures. Pappo's theoretical analysis emphasizes that only when a person nears success or mastery of a task will fear-of-success defenses be engaged and lead to self-sabotage behavior. Due to the unexpectedness of the feedback, subjects might have easily disavowed responsibility for success at the task: They may have reasoned that they hadn't actually developed this ability, but rather just seemed to have it, and perhaps they thought they couldn't do much about it.

We asked ourselves, then, what would happen if we removed the surprise element accompanying the success. We hoped to create a situation that was conceptually quite close to Pappo's theoretical notions about the instigators of fear-of-success defense mechanisms and thus to broaden our knowledge about the conditions under which success-fearing persons will self-sabotage. We conducted another experiment that was very similar to Pappo's—we even used the same reading comprehension test—but it was different in one important respect. Instead of performing the task only twice and receiving feedback only after the first time, participants read, and answered questions about, *four* different sets of reading comprehension passages and received feedback about their reading skill after each set of passages. Again, half of the participants were male, half were female, and half of each of these groups were success-fearers while half were not.

We structured the experiment so that half of the participants would believe they had initially done about average on the reading passages and then gradually increased their skill at the task until they were doing quite well at it. Participants could readily see that they were getting better at the task, and consequently their eventual high performance level should not be so startling. We expected that the gradual improvement in scores would lead all subjects to believe they were gaining competence at the task. For the success-fearing subjects this knowledge should, in turn, trigger self-sabotage mechanisms. Of course, we did not expect the non-success-fearers in this condition to do more poorly at the end of the session.

Half of the subjects participated in this *improvement* condition, and as a comparison, the other half of the subjects participated in a *nonimprovement* condition. In this condition, participants were told that they initially performed at the same average level as those in the *improvement* condition, but their performances, rather than getting better, appeared to remain in the average range over the course of the session. We have no reason to think that this knowledge would encourage subjects to believe they were becoming competent at the task. Hence, the performances of the success-fearers should not be disrupted at the end as they were expected to be at the end of the session in the *improvement* condition, which is what we would expect if Pappo is correct in suggesting that success-fearers sabotage their performances as a result of anxiety about competence when success is imminent.

A somewhat different pattern could be anticipated for our fourth group of participants—the non-success-fearers who continued to perform at an average level throughout the session. Although they could be expected to remain motivated for a while and to concentrate their attention on the task in an attempt to improve, eventually when increased competence was not forthcoming (as reflected in their average performances throughout), they would probably become discouraged or even stressed. Reasoning that their efforts have gone unrewarded and that they are unable to master the task, they might "give up," and they may withdraw psychologically (either consciously or unconsciously) from the task. Regardless of the specific emotions experienced by persons (boredom, discouragement, anxiety, stress), these unpleasant feelings are likely to interfere with their continued motivation and concentration, which could result in poorer performance at the end.

In summary, then, over the course of the first three sets of exercises, we expected all subjects to perform either as well as or better than they had on the previous set, and we had no reason to anticipate differences in performance level among the four groups of subjects. On the fourth set of passages, however, we could anticipate differences in performance of the following sort. If approaching competence is an instigator of self-sabotage behavior for success-fearers, success-fearers should do more poorly on the fourth set of passages in the *improvement* condition but not more poorly in the *nonimprovement* condition. In contrast, if our reasoning is correct, people who do not fear success should react unfavorably to the *nonimprovement* condition, even showing a decrement in performance on the fourth set of passages, but should do as well or better on the last set in the *improvement* condition.

Experimental Procedures

Male and female college students enrolled in the introductory psychology course at a large private university were recruited to participate in this study to fulfill in part the laboratory requirement for their course.[a] All participants had previously completed Pappo's fear-of-success scale and were selected for the study if their scores were at least one standard deviation discrepant from the mean. Here again the mean fear-of-success score for the group from which participants were selected was 37, with a standard deviation of 12. A total of sixty-two students participated in this study, and they were equally distributed between the two experimental conditions (*improvement* and *nonimprovement*). The students were randomly assigned to the experimental conditions.

The instructions and the experimental procedures for this study were adapted from Pappo's study with revisions appropriate to establish the new experimental conditions. Each student participated individually in the experi-

[a]The authors are grateful to Socorro Llubien and Marjory Kessler for their assistance in conducting this experiment.

ment. Students completed four sets of reading comprehension exercises which were timed by the female experimenter. Each set consisted of three passages and twelve multiple choice questions. The presentation of the order of the sets of passages was counterbalanced in a Latin Square design. Before answering the questions for each passage, students wrote down how many questions they thought they would answer correctly in the set. After the subject completed the three passages in a set, the experimenter read the (ostensibly) "correct" answers to the subject while the subject checked his own answers. The experimenter adjusted the feedback so that the subject's final score on the set would conform to the predetermined performance level required by the experimental conditions. Performance level was varied by indicating to students that they had correctly answered a certain number of reading comprehension questions that were shown to correspond to a given percentile equivalent using different tables of (fictitious) group norms.

In the *improvement* condition the feedback given after the first set was represented as being at an average level; after that, it progressively improved. The feedback pattern for the four sets of passages in this condition was as follows: (1) 7 correct corresponded to the 75th percentile, (2) 8 correct corresponded to the 81st percentile, (3) 10 correct corresponded to the 92nd percentile, (4) 10 correct corresponded to the 92nd percentile. In the *nonimprovement* condition, the feedback started at the same level and varied slightly to enhance credibility but it always remained in the average range as follows: (1) 7 correct corresponded to the 75th percentile, (2) 8 correct corresponded to the 78th percentile, (3) 8 correct corresponded to the 79th percentile, (4) 8 correct corresponded to the 77th percentile.

After they received the feedback on each set of passages, the participants answered a short (five questions) reaction questionnaire and then began the next set of passages. After completing all four sets and receiving feedback, subjects completed a longer postexperimental questionnaire and were debriefed.

Results

The performance results are graphically presented in figure 2-1. Because the pattern of results was identical for men and women, the figure graphs the mean number of questions correctly answered on each set of reading passages for success-fearers and non-success-fearers (male and females combined) in each of the experimental conditions. As can be seen, the data strikingly confirm our predictions. Notice the two lines representing the actual performances of the success-fearers in the two experimental conditions. Their performances gradually increased from the first set to the second, and from the second set to the third. At that point, however, there is a radical shift in the pattern of performances. On the average, success-fearers in the *nonimprovement* condition (who believed

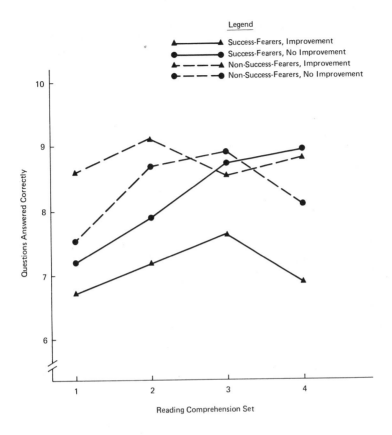

Figure 2-1. Mean Reading Score on Four Sets of Passages.

that they were still performing in the average range on Set 3), performed even better on the last set of passages. Contrast this to the performance of the success-fearers in the *improvement* condition. By Set 3, these people realized that they had gradually improved their mastery of the task from a mere average level to a level that could be considered quite accomplished. At this point, and not until this point, the success-fearers' performances markedly decreased and almost cancelled the gains they had made. This pattern was exhibited by both males and females. The students who do not fear success, on the other hand, exhibited a pattern almost the reverse of that of the success-fearers. The non-success-fearers in the *improvement* condition began at an initially high level of performance and maintained this high level of performance, with minor fluctuations, throughout the four sets of exercises. The non-success-fearers in the *nonimprovement* condition also maintained or bettered their actual performances during the first three sets. In contrast, however, when they were confronted with their apparent inability to improve their performances (which their feedback indicated despite their actual improvement), their actual performances fell off on the last set of passages.

Competence Feelings. Responses of these subjects to our questionnaire reveal patterns of feelings and reactions consistent with the performance data and with Pappo's findings (see table 2-3). A "competence index" was created by combining subjects' responses to five rating scales indicating the extent to which they felt sure of themselves, confident, capable, optimistic, and pleased at the end of the session. In general, non-success-fearers, regardless of experimental condition, indicated greater feelings of competence on this index than did the success-fearers. The reader will recognize this result as being consistent with the success-fearer's general proclivity towards feelings of self-doubt and performance insecurity. More interesting, however, and in line with this characteristic, is the difference between the success-fearers and non-success-fearers in their subjective reactions to improvement and nonimprovement. The non-success-fearers responded as we would normally assume—that is, they reported significantly more positive feelings of competence after the *improvement* condition than they did after the *nonimprovement* condition. The success-fearers, in sharp contrast, did not seem to react differentially to the two experiences; the minor differences in their responses to the performance conditions were not statistically significant and clearly were more negative than those of the non-success-fearers. The success-fearers, then, were not experiencing the heightened positive feelings that might be expected to result from competence attainment. Their reactions are clearly attenuated.

Stress. A number of indicators reveal that the *improvement* condition was anxiety provoking for the success-fearers while the *nonimprovement* condition was distressing for those subjects who do not fear success. Success-fearers reported they felt more pressured due to time constraints and the physical presence of the experimenter and also that they had more difficulty concentrating on the last passages than did the non-success-fearers. Additionally, we created a general "discomfort index" by combining subjects' ratings of the extent to which they felt uneasy, depressed, tired, anxious, and unsociable. The non-success-fearers clearly experienced more discomfort after their nonimprovement experiences, while the success-fearers felt equally uncomfortable after both improvement and nonimprovement. Thus, we have additional evidence that success-fearers react to approaching success and gaining competence with short-circuited enjoyment and with emotional reactions that tend to interfere with their performances.

Table 2-3
Mean Responses of Success-Fearers and Non-Success-Fearers to Improving and Nonimproving Performances

Variable	(A) Success-Fearers		Non-Success-Fearers		Analysis of Variance			
	(B) Improvement	No Improvement	Improvement	No Improvement	F_A	F_B	F_{AB}	MS_e
A. Final Performance[a] (adjusted for covariance with first three performances)	7.5	9.1	8.2	7.9	0.20	2.37	5.42*	2.54
B. Performance Evaluation (higher numbers indicate more positive evaluations)								
1. How well did you do?[b]	6.8	5.3	6.8	5.1	0.09	17.56***	0.10	2.32
2. Competence index[c]	5.5	5.0	6.8	5.8	12.27***	5.80*	0.78	1.35
C. Affective Interference (higher numbers indicate greater interference)								
1. Difficulty concentrating on final set[b]	5.1	6.3	3.4	5.4	6.84*	10.89**	0.60	3.79
2. Pressure experienced from external sources (e.g., time constraints, presence of experimenter)[b]	6.5	5.3	4.3	5.4	5.88*	0.00	5.98*	3.04
3. Discomfort index[c]	5.1	5.0	3.9	5.2	2.74	3.95	6.78*	1.25

*p <.05
**p <.01
***p <.001

[a]Twelve was the highest possible score.
[b]Ratings were made on 9-point scales.
[c]The index was computed by averaging the subject's responses to five 9-point bipolar mood adjective rating scales.

Implications

Pappo's work suggests that the fear of success is not a rarity, but a relatively commonplace occurrence among college students. It suggests also that the fear of success is equally prevalent in males and females in this population. Indeed, in both studies we discussed in this chapter, no major differences existed between men and women success-fearers in the way they reacted to success—neither in their feelings or beliefs about their performances nor in their tendency to self-sabotage their successful performances. In addition to these laboratory experiments to validate the Pappo fear-of-success scale, the usefulness of the scale as a measure of fear of success is further strengthened by the field validation studies presented in chapter 6. In that chapter we show that fear of success affects the everyday lives of people away from the controlled environment of the laboratory.

An argument that the Pappo data can be understood by assuming that the fear-of-success scale "really" measures a fear of failure rather than a fear of success is suggested by the moderate positive correlation between the scale and the Albert-Haber test of performance anxiety. This alternative interpretation of the results of Pappo's study must make two assumptions: that students who received success feedback on the first set of exercises would consider any lesser performance on the second part as a failure and that students who performed only at the average level on the first part did *not* view the possibility that they might perform even more poorly on the second part as a potential failure. If those two assumptions are made, the results can be interpreted as indicating that the anxiety aroused in the *success* condition was failure anxiety rather than success anxiety and that the resulting performance interference was a response to such a fear of failing.

This alternative interpretation is more than a little clumsy; it requires that we think of success as a cue for impending failure rather than for continued success. We believe a more reasonable and less-tortured interpretation is that persons who are fearful of failure (and not fearful of success) would tend to find evidence of success to be a source of relief rather than anxiety and that such persons would be made more anxious by the average feedback than the success feedback. While we cannot altogether refute the "fear of failure" alternative explanation for Pappo's results, then, we do not find it at all persuasive.

The evidence from our second study also seems to argue against such an interpretation. That the gradual improvement in scores—and the mastery of the task such performance connotes—would trigger anxiety about doing very poorly or failing seems very unlikely. Similarly, while consistently performing at an average level (as did the students in the *nonimprovement* conditions) is certainly respectable, many of these college student subjects may have believed such a performance to be below their own standards. Hence, they may have been reacting to the feedback as if it were a "failure" experience. This response did not appear to disrupt the performances of the success-fearers, although it did have an adverse effect on the performances of the non-success-fearers. The issue of reactions to success versus failure will be dealt with head on in chapter 4.

The thinking about the major instigators of fear of success reactions presented in this chapter revolve around ideas about competence development and successful task mastery. These conditions were proposed by Pappo as being important episodes in the childhood development of fear of success. The research discussed here suggests that in the *contemporary* lives of success-fearing adolescents and adults, developing competence does trigger anxiety responses that interfere with their performances. We should note, however, that this research provides no direct support for Pappo's assumptions about the way fear of success develops initially. An alternative view of the origins of fear of success based on ideas about competition is discussed in the next chapter. Indeed, the participants in the studies presented in this chapter may have blown up the competitive implications of the performance norms used for feedback despite the fact that there was no overt competition and no physical competitors involved in these situations. We turn in the next chapter to the work of Dr. Nina Cohen and her Freudian analysis of the origins of fear of success.

Notes

1. Initially, 92 items meeting the criteria were constructed and administered to a total sample of 286 male and female college students from four different colleges. On the basis of an item analysis of the responses of these students, 9 statements were eliminated because their low correlations with the total score suggested they did not contribute to measuring the fear of success.

2. Based on a sample of 126 male and female college students, the correlation coefficients between the Pappo fear-of-success scale and these measures were: (1) Rotter Internal-External Scale, $r = -.24, p < .05$; (2) Rosenberg Self-Esteem Scale, $r = -.47, p < .01$; (3) Alpert-Haber Debilitating Anxiety Scale, $r = .57, p < .01$.

3. Analysis of variance yielded a significant main effect for fear of success category ($F = 92.38$, df 1/81, $p < .001$). For this and all other analyses of the postexperimental questionnaire data, $2 \times 2 \times 2$ unweighted means factorial analyses of variance were performed using the following factors: (1) fear of success category, (2) sex of subject, and (3) experimental condition. All results reported in this section were statistically significant at at least the $p < .05$ level.

3

Early Rivals and Competitors: Another Viewpoint

Shortly after Pappo completed the work we reported in the first part of chapter 2, Nina E. Cohen [15], then a doctoral student at Teachers College, Columbia University, became intensely interested in Pappo's findings. Cohen's neo-Freudian orientation to psychodynamic phenomena (see chapter 1) led her to take issue with two of Pappo's central assumptions: that the fear of success in any given person is restricted to particular spheres of activity (such as academic spheres as Pappo argued) and that anxiety transmission from the "mothering one" to the child is the sole or even the most important process underlying the development of the fear of success. Cohen's [15] work has provided an alternative suggestion of the early childhood origins of fear of success as well as a new and different scale to identify success-fearers. Her research has also provided us with additional evidence that the fear of success is as prevalent in men as in women and with evidence that male and female success-fearers react similarly to success in a competitive context.

The Oedipal Triangle

Cohen took the position that the success-fearing person suffers from a generalized neurotic conflict about the expression of achievement striving and self-assertion. This conflict is not, in Cohen's view, limited to specific areas of activity that have met with parental disapproval. Rather, it is rooted in the person's unconscious equation of any achievement and self-assertion with destructive and/or exhibitionistic motives.

According to Cohen's analysis, fear of success develops when a repeated communication is made by one or both parents that the child's movements toward mastery, individuation, and ultimately separation are threatening to the parent. The parents' concerns can stem from a variety of factors. Among them are the parents' own fears of being outdone by the child, or their need to keep the child dependent. Overtly, in keeping with a conscious wish that the child grow and mature, the parents may encourage independence and competence striving. Actual evidence of the child's success, however, arouses anxiety or anger in the parents. It is unlikely that such parental reactions can be hidden from the child. They may be communicated by a disapproving glance, a nonenthusiastic reaction to the child's success, or by countless other subtle behaviors. In each case, however, the message to the child is that successful behavior is unwelcome.

61

The child who is subjected to this climate is mystified. He may strive toward mastery and independence, but with proximity to a goal he comes to experience a terrible sinking feeling. At such times, avoidance of success will have a tranquilizing effect.

The young child is probably not able to make the fine discriminations for knowing which of his competence-striving behaviors are particularly anxiety-provoking for the parent or which of them will provoke competitive responses. Any instance of his self-assertion or success, then, will be unconsciously equated with aggressive and exhibitionistic impulses and will be fraught with guilt and anxiety. In the attempt to minimize the parent's anxiety and therefore ensure his own continued security, the child is forced to prevent himself and others from understanding that his behaviors have mastery and independence as their goal. By shifting his focus away from mastery and becoming preoccupied with peripheral concerns, such a child permits himself to engage in essential growth activity. The price of this behavior is impaired self-esteem, impaired concentration, and decreased joy in the attainment of competence. Seemingly, the child needs to be sure that he is not engaging in the activity in order to become good at it. The child finally internalizes the implicit parental proscriptions against success as a part of the superego. Once internalized, such proscriptions operate with the same force as the original parental censure even in the physical absence of the parents.

Cohen further suggests that the ramifications of the parental injunction to inhibit success strivings are felt most keenly when the child and the prohibiting parent are of the same sex. She points out that the negotiation of the Oedipal phase of development is strongly implicated in the development of fear of success. The Oedipal conflict emerges when the young child—usually of about four or five years—begins to have desires to possess exclusively the parent of the opposite sex. Presumably, young boys desire the exclusive attention and affection of their mothers—unhampered by their fathers' presence—and young girls desire the exclusive attention and affection of their fathers—unhampered by the presence of their mothers. The parent of the same sex, however, stands in the way of this fantasied incestuous possession. The child thus comes to feel the same-sex parent is a rival for the opposite-sex parent and thus a potential adversary. This feeling leads the child to have intensely competitive and even murderous feelings toward the same-sex parent-competitor. At the same time, however, the child also understands that the parent is the stronger and more powerful person. As a consequence, the child fears that if he or she is successful in gaining possession of the opposite-sex parent, he or she may suffer retaliation and harm at the hands of the rival. The Oedipal conflict, then, consists of an intense desire to possess exclusively the opposite-sex parent and the internal prohibition, based on fear of retaliation, against those impulses. This internal prohibition becomes permanently established in the child's conscience or superego. Eventually the Oedipal conflict is resolved when the child surrenders his desires for the opposite-sex parent and identifies with the parent of the same sex.

If the same-sex parent repeatedly communicates concern that the child is actually seeking to outdo or displace him, the rivalrous feelings normally experienced by the child during this Oedipal phase are heightened. The fantasy of Oedipal victory is lent a greater sense of reality by the anxious reaction of the parent. The child must now intensify his efforts to keep himself and others from becoming aware of his "destructive" intentions, since open recognition of an interest in success carries with it the potential risk of retaliation by the same-sex parental competitor.

Arguing that persons with fear of success problems that have been exacerbated by Oedipal concerns may tend to generalize their success anxiety from the same-sex parent to other people of the same sex, Cohen suggested that such persons are especially threatened by success achieved in competition with same-sex others. To be pitted against an opponent of the same sex is to revive the Oedipal drama, with its associated impulses and anxieties, in the unconscious. Since in her opinion the success anxieties of most success-fearing persons have, in part, developed through Oedipal fantasies involving competition with the same-sex parent, Cohen was able to predict that success-fearing persons will become most anxious when they are competing successfully with same-sex others. Conversely, they should be relatively less disturbed when they are competing against someone of the opposite sex.

Based on the preceding lines of thought, Cohen constructed a new measure of the fear of success. Her scale was not restricted to academic situations, but contained items about a wide range of activities, including intellectual, competitive, interpersonal, sexual, and so on. In designing an experiment to validate her new measure, Cohen built in a test of her predictions that success-fearing persons have the greatest amount of difficulty with success when the success involves competition with same-sex individuals.

Another Measure of Fear of Success

The success-fearing person has been described by Cohen as one who suffers from an inhibition of self-promoting behavior due to an unconscious equation of achievement and competence with aggressive and/or exhibitionistic impulses. In an effort to not notice and to get others off the scent of their success strivings, such persons defensively withdraw from full involvement in goal-oriented activities. Preoccupation with what others may think and feel and impaired concentration are some of the defense strategies at their disposal. Questionnaire items were developed to identify these expected manifestations of success anxiety. Items were constructed to reflect success anxiety that is independent of specific achievement contexts and with the aim of avoiding questions that involve stereotypic behaviors associated with male or female sex roles.

The final version of Cohen's scale contains 64 items in a "yes-no" format.[1] As with Pappo's scale, respondents either agree ("yes") with an item as characteristic of their behavior or beliefs or disagree ("no") with the item, thereby indicating that it is not characteristic of their behavior or beliefs. On the basis of a factor analysis, Cohen identified nine factors that were regarded as meaningful in a description of the responses of success-fearing individuals. These factors are listed below, together with two sample items from each. The answer in parentheses is the answer that is scored as indicative of fear of success. A copy of the full scale is included in the appendix to this volume.

Factor 1: Anxiety over the Expression of Needs and Preferences

It makes me feel uneasy to have to ask other people for things. (Yes)

I often have trouble saying no to people. (Yes)

Factor 2: Reluctance to Acknowledge Personal Competence

I'm pretty competent at most things I try. (No)

I generally feel uptight about telling a boss or professor that I think I'm entitled to a better deal. (Yes)

Factor 3: Impaired Concentration and Distractability

Before getting down to working on a project, I suddenly find a whole bunch of other things to take care of first. (Yes)

I have often "woken up" during a lecture or a meeting and realized that I haven't heard a word that was said. (Yes)

Factor 4: Indecisiveness

I'm reluctant to make a large purchase without consulting someone else first. (Yes)

It pays to check out your ideas with other people before making a final decision. (Yes)

Factor 5: Safety Valve Syndrome—Fear of Loss of Control

It's important not to get too excited about things one really desires. (Yes)

When I notice things have been going particularly well for me, I get the feeling that it just can't last. (Yes)

Factor 6: Illegitimacy of Self-Promotive Behavior

I tend to believe that people who look out for themselves first are selfish. (Yes)

I sometimes have trouble acting like myself when I'm with people I don't know. (Yes)

Factor 7; Anxiety over Being the Focus of Attention

I hate having a fuss made over me. (Yes)

I often feel self-conscious when someone who "counts" compliments me. (Yes)

Factor 8: Preoccupation with Competition and Evaluation

When I'm praised for something, I sometimes wonder if I can do as well the next time. (Yes)

When someone I know well succeeds at something, I usually feel that I've lost out in comparison. (Yes)

Factor 9: Preoccupation with the Underplaying of Effectiveness

I sometimes "play down" my competence in front of others so they won't think I'm bragging. (Yes)

In the lower grades in school, if I got a good grade on a work assignment I often felt that I had fooled the teacher. (Yes)

Although the nine factors that emerged had a high index of factor simplicity and do provide a more detailed picture of the responses to the subparts of the questionnaire that tend to cluster together, we should note that the intercorrelations among the various (unrotated) factors were relatively high, with a mean intercorrelation of .42. This finding suggests that the various thoughts and feelings that comprise the fear of success as measured by the Cohen questionnaire form a coherent whole. We consider it important to note that none of the items in Cohen's scale are descriptions of self-sabotaging behaviors.

The mean score on the revised sixty-four-item questionnaire for 150 female college students was 38.1, with a standard deviation of 10.7. For eighty male college students, the mean was 35.7, with a standard deviation of 10.6. The small difference between the means for the females and the males was not statistically stable.

The Kuder-Richardson Formula 20 split-half reliability coefficient of the revised sixty-four-item scale was .90. Eleven items in the Cohen scale were taken from Pappo's scale. Prior to calculating a correlation between the two measures, these eleven items were eliminated from the Cohen scale. The correlation between the fifty-three remaining items of the Cohen questionnaire and the entire Pappo questionnaire was .74 ($n = 230$, $p < .01$). The magnitude of this correlation lends some support to Cohen's notion that the fear of success is a general characteristic of certain persons and is not restricted to particular spheres of activity that may have been proscribed by their parents.

A Validation Experiment: Men and Women in Competition

In this section, we describe the experiment conducted by Cohen to validate her scale and to test her ideas about the behavior of success-fearing men and women in competition with others. Cohen's theoretical analysis of the origins of fear of success pointed to the important role of the Oedipal stage of development and led her to make several interesting predictions about the performance of people who fear success relative to those who do not when they compete against opponents of the same sex or of the opposite sex. To test her predictions, she staged a contest with a qualifying phase and a subsequent runoff phase. She predicted that after a success experience in the qualifying stage of the contest, the task performances of males and females who scored high on the fear-of-success scale would deteriorate more (or improve less) than the performance of low scorers. This postsuccess performance deterioration was expected to be greater for those high scorers who competed with a same-sex person than with a person of the opposite sex. Such a differential performance pattern was not anticipated for low scorers on the fear-of-success scale.

Cohen wished to evoke competitive and success-oriented concerns among participants, so she presented her experiment as a contest in memory. All participants were high school juniors and seniors in a working- and middle-class suburban school district in New Jersey. Half were high scorers on the Cohen scale, and half were low scorers. Each participant was paid $2.00 for participating after school hours and had the added incentive of a chance to win the $10 prize if he or she won the final contest. Forty-seven males and forty-three females participated in the study.

In the first stage of the contest, students performed a memory task in a group composed of six males and six females evenly divided with regard to their fear-of-success scores. The second part of the study was presented as the runoff between two successful finalists in the contest. Unbeknownst to the students, however, every participant was individually informed that he or she was a finalist and went to a separate room to compete in the runoff contest. Students were paired in the runoff contest either with someone of the same sex or with an opposite-sex opponent. In addition to the performance scores obtained from the two memory tasks, the experiment was designed to provide evidence relating to the contestants' thoughts and feelings about their success, about the memory task and the contest, and about their competitor. The procedures are described in somewhat more detail below for interested readers; a full account appears in Cohen's Ph.D. dissertation [15].

Experimental Procedures

The experimental task involved memory for objects. Using a slide projector, a series of familiar objects in a row (saw, hammer, cup, and so forth) was flashed on a screen. Participants viewed each of eight slides for several seconds (one second of viewing time was allotted for each object depicted in the slide). After each slide, participants were asked to reproduce on an answer sheet the order of presentation of objects in the slide. On successive trials, the number of objects flashed was increased by one. Subjects' scores were recorded as the highest number of objects they remembered in the correct order.

Subjects were told by the female experimenter that they were participating in research on the effects of "various kinds of motivation on memory skills" and that a $10.00 prize was being offered for the person who won the contest on that day. The task was described to them, and they were told that after they had completed it they would be called, one by one, to have their answer sheets graded and that those who scored among the highest in the group would have the chance to compete against other high scorers for the final prize.

Following the eight trials, subjects were told that for those whose scores were not high, the end of their participation had come and that they would go to another room to collect their $2.00 participation fee. Those whose scores were very high, they were told, would have a chance to compete in the "finals." Subjects then waited in their seats to be called outside the room to have their answer sheets scored.

In fact, all subjects received success feedback and participated in the finals. After scoring each subject's answer sheet, the experimenter said: "Mm—you've done quite well! You should stand a good chance in the final competition." The subject then waited outside another room for the runoff.

Each subject was assigned at random to compete against a same-sex or an opposite-sex finalist in the "runoff." The runoffs were conducted by two other female experimenters, who began the session immediately after the second participant arrived, in order to prevent conversation between the participants. After receiving feedback on the first task, each participant saw only his or her own competitor in the runoffs and did not know the fate of the other contestants. As each finalist pair entered the runoff room, they were seated and congratulated on their high scores and told about the importance of short-term memory skills (e.g., "it's a critical ability to have in making judgments about people and in quickly sizing up a situation"). They were then shown eight slides, identical in form to those presented in the first memory task, but containing different pictures.

When the subjects completed the second task they were sent to a third room, where they were asked to respond to a postexperimental questionnaire. After they had completed this questionnaire, all subjects were fully informed about the true nature, purposes, and methods of the experiment, and they were afforded the opportunity to ask questions and give reactions. They were then paid for their participation and asked not to reveal to other students the true purposes of the experiment.

Results

According to the notions discussed above, the proximity of success is what activates immobilizing anxiety for success-fearing persons. With comfortable distance from a goal, strong desires to attain the goal are experienced by such people. At the point at which the goal comes close to realization, however, success-fearing persons are confronted with incontrovertible evidence of their effectiveness in what is perceived as a forbidden task. Their discomfort soars, and success-avoidant behaviors are initiated. If prevented from "leaving the field" by discontinuing working at the task altogether, success-fearers in such a situation are likely to sabotage the very behaviors that are instrumental in goal attainment. Accordingly, high scorers on the fear-of-success scale were not expected to experience undue anxiety on the first memory task before they had received any feedback. After the feedback, however, these participants were expected to show a decrement in performance relative to low scorers on the fear-of-success scale; they were expected to do more poorly on the runoff task.

Table 3-1 presents the performance data for the first and second memory tasks, and for the performance differences from the first to the second tasks. These data clearly indicate that prior to success feedback no differences existed in performance level between the students who fear success and those who do not. The fact that both high and low fear-of-success students performed similarly provides evidence that subjects in the various groups did not differ in their initial ability to perform this task. After success feedback, however, the results are dramatically different. Males and females who scored low on the fear-of-success scale improved their performance markedly, while male and female success-fearers improved far less if at all.

Among the success-fearing students, those who performed the second memory task in competition with a same-sex person improved less than those who competed against an opposite-sex person. This difference is accounted for primarily by the males, however; success-fearing males in competition with other males were the only group whose performances actually worsened after success feedback. For females, the difference between performance changes under same-sex and opposite-sex competition conditions, though in the predicted direction, was not statistically stable. Because other results for female success-fearers (see below) also supported the predictions, however, we are inclined to take the difference for females between same- and opposite-sex competitors seriously despite the fact that it is relatively small and does not reach statistical significance.

We have emphasized that persons who fear the consequences of successful activity become anxious when confronted with evidence of their competence. The intrusion of anxiety serves as a kind of safety valve, since it adversely affects functioning and thereby decreases the likelihood of future successful outcomes—and since anxiety doesn't "feel good," the person experiencing it may

Table 3-1
Mean Performances on the First and Second Memory Tasks

Group	Same-Sex Competitors			Opposite-Sex Competitors		
	Mean	s.d.	n	Mean	s.d.	n
Success-Fearers						
Males						
1st Task	21.3	6.0	12	21.5	8.6	10
2nd Task	20.2	5.4	12	25.9	10.4	10
Mean Difference (2nd−1st)	−1.2	4.5	12	4.4	5.8	10
Females						
1st Task	19.6	6.5	13	21.4	9.1	10
2nd Task	19.6	7.2	13	23.2	10.6	10
Mean Difference (2nd−1st)	0	2.6	13	1.8	5.6	10
Non-Success-Fearers						
Males						
1st Task	19.2	5.9	10	18.3	6.9	11
2nd Task	29.4	6.7	10	29.0	6.8	11
Mean Difference (2nd−1st)	10.2	5.8	10	10.7	5.8	11
Females						
1st Task	20.9	7.4	13	20.2	5.4	11
2nd Task	31.4	8.7	13	30.4	9.7	11
Mean Difference (2nd−1st)	10.5	5.7	13	10.3	7.9	11

Source: This table was adapted from data contained in Cohen [15].

Note: Scores could range from 0, the maximally low score, to 44, the best score possible. Negative difference scores reflect a decrement in performance and positive difference scores indicate an improvement. Analysis of variance of performance scores on Task 1 indicated no significant differences among the groups—all F values were less than 1. An analysis of variance of the difference scores indicated a significant main effect for fear-of-success category ($F = 59.99$, $df = 1$, 82; $p < .001$). A separate analysis of variance on the difference scores was performed for the high scorers on the fear-of-success questionnaire. This analysis yielded only a significant interaction between sex of subject and sex of competitor ($F = 6.89$, $p < .01$), indicating that same-sex competition produced more performance interference after success than competition with opposite-sex others.

feel less likely to be accused of deriving pleasure from the unconsciously prohibited activity. One manifestation of the functioning-impairment effect of anxiety is the impairment of concentration. With concentration interference, effective functioning is disrupted and joy in activity is reduced. Consistent with this notion, success-fearing students reported experiencing significantly more trouble concentrating during the first task and during the second task than the low fear-of-success students. In view of the fact that they had not been exposed to success feedback at the time they did the first task, we might speculate that these persons were generally anxious about performing, being evaluated, and/or competing. Despite their reported difficulty in concentrating, however, their actual test performance on the first task did not differ from that of their non-success-fearing counterparts. For the success-fearing group (but not for the non-success-fearing group), there was a notable increase in reported concentration impairment from the first to the second task, and, as reported above, a considerable impairment of actual performance (see table 3-2, lines A1 and A2).

These results underscore the finding in the performance data that success-fearers, in contrast to their non-success-fearing peers, respond to the awareness of success with behavior that is likely to inhibit performance. Other questionnaire data also show that success-fearers have characteristic ways of evaluating and responding to their competitive successes. Because having confidence in one's ability portends the possibility of success, the success-fearing person, according to Cohen's analysis, may attempt to avoid anxiety by maintaining an attitude of low self-esteem and lack of self-assurance. They may discount their effectiveness in achieving a good performance and might exhibit a preference for attributing success to external rather than internal factors. The existence of such strategies is supported by the data. In retrospective ratings of the perceived likelihood that they would win the contest, success-fearers thought they would be significantly less likely to win than students who do not fear success.[2] Success-fearers also regarded "luck" as more responsible for determining their scores. In contrast, they regarded their "ability" as less important and the unimportance of the task ("low stakes") as more important than non-success-fearing subjects (see table 3-2, lines B1 and B2).

Given a pattern of repeated interference with positive strivings engaged in by success-fearers in order to minimize anxiety, the success-fearing person may come to accept a limited self-view, and a reasonable assumption would seem to be that negative feelings accompany such thoughts of lack of competence. Persons who view themselves as helpless with regard to controlling consequences in their lives are more prone to anticipatory anxiety and to "feeling bad." Accordingly, success-fearers could be expected to report negatively toned feelings with respect to their comfort and displeasure in the task, which was in fact the case. Success-fearers reported they felt greater apprehension and more embarrassment when they were chosen as finalists than non-success-fearers. They also reported feeling greater uneasiness in the presence of others. Consistent with the prediction that success-fearers would tend to use projective defenses against their own feelings, success-fearers also rated the competitor as having a significantly greater competitive orientation than non-success-fearing persons (see table 3-2, lines C1, C2, and D1).

The data bearing on subjects' affective experiences during the competition and their perceptions of the competitors are, for the most part, quite clear in supporting Cohen's predictions. A number of unanticipated sex differences, to which we turn in the next section, also emerged in students' responses to the situation.

Table 3-2
Mean Subjective Responses to the Experiment

| | (A) | | Success-Fearers | | Non-Success-Fearers | | | | | |
| | (B) | Same-Sex ($n = 25$) | Opposite-Sex ($n = 20$) | Same-Sex ($n = 23$) | Opposite-Sex ($n = 22$) | F_A | F_B | F_{AB} | MS_e |
Variable									
A. Concentration Impairment									
1. Difficulty Concentrating on Task 1[a]		27.3	29.7	17.25	16.0	22.42***	0.06	0.53	139.2
2. Difficulty Concentrating on Task 2[a]		34.8	39.95	17.75	13.9	72.9***	0.06	3.16	141.8
B. Performance Evaluations									
1. Likelihood of Winning the Contest[b]		45.1	43.1	31.95	32.35	25.10***	0.10	0.27	126.2
2. Performance Attributions:									
Percentage Attributable to:[c]									
Luck		25.4%	22.6%	16.6%	12.5%	5.15*	0.69	0.02	387.6
Ability		29.6%	39.5%	67.4%	65.0%	40.36***	0.56	1.54	552.0
Low Stakes		28.1%	7.9%	8.2%	6.1%	6.92**	7.28**	4.83*	378.1
C. Affect[d]									
1. Apprehension		38.4	41.0	26.1	16.4	60.66***	2.23	6.72*	124.9
2. Embarrassment		18.4	19.9	7.7	12.6	12.85**	1.66	0.47	138.1
D. Perceptions of Competitors									
1. Competitiveness[e]		42.7	42.1	36.8	29.0	9.9**	1.9	1.4	199.5

Source: This table was adapted from data presented in Cohen [15].

*$p < .05$
**$p < .01$
***$p < .001$

[a]Ratings were made on 61-point dotted rating scales. Higher numbers indicate greater difficulty concentrating.
[b]Ratings were made on 61-point dotted rating scales. Higher numbers indicate greater likelihood.
[c]Subjects were asked to apportion percentage values to indicate the extent to which each of six factors was responsible for their good performance. Values can range from 0% to 100%.
[d]Ratings were made on 61-point dotted rating scales. Higher numbers indicate greater apprehension and greater embarrassment, respectively.
[e]Ratings were made on 61-point dotted rating scales. Higher numbers indicate greater perceived competitiveness.

Sex Differences

It was not expected that males and females would respond differently to the experimental manipulations of the Cohen study. Indeed, the behavioral data suggest that men and women performed similarly in the two experimental conditions employed. Significant sex differences did emerge, however, in subjects' reports of their thoughts and feelings during competition.

The questionnaire findings point to a generalized tendency for women regardless of their fear-of-success category to underrate their ability. Women reported that they had initially viewed the possibility of becoming finalists with less assurance than men. This devaluation of ability was certainly not reflected in actual performances on the first memory task. When asked about their views of their performance following selection as a finalist, women again devalued their performances relative to their male peers. This subjective appraisal, however, did not relate to actual performance differences between the sexes on the second task. Women subjects also felt they were less likely to win the competition than male subjects (i.e., women felt "less certain" about their performance on the finalist test than males).

Consistent with the idealized view of the white American male as hard driving, competitive, and aggressive, the men in Cohen's study showed evidence of a strong investment in winning the competition and particularly in defeating other men. For example, males reported they were significantly more concerned with the importance of winning the competition if they had been in competition with another male than if they had been paired with a female finalist. Men also viewed male competitors as significantly more aggressive than female opponents. Further, regardless of their fear-of-success category, men reported significantly greater discomfort in the same-sex competitive condition than in the opposite-sex condition. A noteworthy aspect is that given the intense emotion apparently attendant upon same-sex competition for males, success-fearing males in same-sex competition evidenced a significantly greater performance decrement from the first to the second memory task than did any other group. For all males, then, male-male victory appeared to be endowed with tension and importance. For success-fearing males, the intensity of these stakes and their internal conflicts about victory seem to have combined to disrupt their performance.

Implications

Cohen's well-conducted experiment adds a good deal of weight to the evidence reported so far: The fear of success is a problem that afflicts both men and women in our society. Cohen's use of high school students in a primarily blue-collar suburb as subjects in her experiment tends to extend the generality of the phenomenon beyond the usual middle-class college student group. In addition,

Cohen's results lend support to her assumption that the fear of success is a general personality disposition rather than one that is restricted to particular idiosyncratic spheres of activity as was assumed by Pappo. The fact that Cohen's fear-of-success scale, which contains items having to do with many spheres of activity (body image, sexual potency, games, intellectual endeavors, and so forth), seems to cohere quite well, and the fact that it correlates highly with Pappo's scale provides some evidence for Cohen's assertion.[3]

The result, predicted by Cohen, that victorious success-fearers tended to have more difficulty if they were pitted against a same-sex competitor than if their competitor was of the opposite sex is a very intriguing one. It tends to refute Pappo's assumption that the fear of success is induced primarily through anxiety transmission by the "mothering one." Pappo's position would probably have led her to predict that success-fearers regardless of sex would have more difficulty in competition with females. Certainly, her conceptual framework would not have been able to predict the result that Cohen obtained.

The results we have been discussing do not shed much additional light on the question of how the fear of success does in fact develop. Cohen's conceptual framework guided her selection of questionnaire items, her choice of experimental procedures and dependent measures, and generated her predictions; the strength and coherence of the results she obtained is impressive and admirable. The same-sex competition finding, however, which Cohen takes as supporting the notion that the Oedipal conflict is strongly implicated in the development of fear of success, can also be explained in another way. If we assume that success-fearing persons are made anxious by competition and if we further assume that competition is experienced as more intense (and for success-fearers, more anxiety arousing) if the competitor is seen as similar to the self in ability and other relevant characteristics, we can explain Cohen's results quite adequately. When other factors are equal or unknown, same-sex others are probably seen as more similar to the self in ability, motivation, and so forth, than opposite-sex others; therefore, if we are in competition with same-sex persons, we will experience the competition as more intense and its outcome as in greater doubt than if we are in competition with persons of the opposite sex. Competing against someone we consider to be much more skilled or much less skilled than ourselves is psychologically not much of a competition. We should note, however, that this post-hoc alternative explanation we have suggested could *not* have been used by itself to generate the questionnaire items or conceive of the basic experiment that Cohen conducted.

The studies reported in this and the preceding chapter have provided us with evidence about how success-fearers feel about, think about, and respond to their performances when those performances are relatively distant from success and when they are quite close to success. In the next chapter we confront directly the issue of how success-fearers respond to performances that can be construed as failures.

Notes

1. Initially 97 items were constructed and administered to a sample of 150 female and 80 male white college freshmen enrolled in undergraduate summer sessions in several public colleges in New York City. Item analyses were performed (an item-total correlation of .2 was selected as a cut off point), resulting in the elimination of 33 items.

2. An interesting finding emerged for subjects' self-ratings of their memory functioning during competition: success-fearing subjects of both sexes rated their memory functioning as having been poorer on the second task if they had been paired with an *opposite-sex* partner than if they had been paired with a same-sex competitor ($F = 4.26$, $p < .05$). This result, considered in combination with the actual performance results, demonstrates that what people feel or believe about these conditions of performance does not always reflect what they actually do. Since these "memory functioning" results for success-fearing subjects are reminiscent of Horner's [42] prediction that success-fearing females perform more poorly under conditions of opposite-sex competition, we should probably note that we must be cautious in assuming a one-to-one correspondence between performance fantasies and performance realities. Along the same lines, we note with interest that subjects in Cohen's study were asked on the postexperimental questionnaire to rate their degree of anticipated comfort or discomfort about competition with same-, opposite-, or mixed-sex finalist groups. Neither high nor low scoring men or women reported feeling more or less uncomfortable in any of the three proposed contexts. Again, since the subjects identified as success-fearers actually seemed to perform less well in competition with same-sex others, we are duly warned of the potential inaccuracy inherent in making predictions about behavior from subjective assumptions or affective responses to the *idea* of performing.

3. An estimate of the test-retest reliability of Cohen's scale has recently been obtained with a sample of 80 male and female college students, using an interval of two weeks ($r = .93$).

4

Do Success-Fearers Fear Failure?

In our discussion of the implications of Pappo's work in chapter 2, we brought up a possible alternative explanation of the results of the experiment she conducted to validate her scale. The argument underlying this alternative explanation was as follows: The high scorers on Pappo's measure of the fear of success performed more poorly on the second reading task after they were told they had done spectacularly well on the first task. These persons could have been made anxious by the possibility that they might not be able to repeat their fine performance and that not being able to repeat this success was tantamount to a failure. Thus, it is possible that these students' performances were disrupted by a fear of failure rather than a fear of success. If so, the argument goes, then the Pappo fear-of-success measure is more properly thought of as a measure of the fear of failure. While this argument is more than a little complicated and indirect, it is not entirely implausible. Our attempt in chapter 2 to suggest a refutation of the argument on the grounds that it is simply less plausible than our own explanation is not entirely satisfactory. When analyzed more thoroughly, however, the entire basis of the controversy between this alternative explanation and ours is questionable, as we shall now attempt to show.

We have been assuming since the beginning of our work on the fear of success that success-fearing persons are highly conflicted about success: On the one hand, they desire it very much, while on the other hand, they fear and avoid it when it is imminent. As we pointed out in chapter 1, this conception was stated quite explicitly by two of the early clinical theorists: Sigmund Freud and Karen Horney. Horney carried the analysis further than Freud by arguing that fear of success was only one expression of a broader underlying conflict about competition. The basic underlying dynamic in the neurotic competitor involves an ambitious desire to win in competition, a fear that winning will lead to envy and rejection, and a fear that failure will lead to painful humiliation. In Horney's view a person with this neurotic conflict over competition is likely to express it either in a fear of success or in a fear of failure [46]. In describing our own position in chapter 1, we agreed with Horney concerning the underlying dynamic but differed from her belief that some persons consistently express fear of failure while others consistently express fear of success. Instead we argued that the same person maintains the three parts of the conflict simultaneously— the desire to compete, the fear of competing successfully, and the fear of losing. Which tendency is expressed depends upon whether winning or losing, success or failure, is in closer proximity to the person in any specific situation.

How Do Success-Fearers Respond to Failure?

What are the implications of this position for the controversy we have raised over the interpretation of the results of Pappo's experiment? If we take Horney's description seriously (as we are inclined to do), we would describe the success-fearing person as someone who strongly desires to succeed, fears success, and fears failure. The central questions that must be asked from this perspective are very different from the question raised in the chapter 2 controversy. The new questions are these: (1) Under what circumstances is a success-fearer's fear of success instigated? (2) Under what circumstances does a success-fearer's desire to succeed become particularly strong? (3) Under what circumstances is a success-fearer's fear of failure instigated? (4) What are the manifestations of the fear of success, the fear of failure, and the desire to succeed? In light of this more thorough analysis, the question we posed earlier in the controversy (Does a person perform more poorly after success feedback because he has a fear of success, or because he has a fear of failure?) is simply the wrong question to ask.

What we already know about the fear of success from our previous research and what we can propose based on our modification of Horney's ideas together permit us to answer at least tentatively the four new questions we have listed above. In answer to the first question, the success-fearer's fear of success is instigated by the imminence of success; when success is near, the person becomes anxious and defensive. In answer to the second question, the success-fearer strongly desires success whenever success is far away—that is, far enough away that anxiety is not raised by it. In answer to the third question, the success-fearer fears failure—or rather feels endangered by failure—whenever failure is an imminent possibility or has actually taken place.

The answer to the fourth question is a bit more complex than the answers to the first three. The fear of success, when instigated by the imminence of success, is manifested by anxiety and a tendency to disrupt or interfere with the performances leading to the success; the anxiety "helps" the person to avoid the success. The desire to succeed manifests itself both in fantasy (thinking about success) and in striving for success, as long as success remains far enough away. The fear of failure is manifested by hard work to avoid failure when failure is uncomfortably close. This final point should make clear that we believe *the fear of failure that is an integral part of the fear-of-success syndrome does not disrupt or interfere with performance.* If anything, it facilitates performance.

In this chapter we report an experiment to test these ideas. This experiment had to include a feature that had not been included in the previous experiments in our program of research: giving success-fearers information either that they were close to succeeding at a task or that they were close to failing at the task. Such an experimental comparison would allow us to test the prediction that success-fearers respond to imminent success with anxiety and self-sabotage and to imminent failure with hard work and improved performance. The experiment we conducted was also designed to provide answers to two additional questions about the fear of success. We discuss these questions below.

Does Self-Sabotage Serve a Function for Success-Fearers?

One of the assertions we have repeatedly made about success-fearers is that they often sabotage their performances when they believe success to be imminent. The use of the word *sabotage* implies a sort of intention—if one can speak of an "intention" that is not conscious. At least, the term implies that performance interference serves a function for the success-fearer and that the person repeatedly behaves in such a way as to allow the quality of his or her performance to deteriorate because of the knowledge at some level that he or she will "feel better." While directly observing an unconscious intention or an unconscious awareness is impossible, obtaining an indirect indication that performance interference after success reduces success-fearers' debilitating anxiety—that is, demonstrating that they then "feel better" and are able to work better at other tasks—seemed a more possible goal.

We believed that we could obtain such an indicator if we asked the following question: What happens to the performance of success-fearers *after* they engage in a self-sabotaging maneuver? If we found that the performance sabotage of success-fearers results in enhanced performance at a new task that requires concentration and effort, we could conclude that the debilitating anxiety that accompanied the impending success had been reduced by the self-sabotage and that these persons had been able to apply their effort to something else, in the service of their desire to succeed. Our experiment, then, had to include an opportunity for participants to perform a different task after they had engaged in behavior that sabotaged their performances on a prior task.

Is the Fear of Success a General Characteristic?

Our final question concerns the generality of the fear of success. As we made clear in chapter 3, Cohen's notions about the fear of success differed from Pappo's in several ways. Among these differences was the notion that since the fear of success has its origin in an early stage of development, it would be experienced and manifested in response to a wide variety of successes—any, in fact, that the person could see as a way of defeating an important other person. Cohen's point of view implies that the fear of success would, for any given person, manifest itself in a wide range of settings in which the person could perceive competition with others, including social situations involving popularity, physical attractiveness, and relational successes as well as athletics, arts and crafts, academic and financial pursuits, and all sorts of exhibitions and contests.

Thus, Cohen's scale was constructed to be general in nature rather than specific to a single category of activities (as Pappo's scale purports to be).

We were interested in providing an initial test of Cohen's notion about the generality over situations of the fear of success. Her ideas would lead us to believe that success-fearers are likely to sabotage not only academic performances but other potential successes as well, including friendships, romances, and explicit or implicit contests involving skills, talents, attractiveness, or popularity. Perhaps success-fearers are people whose important romances start off well and often fail to work out, who lose thirty pounds and then go on an eating binge, or who buy an elegant suit for a big occasion and forget to redeem it from the tailor in time to wear it to the event. Our experiment, then, used a task that was more social in character than the academic ones that had been used in previous studies. Unfortunately, we could not, for practical reasons, stage a beauty contest or a romance. Instead, we settled on a social task involving the communication to others of images and feelings in poetry read and recited aloud. Our college student subjects' task was to memorize and then recite a stanza of a poem before an audience of judges composed of literature and psychology students who were evaluating students' ability to communicate feeling and meaning in poetry. While the task might have had some academic overtones, it was clearly social in that it involved the interpersonal communication of feelings to peers.

An Experiment Designed to Answer Our Three Questions

In the experiment we designed to answer these questions, then, we set success-fearers and non-success-fearers to work on the poetry recitation task: the communication to an audience of the feelings, rhythms, and meaning of a Dylan Thomas poem.[a] Half of the participants were then told that they were succeeding at the task, and half were told they were failing, after which they all performed the recitation task again. Shortly after they had completed the second recitation, participants were invited to do a third, quite unrelated task. When they had completed the third task, they filled out a brief questionnaire about their feelings and reactions to the various aspects of the session. The poetry recitation task permits us to obtain a number of simple indicators of performance quality, such as the frequency of stutters and stammers and forgotten or misplaced words.

If we assume, in accordance with the work of other investigators (and the results of the second experiment reported in chapter 2), that for most non-success-fearing persons success feedback tends to enhance performance and failure feedback tends to induce performance deterioration [14,28,38,59,85],

[a]The authors would like to thank Dr. Dorothy Lekarczyk and Richard Werther for their assistance with this experiment.

our predictions for the experiment become quite clear. Thus, we predicted that: (1) Persons identified as success-fearers will suffer a performance decrement following success feedback, but will improve their performances following failure feedback; (2) relative to other participants, success-fearers who have received success feedback on the first poetry-reciting task will perform better on an unrelated task following their performance on the second poetry-reciting task; (3) persons identified as non-success-fearers will improve their performances following success feedback and will suffer a decrement in performance following failure feedback.

The procedures of the experiment are detailed below for interested readers.

Experimental Procedures

Cohen's fear-of-success scale was administered to 150 students in four undergraduate courses in psychology. The mean score on the scale was 28.9 for females and 26.6 for males. Subjects whose scores were in the top third of the range for their sex were categorized as success-fearers; subjects were categorized as non-success-fearers if their score was in the bottom third of the scores for their sex. Twenty-eight male and twenty female undergraduate students volunteered to participate in a study of communication skills; they were randomly assigned to either the *success* or the *failure* condition. Seven male subjects and five female subjects were assigned to each condition.

Upon arrival at the psychology department, each subject was met by the experimenter and taken directly to a large room, two sides of which held one-way observation mirrors. The male experimenter sat with the subject at a table about six feet away from a one-way mirror. He explained to the subject that the English department and the psychology department were working together in a study of contemporary undergraduates' ability to understand and to communicate aloud the meaning, the music, and the rhythms of poetry. The subject was further told that years ago, when people read aloud a great deal, they were quite practiced in interpersonal expression and were easily able to communicate the sensitivity and subtlety of poetry. The committee would be observing the subjects' poetry recitation from behind the one-way mirrors.

The subject was instructed that he would be given a minute and a half to memorize the first stanza of a poem ("Here in this Spring" by Dylan Thomas), after which he would stand, face the one-way mirror, first read the stanza, and then recite it from memory. The subject was told that the recitation would be tape-recorded for later review and for research purposes.

The subjects in all conditions then memorized, read, and recited the stanza before the mirror. The reading and recitation was recorded. Then the experimenter excused himself to go into the observation room to "find out from the committee members how well they thought the subject had done." He paused momentarily to tell the subject that the poetry committee was made up of two honors English majors and two psychology graduate students and that the committee members were confident that they could tell when someone had the sort of interpersonal sensitivity and communication skills they were looking for in the reading and recitation of poetry.

The experimenter then left the subject and entered the observation room, where he played a recording of a conversation, which was loud enough for the subject to hear that a conversation was going on and yet soft enough so that the content was not discernible. The experimenter returned from the observation room, sat next to the subject, and gave the following evaluations:

In the *success* condition, he said: "Three of the four committee members think that you are in the category of people who can read and recite poetry with a high degree of interpersonal sensitivity."

In the *failure* condition, he said: "Three of the four committee members think that you are not in the category of people who can read and recite poetry with a high degree of interpersonal sensitivity."

Then the experimenter said to all subjects, "But the poetry committee would like to see how well you can do on the second stanza." The procedure used with the first stanza was repeated with another stanza of the same poem.

When the subject completed his second recitation and while the committee was ostensibly making its evaluation, the experimenter introduced "an interesting visual-perception task," the Witkin Embedded Figures Test [118]. After completing a practice example, the subjects completed four cards on the Witkin test (cards A, B, D, and F) on which they were timed; a maximum of two minutes was allowed per card. The Embedded Figures Test was followed by a short recall test on the second stanza, and a postexperimental questionnaire. Finally, the true purposes and methods of the experiment were explained in a full debriefing.

Results

We shall divide our description of the results of the experiment into three sections. First, we present the results for participants' performance on the poetry recitation. Second, we present the results for their performance on the final task, the Embedded Figures Test. In the third section we describe briefly some of the participants' responses on the postexperimental questionnaire.

Poetry Recitation Performance. The aspects of the quality of participants' poetry recitation measured were: (1) the number of stutters, stammers, and slurs and (2) the number of words in each stanza the participants correctly memorized. We expected that the performance of success-fearing participants would deteriorate after success feedback and improve after failure feedback. The performances of the non-success-fearing participants, in contrast, were expected to improve after success feedback and to deteriorate after failure feedback.

Table 4-1 (line A) presents the mean change scores from stanza 1 to stanza 2 on the total frequency of slurring, stuttering, and stammering participants did during the recitation. Positive scores indicate a worse performance on stanza 2—that is, an increased frequency of garbled, awkward, and incomprehensible sounds. Our predictions receive clear support on this measure; the predicted differences were strong and statistically stable. An inspection of these means shows clearly that the success-fearing subjects reacted very differently depending upon whether they were faced with success or with failure. Success led them to sabotage performance—in this instance, to stutter, stammer, and slur more words in the poetry recitation; failure led them to improve the clarity and smoothness of their utterances. The non-success-fearing subjects had reactions to success and failure that were just the opposite; these subjects responded more typically—that is, by improving after success and by doing more poorly after failure. As can be seen in table 4-1 (line A), males and females did not differ substantially from one another in their responses to the experimental conditions.

The second performance measure of interest to us was the change from stanza 1 to stanza 2 in the number of words the participant correctly memorized. While this measure is a more gross and less sensitive one than the "quality-of-speech" measure we have just discussed, we included it in order to provide some additional evidence regarding our predictions about participants' responses to success or failure feedback. The actual measure we used was the change in the percentage of words participants correctly memorized in each stanza. The numbers of words were changed to percentages because the total number of words in the two stanzas is slightly different (25 and 23, respectively, in the first and second stanzas) and we wished to make them comparable. Table 4-1 (line B) presents the mean change: positive numbers represent an increase in words memorized and an improvement in performance, while negative numbers represent poorer performance—that is, fewer words memorized in stanza 2 than in stanza 1. An inspection of these means reveals that while the general pattern of results for this measure is consistent with our predictions and with the results for the stutters and stammers measure (particularly if averaged over men and women), the means for men and women vary much more widely than is the case for the stutters and stammers measure, especially for non-success-fearing participants. A statistical analysis shows that success-fearing participants did perform more poorly in the *success* condition than they did in the *failure* condition. This difference was, however, the only statistically stable one that emerged for this measure. What we can say about this performance measure, then, is that it was less sensitive for our purposes than the stutters and stammers measure and more prone to be affected by extraneous factors. The apparent sex differences that emerged in it for non-success-fearing participants are not statistically stable and should not be taken seriously, due to the small numbers of participants in each

Table 4-1

Performance Responses of Success-fearers and Non-Success-fearers to Success and Failure

| | Success-Fearers | | | | Non-Success-Fearers | | | |
| | Success | | Failure | | Success | | Failure | |
Dependent Variable	Female ($n = 5$)	Male ($n = 7$)	Female ($n = 5$)	Male ($n = 7$)	Female ($n = 5$)	Male ($n = 7$)	Female ($n = 5$)	Male ($n = 7$)
A. Mean Change in Total Stutters, Stammers and Slurs[a]	1.0	1.1	−.6	−.4	−1.0	−.6	1.0	.3
B. Mean Change in Percentage of Words Correctly Recited[b]	−18.6	−4.2	12.5	14.5	7.1	−10.4	−5.4	3.3
C. Mean Time in Seconds to solve Four Embedded Figures[c]	152.8	107.1	232.4	160.9	253.2	183.3	180.6	150.9

[a]Negative scores represent improvement (fewer stutters, and so forth) from stanza 1 to stanza 2; positive scores represent a decrement in performance from stanza 1 to stanza 2 (more stutters, and so forth). An analysis of variance for this measure yielded only one significant effect: the interaction between fear-of-success category and success/failure feedback ($F_{1,40} = 11.66, p < .01$). Planned comparisons of the means show a significant difference (collapsing over sex of subjects) between success-fearers and non-success-fearers in the *success* condition ($p < .01$) and a near-significant difference between these groups in the *failure* condition ($p < .07$). The success-fearers performed significantly more poorly in the *success* than in the *failure* condition ($p < .02$), while the non-success-fearers performed more poorly in the *failure* condition than in the *success* condition ($p < .05$). No significant or near-significant difference emerged in an analysis of the stanza 1 performances.

[b]Positive scores represent improved performance—that is, a greater percentage of correctly recited words; negative scores represent poorer performance or a smaller percentage of correctly recited words. An analysis of variance for this measure yielded two marginally significant effects: the main effect for success/failure ($F_{1,40} = 3.11, p < .10$) and the interaction between fear-of-success category and success/failure ($F_{1,40} = 2.85, p < .10$). The only comparison of the means that showed a significant difference was the difference between the success-fearers in the *success* condition and the *failure* condition (collapsing over sex of subjects) ($p < .02$). We note that in the analysis of variance for the stanza 1 performance, a marginally significant effect for success/failure emerged, suggesting that participants in the *success* condition might have done better prior to receiving their feedback than participants in the *failure* condition. We assume that this difference is a chance difference.

[c]Lower numbers represent better performances on this measure. An analysis of variance of these data showed a marginally significant effect for sex of subject ($F_{1,40} = 3.41, p < .10$) and a significant interaction between fear-of-success category and success/failure ($F_{1,40} = 4.12, p < .05$). Planned comparisons of the means (collapsing across sex of subject) show only that the success-fearers in the *success* condition solved the problems more quickly than non-success-fearers in the *success* condition ($p < .05$). None of the remaining comparisons resulted in statistically significant differences.

of the subgroups. Despite all these problems, however, we see the results for the change in words correctly recited measure as in general agreement with the results for the change in stammers and stutters measure and as providing some additional support for our predictions. Success-fearers do indeed perform more poorly after receiving success information than they do after receiving failure information.

The Third Task. After subjects had completed the second stanza recitation, participants completed a perception task totally unrelated to the communication of poetry. This task—the Witkin Embedded Figures Test—requires the person first to look at and memorize a simple geometric figure and then to identify that simple figure when it is embedded in a more complex pattern of lines and shapes. The relevant measure is the amount of time the person takes to find the embedded figure; the less the time, the better the performance. Participants completed four cards of this test while they were waiting for the "judges' evaluations" of their second stanza performance. Time to solution was recorded, with a maximum limit of two minutes allowed for each of the four cards.

We predicted that success-fearing subjects who had been given success information and who had presumably attempted to sabotage their performance on the second stanza would do particularly well on the Embedded Figures problems. We reasoned that the anxiety of these participants would be reduced by their self-sabotage, and their desire to succeed and their concern about possible failure would mobilize them to work particularly hard at the task.

The results for this task, summed in seconds over the four trials, are presented in line C of table 4-1. A look at the means shows two rather clear and consistent results. First, the men solved the four problems more quickly than the women (a result that is very common in the literature on this test). Second, the success-fearers in the *success* condition (regardless of sex) did indeed do somewhat better on the task than any other group of participants; in fact, the comparison between their average performance and that of the non-success-fearers in the *success* condition is statistically stable. We should point out that while the non-success-fearers in the *failure* condition also appeared to do rather well, the difference between their performances and those of other groups of participants were not stable in a statistical sense. Thus, we do have some support for our notion that the performance sabotage of success-fearers following success leads to a reduction in their anxiety and an increase in their desire to do well on subsequent tasks.

Reports of Feelings. After they completed the Embedded Figures Test, participants answered a few questions about the session and their reactions to it. We were interested in finding out whether the feelings of success-fearers in response to this social task were similar to their feelings in response to the more academic tasks we had used in earlier studies. Results for this questionnaire were indeed very much in line with the responses of success-fearers in previous research. Success-fearers reported more trouble concentrating on the poetry task, both on stanza 1 and on stanza 2, than non-success-fearers did. They also complained, more than non-success-fearers did, that their memories were functioning more poorly than usual. Furthermore, they reported, more than non-success-fearers did, that they felt uneasy being observed during their two recitations and that they felt "detached" during their recitations of the poem.

Conclusions

Taken as a whole, the results of the study we have reported support the hypotheses that led us to undertake it. Success-fearers expressed their motive to avoid success by sabotaging their performance after a success and expressed their motive to avoid failure by improving their performances in response to a failure. Non-success-fearers, on the other hand, responded favorably to success by improving their performance and responded unfavorably to failure with performance deterioration. The argument that our fear-of-success scales really identify people who fear failure rather than success is effectively refuted by these results. According to that position, high scorers on our scales become anxious when threatened with failure, and this anxiety interferes with their performance. Thus the prediction that would be made from that perspective is that high scorers on our scale who were informed they had probably failed on the task would respond by performing more poorly. Instead, they performed better.

This study's findings also make clear that the fear-of-success phenomena manifested themselves in this more social situation much as they did in the academic situations of our previous studies. We have found, then, preliminary support for Cohen's assumption that fear of success is a personality trait that has consequences over a wide range of endeavors and situations. We call this support preliminary because we have not yet shown that the same persons respond to different kinds of successes in different ways. We have, however, made a reasonable beginning.

Our data also show very clearly that success-fearers respond quite differently to success and failure feedback and that they respond to success and failure feedback rather differently than non-success-fearers do. The performance of success-fearers does not appear to be disrupted by failure; on the contrary, failure seems to mobilize them to greater effort. Finally, we have developed some evidence for the proposition that performance sabotage serves a function for success-fearers when they feel they are succeeding. Our results allow us to infer, with some caution, that the performance sabotage of success-fearers reduces their success anxiety and permits them once again to work hard in the service of their desire to succeed and their abhorrence of failure.

Our experiment has, then, provided beginning answers for each of the questions we asked of it. We now know considerably more about the complexity of success-fearers' motives than we did before. The conflict that success-fearing persons must repeatedly live through is plainly frustrating and painful. Their desire to achieve consistently pushes them into the achievement arena and effectively prevents their escaping the conflict. Once in an achievement situation they are driven forward not only by the desire to achieve but also by the humiliating spectre of failure. As they come closer to success, success anxiety appears, and they must find a way to withdraw from that as well.

In the next chapter we address the issue of whether the fear-of-success phenomena we have investigated in adults can also be observed in children. This question must be answered before we can pay serious attention in our research to the question of how fear of success develops.

5 Do Children Fear Success?

All participants in the research we have reported in previous chapters were students from either high schools or colleges. Although we had no reason to assume that fear of success would operate any differently for other age groups—either younger or older—we had no concrete evidence to support our intuitions. Consequently, in this chapter we report research conducted with two major purposes in mind. First, in order to extend our research program to younger age groups, we needed to develop a questionnaire to identify success-fearing children—that is, a questionnaire elementary school children would be able to understand and to which they could respond. In the first part of this chapter we discuss the development of our fear-of-success scale for children. Our second and closely related purpose was to explore whether success-fearing children would respond to performance feedback in ways similar to those of the late adolescents and young adults who participated in the earlier studies. In the second section of this chapter, then, we discuss an experiment with fourth-, fifth-, and sixth-grade boys and girls conducted to validate this scale. This study demonstrates that the children's scale has adequate validity for use with elementary school age children and provides us with a fuller understanding of how success-fearing children interpret, evaluate, and respond to their successful and nonsuccessful task performances. In later chapters (9 and 10) we report preliminary findings from a study using this scale to explore the interaction patterns between parents and their success-fearing and non-success-fearing children.

Fear-of-Success Scale for Children

The task of developing a fear-of-success scale suitable for children was a relatively simple one and primarily involved rewriting the items included on the final version of Cohen's fear-of-success scale (see chapter 3).[a] Our intention was to adapt the items so they contained only vocabulary and concepts that young children could read and would understand. In general, our approach involved making only minor changes in wording that simplified the vocabulary of the item but left the content essentially the same. For example, Cohen's item "I frequently find myself making a date or appointment and then dread having to

[a]The authors are grateful to Karen Kurlander for her assistance in adapting the items for this scale and to Ms. Kurlander and Yohel Camayd for their assistance in conducting the validation experiment.

go through with it" was changed to "I often tell kids I'll do something with them and then I don't feel like doing it." In a few instances, we judged the content of an item to be inappropriate for young children and major changes were made in the item or it was eliminated altogether. The items that were omitted generally dealt with sexual or body-image issues or activities we felt most children would not have experienced. A few items were adapted from the Pappo scale, and a few were written by us especially for the children's scale.

Our adaptation resulted in a questionnaire consisting of 58 items. Respondents either agree ("yes") with the item as characteristic of their behaviors and beliefs or disagree ("no") with the item, thereby indicating that it is not characteristic of their behavior and beliefs. The scale was completed by over 1,300 fourth-, fifth-, and sixth-grade children,[1] and a factor analysis was computed. The factor analysis of the scale resulted in four main factors. Not surprisingly, this factor structure is similar to the one Cohen found for her original sample of adolescent high school students, although it is somewhat simpler (Cohen's factor analysis yielded nine factors). Our four factors are listed below, together with two sample items from each. The answer in parentheses is the answer that is scored as indicative of fear of success. A full copy of the children's scale is included in the appendix to this volume.

Factor 1: Impaired Concentration and Distractability

When I have to do an important homework assignment in a hurry, I get so scared that I can't keep my mind on it. (Yes)

As I get close to winning a game, I often start thinking about something else. (Yes)

Factor 2: Reluctance to Express Needs and Preferences

If someone wants to be your friend it is hard to say no without hurting their feelings. (Yes)

If I have to ask someone to help me I feel like I am bothering them. (Yes)

Factor 3: Indecisiveness

It is a good idea to talk to your friends before deciding something. (Yes)

I often tell kids I'll do something with them, and then I don't feel like doing it. (Yes)

Factor 4: Reluctance to Acknowledge Personal Competence—Tendency to Underplay Effectiveness

I believe I'm very good when it comes to sports. (No)

I've done as well as I have partly because I've had some pretty good luck. (Yes)

Items that were intended to indicate the person's tendency (1) to view accomplishment as equivalent to competitive defeat of another, (2) to be highly concerned about the evaluations of others, (3) to view exhibitionistic impulses with uneasiness, and (4) to sabotage success all loaded on two or more of the four factors described above.

The reliability of the scale was satisfactorily high. A small sample of about 100 children also completed a self-esteem questionnaire and a stability-of-self-esteem questionnaire [95]. The relationship between fear-of-success score and low self-esteem was very weak; the relationship with self-esteem instability was somewhat stronger. Another subsample of about 450 children completed a measure of test anxiety [97]. The relationship between fear of success and test anxiety was quite strong, and we shall discuss its implications later in this chapter.[2]

A Validation Experiment

In order to validate the fear-of-success scale for children, elementary school boys and girls participated in an experiment similar in general characteristics to the studies presented earlier in which students performed a task, received pre-established feedback about the quality of their work, and then performed a comparable task. The study we are reporting here was modeled most closely after Pappo's validation study (chapter 2). As in that study, the children first read and answered questions about a set of reading comprehension passages adopted from a standardized test. When they completed this first set of passages, half of the students were informed they had done very well (the *success* condition), and half were informed they had done work at an average level (*average* condition). Half of each of these groups were boys and half were girls; half of each of the gender subgroups were success-fearers while half were not. After receiving the feedback, all students completed a second set of reading comprehension passages of similar length and difficulty. Self-sabotage would be indicated by poorer performances on the second set of passages relative to the first set. Again, we expected that self-sabotage would emerge only for the success-fearing children who received success feedback. Theoretically, the performances of the other groups of children on the second set of passages should not be adversely affected by the experimenter's evaluation of their initial performances. The experimental procedures are discussed more fully below for interested readers.

Experimental Procedures

In order to select subjects for this study, the children's scale was administered to all fourth-, fifth-, and sixth-grade children attending two elementary schools in a suburban Boston school district. A total of 459 boys and girls ranging in age from nine to thirteen years old completed the children's scale in their classrooms. Students who scored in the top 25 percent of the distribution of scores for their sex and in the bottom 25 percent of the distribution of scores for their sex provided the pool from which subjects for the validation experiment were selected. Altogether eighteen male and seventeen female success-fearers and sixteen male and sixteen female non-success-fearers participated in the experiment; they were randomly assigned to the two experimental feedback conditions.

Each student participated individually in this study. The female experimenter introduced the study by telling the students that she was interested in "studying how people make predictions" and explained that in order to do so, they would be required to read a series of four short passages and answer multiple-choice questions on each passage. Before answering the comprehension questions, they would make predictions about how many questions of the total nineteen they would answer correctly. Students were told they would be given two tests; the first set of passages was represented to the student as "practice problems" to help them make more informed predictions on the second set, which was referred to as the "real task."

The passages for the reading comprehension task were taken from the Metropolitan Achievement Test, Forms Bm and Cm. For all students (fourth, fifth, and sixth graders), the first three passages and questions in both the first and second sets were identical. The particular passage that appeared last in each set, however, depended upon the grade level of the student. For sixth graders, the last passage was somewhat more difficult than the one used for fourth and fifth graders. A more difficult final passage was substituted for the older children to minimize the possibility that the passages would be substantially easier for them overall than for the younger students, which could lead either to their actually performing better or to their suspecting the credibility of the preestablished feedback. Since there was no appreciable correlation between grade level and students' scores on the first set of exercises, we assume that this procedure accomplished its aims.

After the student had completed the four passages in the first set, the experimenter pretended to score the answers and gave the student predetermined feedback according to the experimental condition. The intended interpretation of the performance was varied by presenting students with bogus percentile norms graphically illustrated by impressive-looking charts and bar graphs. Students assigned to the *success* condition were informed that they had correctly answered sixteen of the nineteen questions, which thus placed them at the 95th percentile among students their age in the state, and they were further told that they could reasonably expect to do as well or better on the second part. Students assigned to the *average* condition were informed they had correctly answered fourteen of the nineteen questions, which placed them at the

60th percentile among students their age in the state. The experimenter commented simply, "That's all right," and remarked that the student would probably do similarly on the second part. After receiving their performance feedback, students completed the second set of reading passages and subsequently answered a questionnaire designed to elicit their subjective reactions to the experience.

Results

Self-Sabotage. By now the reader is familiar with our theoretical analysis of fear of success and what many may consider the most striking behavioral manifestation of this phenomenon: performance self-sabotage. To summarize briefly, as in the previous studies we expected that the success-fearing children (boys and girls) who received success feedback on the practice reading passages would become anxious and that this anxiety would interfere with their performances on the subsequent set of reading comprehension passages and thus result in their having lower scores relative to those of the success-fearing children who believed they had performed at an average level on the first set of passages. Additionally, we expected that the nature of the feedback would not differentially affect the performances of the non-success-fearing children; they could be expected to do equally well after either an initial success or an average performance. This is precisely what occurred. The lowest scores on the second set of reading passages (statistically adjusted to take into account scores on the first set of passages) were obtained by the male and female success-fearing children who received success feedback. These children performed significantly more poorly on the second set of passages than children in any of the other groups (see table 5-1, lines A1 and A2).

Anxiety and Other Feelings. The children's own reports following the second reading task show clearly that the success-fearing children felt worried, concerned, and anxious after their performances on the reading tasks. The success-fearing students indicated that they felt significantly less self-assured after the experiment; they were also more worried after learning how they had done on the first part than their non-success-fearing peers (see table 5-1, lines C1 and C2). Theoretically, we might expect success-fearing students to be more worried by the success feedback than by the average feedback and non-success-fearing students to be more worried by the average feedback than by the success feedback. In fact, a statistically nonsignificant tendency existed for this pattern of responses to occur despite the strong normative and social desirability pressures working against such admissions (see table 5-1, line C2). Because the differences are small, we hesitate to place full confidence in this finding; we nonetheless mention it to alert other researchers to this possibility.

Table 5-1
Results of Children's Scale Validation Study

	Group				Analysis of Variance			
	(A) Success-Fearers		(B) Non-Success-Fearers					
Variable	Success (n = 19)	Average (n = 15)	Success (n = 16)	Average (n = 16)	F_A	F_B	F_{AB}	MS_e
A. Reading Comprehension Scores[a]								
1. Mean Part 1 score	12.2	11.8	12.8	12.9	1.10	0.06	0.10	10.6
2. Mean Part 2 score (adjusted for covariance with Part 1 score)	12.6	14.4	14.4	14.0	1.88	1.97	4.19*	4.6
B. Performance Evaluation[b]								
1. General evaluation	16.2	29.3	18.1	30.0	0.28	25.59***	.006	99.7
2. Evaluation compared to others' performances	48.6	34.7	49.1	35.1	0.04	39.68***	.001	80.5
3. Evaluation compared to own expectations	16.5	33.2	22.1	31.6	0.39	17.01***	1.29	163.1
C. Affect Responses								
1. Self-assurance[c]	31.4	33.6	38.6	38.4	5.41*	0.16	0.20	109.4
2. Worry experienced after learning first score[c]	37.9	34.7	21.2	24.6	11.74**	.001	0.70	245.9
3. Confidence that score will improve[c]	33.0	42.7	36.2	37.4	0.18	5.11*	3.03	93.4
4. Competence anxiety index[d]	40.9	37.5	31.9	34.0	3.29	0.04	0.63	187.9
5. Competition anxiety index[d]	41.3	36.1	34.5	26.3	9.14***	6.02	0.30	120.6

*p <.05
**p <.01
***p <.001

[a] The highest possible score was 19.

[b] Ratings were made on 61-point dotted scales; higher numbers indicate more positive evaluations.

[c] Ratings were made on 61-point dotted scales; higher numbers indicate greater self-assurance, greater worry, and more confidence of improvement, respectively.

[d] The index was computed by combining Ss' responses to two questions (see text); higher numbers indicate greater reported concern about these issues.

The overall tendency for the performance feedback—regardless of whether it was success or average—to worry the success-fearing students more than the students who do not fear success (table 5-1, line C2) is understandable in light of the approach-avoidance conflict success-fearing persons experience in achievement situations. Since they are consciously motivated to strive for successful achievements, the degree of worry that the success-fearing students reported experiencing after receiving average feedback may well have been a result of their desire to do well and their concern that their average performance meant they might fail to accomplish this goal. In line with this interpretation, the success-fearing students receiving average feedback also reported they were the most certain they would do better on the second set of passages, which probably reflects their motivation to succeed (see table 5-1, line C3). We are suggesting, then, that the greater overall degree of worry and concern expressed by success-fearing students regardless of their experimental condition reflects worry and concern about qualitatively different aspects of the situation. On the one hand, these students were apparently anxious that they would be successful; on the other hand, they were also worried that they would not be successful.

Clearly, then, for children who fear success, successful performances are accompanied by anxiety responses that interfere with their subsequent performances. We have already mentioned another set of strategies available to success-fearing persons to help them deal with confrontations with their successes—that is, the tendency to rationalize or excuse high-quality performances by assuming such results are attributable to factors external to themselves or factors over which they have little control. Such a view of the reason for their successes allows success-fearing persons to continue, despite success, to deny their competence and their responsibility for their accomplishments. Like the late adolescents in our other studies, the children in this study also demonstrated such biases in their interpretations of their performances. The success-fearing children who received success feedback on the first set of reading passages were the most likely to report that they had done "much better" than they had originally expected, suggesting they had begun the task expecting not to do very well (see table 5-1, line B3). When they were confronted with their unexpected success, however, they were as likely as non-success-fearing children to admit, perfectly realistically, that their ability and effort played a role. However, these success-fearing children were also significantly more likely to say they believed a scoring mistake had been made and that their mood while they were doing the test was important in influencing their final score, as is consistent with the general tendency of success-fearers to downplay responsibility for their successes. Although we do not have information concerning precisely how the children believed these factors were important, we can reasonably assume that the success-fearing children who received success feedback on the first part believed that if a mistake had not been made in scoring the test, they would have received a lower score, while the success-fearing children who received average feedback initially, believed they would have received a higher score if no mistake had been made.

Competence or Competition Anxiety? In earlier chapters we have presented two quite different theoretical perspectives concerning the development of fear of success: one that emphasizes the importance of competence and independence strivings (chapter 2) and the other that emphasizes the role of competition (chapter 3). Students' questionnaire responses in this study suggest that both competence issues and competition issues contribute to triggering anxiety in success-fearing persons. After the testing, students were asked to reflect on how they felt "before you actually began the test, while you were being told about what you would have to do." They responded on four separate dimensions indicating worry about the quality of their predictions, worry about the quality of their reading comprehension scores, worry about how well they would do compared to others, and finally, curiosity about how well other children in the class would do. We combined their answers to create two new indices. The first index, computed by averaging students' responses to the first two items, reflects their concern with how well they themselves perform at the tasks involved in the experiment; we, therefore, consider it a "competence anxiety index." The second index, computed by averaging students' responses to the last two items, reflects their concern with how other people are performing and how their own performances measure up to those of the others; we consider it a "competition anxiety index."

Students who fear success, regardless of their experimental condition, reported both greater competence anxiety and greater competition anxiety than did the students who do not fear success. Indeed, we are not surprised that the success-fearing students who experienced an initial success reported the highest degree of anxiety from both of these sources. Although the questions asked them how they felt prior to beginning the reading comprehension passages, no doubt their recollections had been colored by their experiences during the experimental session. The fear-of-success variable actually accounted for more than twice as much variance for the competition anxiety index than for the competence anxiety index (12 percent versus 5 percent), thereby indicating that the fear-of-success factor was substantially more important in determining students' reactions to the competitive aspects of the situation than to the competence aspects of the situation. Clearly, however, both issues seem to be important sources of anxiety for these success-fearing children (see table 5-1, lines C4 and C5).

Implications

Our attempt to devise a questionnaire measure for use in fear-of-success research with children of elementary school age appears to have been quite successful.

The scale is appropriately geared to the concerns and vocabulary level of children of this age; it has adequate reliability and a factor structure similar to that reported for the adult scales; and it has gained a measure of predictive validity from the results of the experiment we have described in this chapter.

The data from the experiment also give us confidence that the dynamics of the fear-of-success syndrome in children of this age range are similar to its dynamics in late adolescence and early adulthood. The performance decrement following success, which we have called self-sabotage behavior, was clearly demonstrated by the success-fearing children in the experiment. Both success-fearing boys and girls performed more poorly following initial success feedback than after initial average feedback, while non-success-fearing children performed equally well after success or average feedback. The students' responses to a number of questions following the reading comprehension exercises indicate that the success-fearing children in our study experienced anxiety following success in much the same way the older students in our other studies did and that they used similar defense mechanisms to guard against success anxiety. The overall pattern of responses to a successful performance and an unremarkable one by younger and older success-fearers is remarkably similar.

As in the other studies we reported in this book thus far, no important sex differences emerged between the reactions of boys and girls who fear success. The few minor sex differences that did show up in the experiment probably were due to differences in the degree to which boys and girls considered reading comprehension skills to be important; girls might have been somewhat more involved in the task. Thus, their reactions appeared slightly more intense relative to the reactions of the boys in the experiment.

The Recurring Issue of Fear of Success and Fear of Failure

The strong relationship that emerged between the children's scale and the test anxiety scale leads us once again to the relationship between fear of success and fear of failure. The Sarason et al. Test Anxiety Scale for Children, which served as our measure of test anxiety, has often been used by researchers other than Sarason as a measure of fear of failure in children. Someone interested in incorporating our research into previous studies of fear of failure [12,39] might still be tempted to argue, on the basis of the strong relationship between our scale and the Sarason et al. scale, that our scale is "really" measuring fear of failure. We shall say a few more words about this apparent confusion.

The Sarason et al. test is a measure of anxiety about performance, evaluation, test taking, and the like. The respondent is asked to say "yes" or "no" to a variety of questions such as the following: "Do you worry when the teacher says that she is going to ask you questions to find out how much you know?" "Are you afraid of school tests?" Clearly, such questions as these are not specific to failure; they are about reactions to performing and being evaluated in general. The argument that we have "really" been investigating the fear of failure because our measure is correlated with this one is an argument that mistakes Sarason's measure of the concept of test anxiety for a measure of the concept of fear of failure. As we have pointed out before (see chapters 2 and 4), distinguishing the fear of success from the fear of failure both conceptually and empirically is important in order to know how particular identifiable categories of people respond to particular identifiable categories of circumstances. This distinction cannot be made simply by using a measure of test anxiety as a measure of fear of failure, however. We will return to this issue in chapter 11 with further discussion of the relationship between the research conducted by Sarason and his colleagues on test anxiety and our own research on fear of success.

We now turn to a different issue in research on fear of success. The preceding chapters have demonstrated that fear of success is manifested in the controlled environment of the laboratory; but do success-fearing persons differ from other persons in natural settings? In the next chapter we examine differences between success-fearing and non-success-fearing college students in everyday situations.

Notes

1. Children from three elementary schools in the Boston area completed the children's fear-of-success scale. The mean scores for boys and girls in each of the three schools were: (1) socioeconomically heterogeneous suburban school: Males ($n = 460$, Mean = 30.6, s.d. = 7.68); Females ($n = 455$, Mean = 34.1, s.d. = 7.45); (2) upper middle class suburban school: Males ($n = 109$, Mean = 26.0, s.d. = 8.06); Females ($n = 121$, Mean = 34.4, s.d. = 7.68); on a military base: Males ($n = 110$, Mean = 34.4, s.d. = 7.68); Females ($n = 119$, Mean = 35.6, s.d. = 7.86). In all three samples of children tested, a small but statistically stable difference existed between the scores of male and female children. This difference is probably due to the greater willingness of girls than boys of this age to recognize and report their personal feelings. No differences emerged among the three grades tested, and no differences were detected between children whose classroom teachers were women and children whose classroom teachers were men.

2. Coefficient Alpha was computed to be .83 based on the questionnaire responses of 814 boys and girls. Based on a sample of 110 boys and girls the correlation between responses to the children's scale and these other measures were: (1) Rosenberg Self-Esteem Scale, $r = .14$; (2) Rosenberg Self-Esteem Stability Scale, $r = .28$, $p < .05$; (3) Sarason, et al. Test Anxiety for Children, $r = .63, p < .001$.

6 Success-Fearers in Everyday Life

The results of the experiments we have presented thus far to validate our various questionnaire measures of fear of success are clear and impressive. The results of any laboratory experiment, however, leave a major question unanswered: In real-life terms, how important or robust is the variable under investigation? Is the variable strong enough to influence behavior in natural, real-life settings? Experiments, after all, are designed to provide optimum circumstances for detecting the consequences of the theoretical ideas that underly their independent variables. Extraneous factors are removed or brought under careful control so that their effects are minimized. More ordinary environments, on the other hand, are not so conveniently "purified." People in real life are under many pressures, have a variety of interests and goals, and are subject to distractions, accidents, and hosts of other factors that can otherwise interfere with the operation of variables that may work quite successfully in experiments. Only the more powerful influences on human behavior can be observed to affect people in complex, real-life circumstances. In this chapter, therefore, we present the results of several investigations of the fear of success conducted in natural settings. These data confirm the everyday operation of the fear-of-success variable and provide us with interesting insights into the experience of fearing success in day-to-day life.

A Brief Note on Procedures

The information we will be discussing in this chapter is based on data collected several years apart from three different groups of male and female college students enrolled in two large coeducational universities. All students had completed the Pappo fear-of-sucess scale. The samples used for the analyses were selected on the basis of scores on this scale approximately one standard deviation discrepant from their respective group mean. In actuality, the means and standard deviations of the larger groups from which the samples were drawn were virtually identical with a mean of approximately 37 and a standard deviation of 12. Therefore, for all samples, the distribution cutoff score to define success-fearers was 49 or above, and for non-success-fearers, it was 25 or below.

The first sample consisted of 200 students at all grade levels attending a public university. The computerized academic transcripts of approximately three-fourths of these students were made available to us (after students' names were replaced with identification numbers) two years after these students had originally completed the Pappo scale. Analysis of these records uncovered interesting patterns in the overall academic histories of these students. The second sample included 219 students enrolled in the introductory psychology course at a private university during three consecutive academic semesters. The large majority of these students were freshmen; some were sophomores, but only a handful were upperclassmen. Analysis of detailed records of these students' within-class progress during one of the semesters provided more specific clues to the actual process of learning for success-fearing persons. The third sample was drawn from a larger group of students at all grade levels from the same private university who volunteered to participate in a questionnaire survey about "achievement-related motivation" for a small remuneration. Although this survey was designed with other purposes in mind, much of the information is relevant to the issues we present here. Numerical descriptions of these samples are contained in table 6-1.

Indecisiveness

We have discussed a variety of defense mechanisms used by success-fearers to ward off or cope with the anxiety generated by imminent success. One of the general characteristics of success-fearers discussed in this context is their tendency to focus their attention away from information that indicates competence or mastery, such as by attending to the evaluations made by others in a performance situation or by delaying the acknowledgment that success has been or will be attained. College students may manifest success-avoidant mechanisms in a variety of ways. For them, the ultimate indication of success at college is graduation, after which the person is expected to change from the role of "student" to that of "adult job holder." One way the success-fearing college student may deal with this impending transition, this evidence of success, competence, or independence, is by not attending to it and/or by not planning for it. Thus, we might expect that success-fearing persons would delay making a decision about what career or occupation they intend to enter after graduation, or they might frequently change their minds about their future plans. Both behaviors could serve the function of allowing them to not commit themselves to a particular career choice, since such a commitment might constitute an acknowledgment that they will in fact be graduated one day.

Such choice delaying or choice shifting may also be manifested around decisions relating to the college career itself. For instance, students who fear success might put off making a decision about their "major" area until forced by the school to declare a major, or they might frequently change their majors. Delaying or shifting the choice of major also conveniently allows persons to delay or shift their choice of career specialization.

Table 6-1
Description of Samples Used in Field Studies

| Sample or Subsample Number | Source of Sample | Fear-of-Success Scale Scores | | | Sample Sizes Used in Analyses Reported | | | |
| | | | | | Success-Fearers | | Non-Success-Fearers | |
		Mean	s.d.	Total n	Males	Females	Males	Females
1	Public University	37.0	12.0	516	64	54	37	45
1a	Transcripts available				54	40	22	28
2	Private University							
2a	Introductory Psychology students (a)	37.6	11.4	631	51	62	51	55
2b	Introductory Psychology students (b)	36.7	11.0	333	26	27	23	31
3	Private University (General)	37.0	11.7	409	41	47	25	41

These behaviors, which we speculate are particularly characteristic of success-fearers, may appear to an outside observer as indecisiveness. Success-fearing persons may seem unable to commit themselves to particular courses of action, or they may choose courses of action, apparently pursue them vigorously, but before ever fully realizing their goals, switch to other paths of action that they ambitiously pursue, only to drop those before reaching their goals. A number of indices suggest that such apparent indecisiveness, vacillation, and disillusionment with choices once made are indeed more characteristic of success-fearing persons than of those who do not fear success.

Embedded within a "background information" questionnaire completed by students at the public university was a question asking them simply to state their "future occupational goal." In order to ascertain whether success-fearing persons are in fact more unclear or indecisive about their future plans, students' responses were categorized according to whether they reported an occupational goal or did not report one. Included in the latter category were all students who left the answer blank or answered with a question mark, wrote "undecided" or "unknown," or in some other way indicated that they were vague or unsure of their career goals, such as by writing a goal and then qualifying it by one or more question marks or by specifying several quite different occupational goals. Over half of both male and female success-fearers lacked clarity concerning their future plans while only a minority of non-success-fearers lacked such clarity, as can be seen in table 6-2. In the entire sample, fully 56 percent of all success-fearers failed to indicate a future goal while less than half that number (27 percent) of non-success-fearers were ambiguous about their goals. The same question was asked of the private university students, and here again, a similar pattern emerged: both male and female success-fearers were less likely to report an occupational goal than were their non-success-fearing peers. The difference between success-fearers and non-success-fearers is much less pronounced for the women than men in the private university, however.

When asked directly how definite were their plans for the period after college, success-fearers who participated in the questionnaire survey at the private university reported being significantly less definite about their plans. They also reported that they experienced significantly more difficulty making decisions in general and more difficulty making the specific decisions about which college to attend, about what area to major in, and about what to do after they are graduated from college. Moreover, for each of these specific decision areas, success-fearers reported they were significantly less satisfied with the choice they had made.

Clearly, then, high scorers on the Pappo fear-of-success scale are more reluctant than low scorers to admit to having clearly defined occupational goals. Success-fearers also report greater difficulty in making important life decisions (such as choice of college and major subject) and less satisfaction with these decisions once they are made. But these are questions having to do with the respondents' subjective states. As important as these subjective-state questions may be, we can argue that if they have no implications for actual behaviors and performances, they need not be taken so seriously.

Table 6-2
Indicators of Indecisiveness among Success-Fearers and Non-Success-Fearers: Mean Ratings and Percentages

Dependent Variable	Sample Number (From Table 6-1)	Success-Fearers		Non-Success-Fearers	
		Male	Female	Male	Female
Future Goals					
Percent not specifying an occupational goal	1	55%***	57%	30%	24%
Percent not specifying an occupational goal	2a	49%***	31%	13%	22%
Mean rated definiteness of future plans[a]	3	5.7*	5.1	6.9	6.1
Interference with Decision Making					
Mean rated difficulty of decision making (in general)[b]	3	4.5***	5.3	2.8	2.7
Mean rated difficulty of decision regarding:					
a. which college to attend[b]	3	5.2***	4.4	3.2	2.7
b. major subject[b]	3	5.3***	5.0	3.4	2.2
c. career[b]	3	5.9***	5.5	3.6	3.2
Mean rated satisfaction with decision regarding:					
a. which college to attend[c]	3	5.7*	6.4	7.1	7.3
b. major subject[c]	3	7.1	6.7	7.2	7.7
c. career[c]	3	6.7***	6.2	8.0	8.0

Note: The percentages in the table were analyzed using the arcsin transformation procedure suggested by Langer and Abelson [58]. Asterisks denote probability levels associated with the difference between the responses of success-fearers and non-success-fearers, without regard to sex.

*$p < .05$
***$p < .001$

[a]Ratings were made on a 9-point rating scale. Higher numbers indicate greater definiteness of future plans.
[b]Ratings were made on a 9-point rating scale. Higher numbers indicate greater difficulty in decision-making.
[c]Ratings were made on a 9-point rating scale. Higher numbers indicate greater satisfaction with the decision.

Self-Sabotage

A veritable munitions factory of self-sabotage behaviors is available to college students to cope with their battle against success-induced anxiety: "forgetting" to do assignments or to attend exams, getting ill just before an important class presentation, deciding at the last minute that a final paper needs more library research, performing less well in a course at the end of a term, delaying studying or paper writing until the pressures of time and material force "cramming" at the last minute, finding ending papers difficult, and so forth. The ultimate self-sabotage behavior is dropping out of school altogether. A less drastic maneuver, but one that may serve a similar psychological function, is transferring to another school. We discuss these various forms of self-sabotage in the next three sections.

Academic Performance Records

"Spotty" Records. Interferences in the process of studying or completing assignments may actually result in success-fearing students' obtaining lower grades than students who do not fear success. Although this pattern would not necessarily be true for each and every course in which the student enrolls, we suspected that success-fearing students would show greater variability in their overall performances than students who do not fear success. In other words, we expected success-fearers, more than non-success-fearers, to have what we call "spotty" records—that is, records indicating a lack of consistent performance, with the student earning both good grades and poorer grades. This performance variability or inconsistency might sometimes also be reflected in a lower overall grade-point average for success-fearing students when compared to students who do not fear success.

One rather simple indication of performance variability we computed from the transcripts available from our public university sample takes into account all the courses in which a student had enrolled. We simply counted the number of different grade categories necessary to describe each student's academic transcript. The possible categories included the letter grades A, B, C, D, and F (grades at this school were not modified by pluses and minuses), and nongraded categories of pass, withdrawal, incomplete, and no credit. Significantly more categories were necessary to describe the academic transcripts of success-fearing students than those who do not fear success (see table 6-3).

Since the number of categories necessary to describe a transcript includes nongraded as well as graded courses, we developed a more specific "spotty record index." This index summarizes the amount of performance variability in those courses the student completed and for which he received a letter grade. Thus, all courses for which the student elected a pass or no credit option or

Table 6-3

Indicators of Self-Sabotage and Competence Derogation among Success-Fearers and Non-Success-Fearers

Dependent Variable	Sample Number (From Table 6-1)	Success-Fearers Male	Female	Non-Success-Fearers Male	Female
Academic Records					
Mean number of grading categories to describe transcript	1a	5.4**	5.1	4.4	4.3
Spotty record index	1a	0.96*	0.80	0.76	0.64
Actual grade-point average	1a	2.67**	2.92	3.05	3.23
Self-reported grade-point average	1	2.69*	2.91	2.91	3.21
Procrastination					
Mean number of mastery units completed by mid-term	2a	5.6**	5.6	6.3	6.8
Self-Sabotage					
Percent repeating mastery units	2a	57%[a]	57%	39%	39%
Percent endangering honors credits	2a	56%	56%	39%	45%
Percent "dropouts"	1a	23%	34%	18%	20%
Percent considering changing major subject	3	58%*	38%	41%	22%
Percent considering dropping out or transferring	3	44%**	29%	12%	16%
Competence Derogation					
Number of own skills reported	3	4.3***	5.1	6.2	7.3
Percent reporting sarcastic-derogatory skills	3	44%***	28%	6%	10%

Note: The percentages in the table were analyzed using the arcsin transformation procedure suggested by Langer and Abelson [58]. Asterisks denote probability levels associated with the difference between the responses of success-fearers and non-success-fearers without regard to sex.

*$p < .05$
**$p < .01$
***$p < .06$

[a]$p < .06$

those the student did not complete and received a grade of incomplete or withdrawal are not included in tabulations of the spotty record index.

In general, then, the spotty record index (SRI) is a measure of the average variability of a student's performance in graded courses. The particular grade range in which the student usually performed was taken into account by using each student's most frequently obtained grade as the baseline and differentially weighting grades above and below this base according to how discrepant they were. Since performing more poorly than usual is more likely to indicate anxiety interference than performing better than usual, grades below the base grade were weighted slightly more heavily than those above the base grade. The actual mechanics involved in computing the SRI for each student were as follows: The total number of credit hours earned in each grade category (A through F) was determined and the modal grade (that grade in which the highest number of credits was earned) was identified. The number of credit hours earned for each grade above and below the modal grade were then multiplied by a constant. The number of credit hours one grade higher than the modal base was multiplied by 1; those one grade below were multiplied by 1.5. Credit hours two grades above or below the modal base were multiplied by 2 and 2.5, respectively; those three grades deviant by 3 if above and 3.5 if below, and those four grades above or below the mode by 4 and 4.5, respectively. The SRI was then computed by summing these weighted credit hours and dividing by the *total* number of graded credit hours (including the credit hours of the modal grade). A higher numerical index reflects greater performance variability.

Let us illustrate this method with two examples. In our manner of computation, a hypothetical student who earned thirty credits of grade A and ten credits of grade B would be assigned the same index score as a student who earned thirty credits of grade B and ten credits of grade C (SRI = .375). The fact that the second student has grades that are generally lower than those of the first does not alter the spotty record index. On the other hand, a student who earned thirty credits of B and ten credits of C would have a lower index than a student who earned thirty credits of B, five credits of grade C, and five credits of grade D (.375 versus .50). The latter student's record is intuitively less consistent than the former's, which is reflected in a higher spotty record index assignment for that student.

If our reasoning is correct, we would expect the success-fearers to obtain a higher SRI score on the average than the non-success-fearers, which is precisely what we did find. In the total sample, success-fearers obtained significantly higher SRI scores on the average than non-success-fearers (see table 6-3).

Grade-Point Averages. Since success-fearers have been shown to have more variable academic performance records than non-success-fearers, not surprisingly, their cumulative grade-point averages (GPAs) for their college careers as reported on their transcripts were also somewhat lower. The difference in grade-point average between success-fearers and those who do not fear success, although statistically stable, was quite small in magnitude, however. For this reason, we are persuaded that success-fearers are not inherently less able than non-success-fearers. Success-fearing students are clearly capable of earning high grades because many As do appear on their transcripts. Their lower GPAs are not because they *always* earn low grades, but rather because they are less consistent than non-success-fearing students in earning high grades.

Since success-fearing persons have been shown to obtain slightly lower grade-point averages, it might be reasonable to suggest that perhaps the demonstrated difference in goal clarity between students who fear success and those who do not is due to the realistic perception among students with lower GPAs that fewer career options are open to them. This interpretation would rationally explain why success-fearers (who obtain lower GPAs) are also less likely to have clear goals without having to postulate an interference in the decision-making process due to their fear of success. This alternative explanation would imply that students who specify a goal should report higher GPAs than those who do not specify a goal. However, the evidence rules out this interpretation. The reported GPAs for students in the public university who specified a goal and those who did not were compared. In none of the four sex by fear-of-success subgroups was this difference statistically significant.

Procrastination: Performance in a Self-Paced Course

Analysis of the spotty record index confirms our expectation that success-fearing males and females are likely to be less consistent in their overall college records than are students who do not fear success. By examining detailed class records of students' work in the introductory psychology class at our private university, we can begin to understand more clearly how success-fearing students progress through a course. This information allows us to make inferences about the study habits of success-fearing students that partially explain their inconsistent course performances. The organization of the introductory psychology course was ideal for our purposes since students could move at their own pace through the material. This flexibility would allow individual differences among students in their approach to the course to emerge more freely than if all students were forced to adhere to rigid course deadlines.

The subject matter of this course was divided into small units of material, and each student was required to pass a "mastery test" at the end of each of fourteen units with a perfect score. Students could not proceed to another unit until complete mastery on the preceding unit had been demonstrated, but they could take a test on any given unit as many times as was needed to achieve the necessary mastery level. Having to repeat units did not directly affect a student's final grade. To obtain credit for the course, students were required to complete the fourteen units satisfactorily, pass a final exam with a grade of at least "C," and participate in five hours of research in the department. Course grades were based on the grade obtained on the final exam (maximum B) and the number of "honors credits" earned from three additional and voluntary exams given at scheduled times during the term. Honors credits incrementally raised the grade on the final exam to determine the final course grade. A progress report was kept for each student to record the date each unit mastery test was taken, the performance on each mastery test, and how many credits were earned on each of the honors tests. Thus, we were able to analyze a fairly detailed record of the in-class performances of students in a course for which students had to take a great deal of responsibility and initiative for the scheduling and completion of the course work.

We first examined the final course grade earned by students in our sample and found only a slight and nonsignificant tendency for success-fearers to obtain lower final grades on the average when compared to non-success-fearing students. We were not surprised at this finding. Although we had seen that grade-point averages were somewhat lower for success-fearers, the differences, as we noted, were small. Because the GPA takes into account a student's performance over a wide range of courses—and different courses for different students—the performance variability demonstrated for success-fearers would not be expected to result in lower grades in any one particular course we might select to study.

We did, however, expect fear of sucess to be evidenced in the *process* by which students obtained their grades in this self-paced course. Mastery of the required fourteen units could be achieved in a variety of ways. The most straightforward would be for students to pace themselves at the rate of one unit per week during the fourteen-week semester. Obviously, though, variations in the rates at which students proceeded through the units could be expected. Some students might work rather consistently at an even rate; others might work rapidly at the beginning of the term and complete all the units in a short period of time; and still others might procrastinate and leave the bulk of the work to the end of the term. In fact, we expected success-fearers to demonstrate more procrastination than the non-success-fearing students. We reasoned that if success is anxiety producing for students who fear success, then in the early weeks of the course, when the end of the term seems quite distant and time pressures are minimal, they would cope with anxiety that might be aroused by successful completion of early units by delaying the completion of additional units that could potentially arouse more anxiety. However, the amount of procrastination and delay that would be feasible had an upper limit; the reality constraint of the term's end would force success-fearers to speed up in order to complete the required units by the end-of-term deadline.

We therefore expected that the success-fearing students would complete fewer units by the midsemester point than the non-success-fearing students. Each student's progress report was examined to determine the number of units successfully completed by the end of the seventh week of classes. As predicted, students who fear success completed significantly fewer units on the average by the middle of the term than students who do not fear success, and this difference was demonstrated by both males and females (see table 6-3).

Other Self-Sabotaging Behaviors in the Self-Paced Course. Delaying completion of mastery units might be considered an indirect form of self-sabotage behavior, for if students delayed too long they could conceivably not complete the course requirements by the end of the term. This ultimate self-sabotage was not characteristic of students in our sample, however; only three students failed to complete the course requirements. Two other indicators of self-sabotage behavior in this course were available, however: repeating mastery units and undermining the accumulation of honors credits.

The first self-sabotage indicator we examined was the number of students who had to repeat one or more mastery units. Recall that repeating units did not directly affect the students' final grades, although it could influence the rate of their progress through the material. Failing to pass a mastery test after having passed a previous one, and consequently repeating it, is analogous to our previously reported experimental findings that following success success-fearers do more poorly than non-success-fearers. We expected, of course, that more success-fearers would need to repeat units than non-success-fearers, and this prediction was confirmed. Approximately 57 percent of the success-fearers had to repeat one or more units following a successful unit mastery, while among the non-success-fearers, only 39 percent had to repeat units.

Since the final grade students earned in this course depended in part upon the total number of honors credits they earned and since taking honors tests was voluntary, another potential self-sabotage strategy available to students who fear success involved undermining their accumulation of honors points. Earning as many of the possible nine honors points as a student could was to his or her advantage because these points incrementally raised the grade on the final exam to determine the final course grade. For instance, a grade of C+ on the final exam could be raised to a course grade of A if the student earned at least eight of the nine honors points; however, since only three honors tests were given, the student could achieve such a score only by taking all of them.

To determine whether success-fearing students would self-sabotage with respect to the honors credits more frequently than non-success-fearing students, we identified those students who failed to take the third honors test or who earned fewer points on it than they had on the preceding honors exams. Since there was only a slight tendency for success-fearers to obtain lower course grades than students who do not fear success, we did not expect this measure to produce large differences. Nonetheless, there was a tendency for a higher proportion of success-fearing students to self-sabotage on the last honors exam than non-success-fearing students. In the entire sample, 56 percent of the success-fearers either failed to take the third honors exam or received fewer credits on it than on preceding exams, while only 43 percent of the non-success-fearing students did so. The proportions within the male and female subsamples are nearly identical.

Because of the organization of this particular course, undermining one's score on a unit test—which would have to be repeated—and delaying the completion of one's course work were behaviors that would not necessarily affect the student's final course grade. However, in more "traditional" courses in which students obtain test grades and must meet assignment deadlines throughout the term, such processes might sometimes be expected to actually lower their final grades and thus result in the lack of overall performance consistency demonstrated above. The tendency for success-fearing students more often to undermine their honors credit exams—which could affect their final grade—suggests that self-sabotage behaviors occur not merely with respect to situations that have no evaluative consequences and that can ultimately be rectified, but also with respect to tasks that do have evaluative implications and potential long-range consequences.

"Dropping Out" and Switching Majors

Our reasoning about fear of success led us to suggest earlier that success-fearers would be more likely than students who do not fear success to drop out of school or transfer to another school. We were able to test this prediction by examining the academic transcripts available for students from our public university to determine whether the students were in attendance every term. Although we have no way of knowing whether or not a student actually transferred to another school, his or her absence from school for one or more terms was indicated to us by a lack of entries on the transcript for a given term after the student's matriculation. In such cases we assumed that the students had withdrawn from the school either temporarily or permanently and thus classified them as "dropouts." Since study abroad or through exchange programs with other universities was specified on the transcript, our "dropout" figures include only those students who had interrupted their studies or transferred permanently to another university; they do not include those students who remained matriculated but took courses elsewhere during any given term.

We found a tendency for success-fearing students to drop out more frequently than students who do not fear success although the differences do not reach statistical significance. The differences are most pronounced among the females, where approximately 34 percent of the success-fearing students were classified as dropouts and only about 20 percent of the non-success-fearing students were so classified. Among the males, this pattern is still evident, but it is much less pronounced, with only about 23 percent of success-fearers being classified as dropouts and approximately 18 percent of non-success-fearers so classified (see table 6-3).

Additional evidence supports these observations. Among respondents to our private university survey, success-fearers were more likely than non-success-fearers to report that they had "very seriously" considered taking a leave of absence or transferring to another school. They were also significantly more likely to report that they had either switched majors sometime during their college experience or had "very seriously" considered doing so. In the total sample, 47 percent of the success-fearers said they had either changed their majors or had seriously considered doing so, while only 29 percent of the non-success-fearers reported that they had done so (see table 6-3).

Competence Derogation

One of the characteristics we identified for success-fearers is their tendency to repudiate, deny, or downplay their competence at various tasks. We have all known the student who reports to his classmates that he did "lousy on the exam" when he obtained "only" an A—. Such a statement may be more than a consciously adopted reporting style; the student may in fact genuinely believe that his performances have not measured up to his standards. The defense mechanism of underevaluating one's competence, denying or distorting successes, or disparaging achievements, then, may very well reflect the operation of the more subtle psychological process of standard elevation. In other words, the success-fearing student may set his standards so high that his actual performances must necessarily fall short. The adoption of high standards is consistent with the success-fearer's high motivation to attain success, but it also functions to ensure that the person never has to acknowledge that his or her performances are at an objectively high level—that is, that he or she has been "successful." Because of their high motivation to succeed, success-fearers may very well even attain levels of performance that outsiders would evaluate very positively. However, by setting their own standards at a sufficiently high level, success-fearing persons never have to acknowledge personally that they have done well. We suspect that success-fearing persons are rarely able to say "good enough"; no matter how well they perform, they are likely to think their performances are inadequate or that they could have done better. Thus, they can deny that they have actually succeeded.

The questionnaire survey of our private university students provides us with data illustrating competence derogation on the part of success-fearers. A space was provided for students to "list all the things you do well." Initially we simply counted the number of skills the student reported. Overwhelmingly, both male and female success-fearers mentioned significantly fewer skills than their non-success-fearing peers. Success-fearers mentioned only 4.7 skills on the average, while non-success-fearers mentioned fully 6.7 on the average. As telling as this quantitative indicator is, however, it masks some very interesting qualitative differences in the reporting of one's perceived skills by these students. Many of the students listed what we have called sarcastic or self-derogatory skills—that is, activities most people would not consider to be competence areas but seem instead to be self-inflicted "put-downs." We categorized the following examples taken from students' questionnaires as sarcastic-derogatory skills: "watch TV," "eat," "daydream," "tying shoelaces," "blab," "lie," "worry," "sleep," and "goofing off," among others. Not surprisingly, success-fearers—both males and females—were much more likely to include such activities in their lists of what they do well. In the entire sample, over one-third (35 percent) of the success-fearers mentioned at least one such "skill," while only 9 percent of the students who do not fear success did so.

Some anecdotal evidence points to further interesting differences between the way success-fearers and non-success-fearers think about their skills. Several of the students responded to this question by saying that they did "nothing" well. Although this response was characteristic of less than 2 percent of our sample, the fact that every single person who claimed no skills was a success-fearer is noteworthy. The opposite response—referring to themselves as being generally competent—occurred only among the students who do not fear success. For instance, a non-success-fearing male wrote: "I do anything well that I want." Another student—a female—remarked: "When I have a job, I *always* do quality work."

Success-fearers were more apt to qualify their statements or make them conditional by claiming that "sometimes" they did a given task well or that they do it "fairly" well. Contrast the confident tone of the quotes from the non-success-fearers above with these statements made by success-fearers:

Although I consider myself fairly confident, I can't think of specific things I do well. (female)

I like to think there is little I do well, but several things I do above average. (male)

I have no idea what I can do well. I guess if I try, I would be able to do well in any field I want to, if I have the concentrated effort to do it. (female)

I organize things that have a low priority; academic and other pressing matters are put off and left disorganized. I can write reasonably well when I try hard enough. (male)

Admittedly, only a small proportion of success-fearers thought they did "nothing" well, and only a handful of non-success-fearers spoke in global terms of their competence. Most students listed some specific activities they were good at, covering the broad spectrum of human activity: athletics, the arts, interpersonal relationships, intellectual activities, domesticity, and so on. Nonetheless the above examples help to highlight the experience of fearing success.

Conclusions

Taken together, the data presented in this chapter give abundant support to the notion that the fear of success has important real-life consequences for a rather large group of people—for their inner lives (e.g., what they think and feel about their abilities, their competencies, and their future prospects) and for what they actually do and obtain in life. The fear-of-success concept has shown itself to be a sturdy and practical one that predicts behaviors and feelings not only in the controlled environment of the laboratory, but also in the richer and more varied environments of everyday life. Thus, our laboratory studies gain some additional significance from the field studies we have reported in this chapter. Clearly, it is more consequential to study in detail an idea that is robust and predicts behavior in everyday life.

**Part III:
The Social Psychology
of Achievement and the
Fear of Success**

Introduction to Part III

A set of theoretical ideas about a phenomenon such as the neurotic fear of success becomes more useful when those ideas are embedded in a larger framework of ideas. The larger framework provides connections between the phenomenon of interest to us and other phenomena and guides researchers toward investigating these connections. The notions about the fear of success we developed in earlier chapters were rooted in a more general network of ideas about neuroses and their origins. These connections led us toward a line of investigation we might otherwise not have followed.

Although the kinds of constraints that a theorist must work with are somewhat different than those accepted by poets, sculptors, or composers, a scientific theory is just as much a human invention as a sonnet, a statue, or a string quartet. The directions taken by the scientific theorist are in large part dictated by that person's interests, predilections, and personal experiences. We chose to think about the fear-of-success phenomenon in personality development and clinical terms, and to some degree, that choice was arbitrary. We could have taken the theory in a very different direction. Matina S. Horner, for example, has studied a phenomenon that is something like the one we have been talking about—that is, a tendency or motive to pull back from success. Horner chose to embed her ideas in the general framework of achievement motivation proposed by one of her former teachers, John W. Atkinson. She postulated a motive to avoid success among women not only because she had herself observed success avoidance in women, but also to help explain the failure of Atkinson's theory to account for the behavior of women in certain achievement situations. Her idea was interesting, ingenious, and potentially very useful; thinking about fear of success phenomena in connection with other notions that have to do with work, striving, achievement, and so on seems highly appropriate.

In the three chapters that follow, then, we explore various general ideas about accomplishment and achievement as a potential network in which the fear-of-success phenomenon as we know it can be contained. This alternative leads us in a direction very different from the one we have taken so far and extends our thinking about the fear of success a great deal, in ways that seem to us to be practical as well as intellectually interesting.

As we began to think carefully about people's desire to accomplish and achieve, we embarked upon a close examination of the voluminous literature on achievement motivation written or stimulated by John W. Atkinson and his colleagues and students. This point of view has essentially dominated the scholarly literature on achievement motivation for twenty-five years, and has stimulated a large body of empirical research. Our examination of this literature has led us to the conclusion that the theory has certain difficulties that reduce its usefulness for our purposes. We have, therefore, moved in the direction of an alternative theoretical perspective. In chapter 7, then, we present and examine the ideas about achievement motivation of Atkinson and his associates, and some of the research conducted to test these ideas. Horner's ideas and research on fear of success in women are also discussed in some detail. In chapter 8 we ask broader questions about sources of the motivation to accomplish, and deal with situational as well as intrapersonal sources of the desire to do productive work. Chapter 9 examines the influence of certain social arrangements on accomplishment motivation and finally connects what we know about fear of success with the theoretical notions toward which we have moved in part III.

7

Achievement Motivation and Achievement Conflict in Women

In our search for a network of general ideas about achievement motivation that could be used to extend our understanding of fear of success, we began with a close examination of the theories of achievement motivation developed by David C. McClelland and John W. Atkinson. These ideas have been dominant in the literature on achievement motivation for nearly three decades and have generated a great deal of empirical research. Atkinson's version of the theory, which was designed to investigate achievement motivation as a personality disposition and to examine its consequences for individual behavior in achievement-related situations, appeared most promising. Atkinson's theory has been used by Matina S. Horner and others as a framework within which to study success avoidance in women, which made the theory particularly intriguing to us. This chapter, then, is primarily devoted to an examination of Atkinson's theory of achievement motivation and Horner's work on achievement conflict in American women. We ask whether Atkinson's theory is useful for our purposes, and examine whether the theory deals with a variety of motivational phenomena that we believe are of importance in the study of achievement motivation. Our examination of Atkinson's theory is followed by a detailed discussion of Horner's intriguing work on what has been termed fear of success in women.

Atkinson's Theory of Achievement Motivation

The theory of achievement motivation dates back to 1948, when Atkinson and McClelland published a paper on the effect of variations in hunger on responses to the Thematic Apperception Test (TAT) and other projective stimulus materials [9]. Armed with this evidence that they could measure the strength of motives in humans, McClelland and Atkinson proceeded to demonstrate that TAT measures were responsive to situational manipulations of the general level of achievement motivation in people and that stable individual differences in achievement motivation could also be measured in this way [4,69,71].

Although they have generally been in agreement with one another about the basic assumptions underlying their work, Atkinson and McClelland have followed rather different investigative paths. McClelland chose to concentrate on providing a sociopsychological explanation for rather major political and economic events. He measured the level of achievement motivation characteristic of modern and ancient nations and cultures and related the amount of

117

achievement imagery found in their folk tales and children's books to indices of their level of economic productivity or economic development [70] and to their child-training practices [70,72]. McClelland has been concerned also with the achievement motivation of groups of entrepreneurs and business managers [70]. Atkinson, whose work will be examined in detail in the following pages, took a more "micro" path by concentrating on the development of a tightly formulated theory of the achievement-related behavior of individual people. His earliest interest [3] was in making precise predictions about the behavioral consequences of the need for achievement versus the fear of failure as stable characteristics of people. Among these behavioral consequences, he included, in line with an earlier literature on level of aspiration (see chapter 8), differences in risk preference, persistence, and level of performance. Subsequently Atkinson and his colleagues have extended their predictions to include academic performance, career choice, and occupational success [6,8,10].

A Description of Atkinson's Theory

Atkinson's basic assertion concerns the various determinants of a person's "tendency to approach success" (T_s). This tendency is, in any given instance, influenced by three factors. The first, a relatively stable disposition of the person, is the person's motive to achieve success (M_s). The remaining factors represent the effect of the immediate environment: The person's estimate of the probability that task performance will yield success (P_s) and the attractiveness to the person of success at the task—that is, the incentive value of the success at hand (I_s). The three factors combine multiplicatively to determine the tendency to approach the task: $T_s = M_s \times P_s \times I_s$ [5]. The "tendency to avoid failure" (T_{af}) is similarly derived, and conceived of as independent of the tendency to approach success. It is expressed as a multiplicative function of the motive to avoid failure (M_{af}), the subjective probability of failing at the task (P_f) and the negative incentive of failing at the task; thus, $T_{af} = M_{af} \times P_f \times I_f$. The motive to avoid failure is, again, an enduring personal disposition, usually measured by a test-anxiety questionnaire such as the one developed by Mandler and Sarason [74]. The motive to avoid failure (or fear of failure, as it is often called) represents an inhibitory or avoidance tendency with respect to all activities involving the possibility of failure.

An elegant simplification is now introduced into the model. Assuming, as was suggested by the level-of-aspiration theorists (see chapter 8), that in the domain of achievement-oriented activity the attractiveness of a success tends to increase with greater task difficulty, Atkinson defined the incentive value of success entirely in terms of the subjective probability of success; thus, $I_s = 1 - P_s$. Similarly, the negative incentive value of failure at a task (I_f) is greater the *easier* the task; presumably failing at an easy task is more unpleasant than failing at a difficult one. Thus, Atkinson expressed the negative incentive of failure as $I_f = -P_s$. Atkinson assumed also that the subjective probabilities of success and failure sum to unity—that is, $P_s + P_f = 1$. We can now see that both the strength of the tendency to approach success and the strength of the tendency to avoid failure on a given task are determined by only three factors: the person's stable motive to approach success (or need for achievement, as measured by the TAT); the person's motive to avoid failure (or fear of failure, as measured by test anxiety); and the person's subjective probability of success at the task.

Atkinson assumes that all people have acquired some motive to achieve success, M_s (an approach tendency), and some motive to avoid failure, M_{af} (an avoidance tendency). These conflicting motives combine additively and yield a tendency either to approach or to avoid achievement tasks. The resultant tendency is expressed $(T_s - T_{af})$, or alternatively as $(M_s - M_{af})$. If the T_s or M_s is the stronger tendency, the person will approach the task, and if the T_{af} or M_{af} is the stronger, then the person will wish to avoid the task. Thus, predictions about whether people will approach or avoid achievement tasks are based solely on the premeasured personality differences represented by M_s and M_{af}. A person dominated by M_s tends to approach all achievement tasks, while a person dominated by M_{af} would, given free choice and no external constraints, prefer to avoid achievement tasks altogether.

If we constrain the M_{af}-dominated persons (whom we will call high in fear of failure) to choose some achievement task, the theory permits us to predict the level of task difficulty that will be chosen both by them and by persons dominated by M_s (those high in need achievement). Since the measurement of need achievement and fear of failure allows one to determine only *whether* the person is dominated by the motive to approach or the motive to avoid achievement tasks (and not the strength of either motive), *the strength of a person's tendency to approach or avoid an achievement task at a particular level of difficulty is determined entirely by the subjective probability of success or failure at that level.* The reason, of course, is that the incentive value of success or failure is assumed to be tied to its respective subjective probability $(I_s = 1 - P_s$ and $I_f = -P_s)$, and the subjective probability of failure is assumed to be tied to the subjective probability of success $(P_f = 1 - P_s)$. A moment's reflection will make clear that the expressions $P_s \times I_s$ and $P_f \times I_f$ are at their maximum value when P_s and P_f are 0.50; $P_s \times I_s$ and $P_f \times I_f$ in this instance are equal to 0.25 and in any other instance would be lower. Thus, both the strength of the approach tendency *and* the strength of the avoidance tendency are maximized when P_s and P_f are 0.50. This statement predicts that people who are dominated by need achievement will be most *attracted* by a difficulty level in which the subjective probability of success is 0.50 and that people who are dominated by fear of failure will be most *repelled* by a difficulty level in which the subjective probability of failure is 0.50, and least repelled by tasks of extreme difficulty and extreme ease.

The $P \times I$ products for different levels of difficulty can be plotted to produce a symmetrical bell-shaped curve. This curve, which peaks at $P_s = 0.5$, shows the theoretical instigating power of tasks at various levels of difficulty. The 0.5 point (which Atkinson calls "intermediate" difficulty or intermediate risk) is predicted to have the greatest instigating power for both high need achievers and for those high in the fear of failure. The high need achievers are predicted to see the $P_s = 0.5$ level as most attractive, with the attractiveness of more or less difficult tasks falling off symmetrically from the peak. For persons high in the fear of failure, the "intermediate" difficulty or risk level is predicted to be most repellent; these persons are predicted to choose either higher or lower levels of difficulty, if they are constrained to make a choice.

The model is simple and elegant and is especially interesting in light of McClelland's earlier and more vaguely stated assumption that successful entrepreneurs tend to choose risks of an "intermediate" level rather than extremely high or extremely low risks [70]. Extremely low risks generally have a correspondingly low rate of financial returns, and extremely high ones have too great a probability of failure; "intermediate" risks, then, are most likely to lead to financial success. If we further assume (as Atkinson does) that risks having a subjective probability near 0.50 are of this "intermediate" variety, we can predict that persons high in achievement motivation will be more likely to succeed in such situations, since they are attracted to the very risk levels that are most likely to pay off.

Achievement Motivation Research Procedures

The basic outlines of the experimental procedures used by Atkinson and his colleagues in the study of achievement motivation are very similar to those we have used in our investigations of fear of success in part II. First, persons who are high and low in resultant achievement motivation are identified, and then the persons in these groups are assigned to one or more conditions in which their behavior can be observed. We detail some of these procedures in this section because they help to make clear some of the general problems we see in this work.

Identifying Persons as High or Low in Achievement Motivation

A typical study on the achievement motive begins with the administration to a pool of persons of four TAT (Thematic Apperception Test) cards and a test-anxiety questionnaire, usually the Mandler-Sarason TAQ [74]. Achievement is the theme of each of the four TAT cards; for example, one of them may depict a youngster in an empty classroom. The task of the person is to write an imaginative story about each picture that includes answers to four questions: What is going on? What led up to this situation? What is going to happen? What are the people in the picture thinking and feeling? The person has about five minutes for each card. The text-anxiety questionnaire, used as a measure of fear of failure, requires the respondent to answer a series of questions about his or her anxiety about taking tests, giving answers in the classroom, and so on.

Responses to the TAQ yield a simple numerical score based on the number of items on which anxious responses are given [73]. The scoring of the TAT cards is far more complex and requires the scorer to undergo many hours of training to reach an acceptable standard of agreement with other trained scorers. The scoring rules are very complex [71]; only the main points are summarized here to give the reader a sense of the kinds of stories that are scored as high in achievement motivation. In order to be eligible for any achievement scoring, the respondent's story must be about a person who is striving to succeed in competition with some standard of excellence. According to the authors of the manual, competition with a standard of excellence is clearest when winning or doing as well as or better than others is a stated goal. Feeling proud because of winning, feeling bitter because of losing, and the anticipation of glory for winning also qualify as the kind of affective concern over goal attainment from which a competitive goal can be inferred.

Three other kinds of stories also qualify to meet the criterion of competition with a standard of excellence: A story in which the central character is involved in a unique accomplishment like an invention or an artistic creation that will mark him or her as a personal success; a story in which the person is meeting self-imposed standards for good performance; and a story that indicates long-term involvement in an achievement goal like becoming a doctor, lawyer, or "a success in life." Here we quote the authors' explanation:

... We are able to include long-term involvement as evidence of achievement motivation only because we have knowledge that in contemporary American society success in the career usually demands successful competition with a standard of excellence. Not everyone can be a doctor, lawyer ... [71, p. 184].

If the story qualifies according to any of the four criteria above as indicating competition with a standard of excellence, then the other parts of the story are scored for additional achievement imagery. Some of the additional contributions to a high achievement imagery score include indicators of feelings of need, and the description in the story of instrumental acts for, obstacles to, and resources for goal attainment. The respondent's total score for need achievement is the sum of the scores on each of the four stories.[1]

Once the scoring is completed, two groups of respondents are formed: those who score above the median on TAT achievement imagery and below the median on test anxiety are called high in resultant achievement motivation or simply achievement-oriented, and those who score below the median on TAT achievement imagery and above the median on test anxiety are called low in resultant achievement motivation or simply failure-oriented. The remaining two groups (half the original pool of respondents) are often not considered further[2]; participants in the experiment to be conducted are selected from the groups high and low, respectively, in resultant achievement motivation.

Experimental Procedures Using the Ring-Toss Task

The ring-toss task, in which the experimental participants attempt to toss a series of rubber or rope rings to encircle a short post some distance away, has been used in a number of achievement motivation experiments [8,68] and will provide an illustration for this section. Participants (about half of them high and half low in resultant achievement motivation) go through the experiment in groups. The experimenter typically explains that he is interested in seeing how well the participants can do at this game and exhorts them to do their very best. On each turn, each participant must choose to stand at one of a number of lines representing distances from the target and usually makes ten tosses from whatever distances he or she chooses. Participants take turns tossing their rings in one another's presence. The experimenter's instruction to "see how good you are at this" is typically repeated to each participant just before he begins to play the game. In some experiments, some or all participants are asked to give estimates of their subjective probability of success and/or the value of succeeding from each distance, before or after playing the game [67].

Assessing the Results

We might usefully remind the reader here about the major prediction made by achievement motivation theory for an experiment such as the simple one described above. Participants who are high in resultant achievement motivation are predicted to prefer doing the task whose subjective probability is .50—the "moderate" risk—while those who are low in resultant achievement motivation are predicted to prefer avoiding just that risk level, and to prefer choosing extremely high or extremely low risk levels, with neither of these preferred over the other. The assumption is that persons who are primarily oriented to avoid failure are strongly repelled by the very risk levels that must strongly attract people who are primarily oriented to achievement.

If the participants are asked appropriate questions, such as their estimates of the probability that they will succeed from each of the distances or the monetary prizes they would award to a successful toss from each distance, then some of the basic assumptions of the theory may be tested also, as for example the assumption linking the incentive value of a success to its subjective probability.

The risk preference predictions were tested in a study using the ring-toss task (among others) by G.H. Litwin [68]. Litwin constructed three indices of deviation from the "moderate" risk. The first was a measure of the extent to which participants' risk choices differed from one estimated by a different group of people to have a subjective probability of success of .50. The second was a measure of the extent to which each participant's risk choices deviated, without taking account of direction, from the median risk chosen by all the participants. The third was a measure of the extent to which participants' risk choices differed from the geographical mid-point of the various distances in the game, again without consideration of the participant's direction of deviation from the mid-point. The risk prediction received some degree of support in Litwin's study. For the ring-toss game and a similar penny pitch game, however, statistically stable differences between achievement-oriented and failure-oriented participants emerged only for the second measure: the absolute differences between the participants' risk choices and the average risk choice made by all participants.

Some Problems of the Atkinson Model

The description given above of research procedures in a typical risk preference experiment conducted in the Atkinson tradition highlights some of the central difficulties and limitations we believe the theory to have. We shall begin with a discussion of the test of the risk choice prediction and its implications and then turn to an examination of the general experimental procedure and, more fundamentally, the method of measuring achievement motivation.

The prediction for risk preference in the experiment is that achievement-oriented persons prefer risks having a subjective probability of success of 0.5 and that failure-oriented persons gravitate equally toward risks having a very high or a very low subjective probability of success. None of the measurement techniques described for Litwin's experiment actually test that prediction. The first index described above measures not the relationship between the person's own *subjective* probability of success and his or her risk choices, but rather the discrepancy between the person's risk choices and the risk choices that observers have estimated to be the distance representing a 0.5 probability of success. The implication here is that the subjective probability of success is equal for all participants, regardless of their high or low resultant achievement motivation, or their self-perceived skill at such games. This implicit assumption, we should add, is generally made in the achievement motivation research.

The second index, which assesses the absolute difference between the participant's risk choices and the median risk choice made by all participants, has the same problem as the first index. It also disregards the 0.5 quantity by assuming that the "moderate" risk is best estimated from the behavior of participants. Since it uses the absolute difference between a person's risk choice and this overall median and disregards the direction of the difference, it obscures the possibility that failure-oriented participants may be choosing risk levels that are systematically lower than those chosen by achievement-oriented participants—which is hardly an implausible result—or even that they may be choosing higher risk levels. The third index used in the analysis of the results suffers from the same kinds of problems. In any event, the meaning of "moderate risk level" is not very precise in Atkinson's model as the term is actually used in research.

One of the details of the procedure in the experiment described above presents an additional problem for the testing of the theory's risk preference prediction, particularly in regard to failure-oriented participants. Let us for the moment make the assumption that failure-oriented persons—those who score high on a performance anxiety test—are generally less confident of their abilities than achievement-oriented persons. If this assumption were true, the failure-oriented people would be relatively cautious in the face of possible failure and thus perhaps prefer easier, less risky tasks. In the Atkinson experiments using ring-toss and other experimental games, a competitive environment is almost always set up; participants play the game in groups and are exhorted, in effect, to try to compete successfully. For the presumably cautious and unconfident failure-oriented persons, this situation presents a serious problem: a potential loss of social face. They may be reluctant to stay with the easy tasks they really prefer since they fear the ridicule of other participants or the experimenter if they fail to score from a very short distance. Thus, choices of high levels of risk under competitive conditions by such persons may well be predicated on the idea that failure is less socially humiliating if the task appears very difficult than if the task appears easy or even moderate.

At this point the achievement motivation theorists may accuse us of agreeing with their analysis without realizing it. Why, this is precisely the point, they might say; failure-oriented persons under achievement conditions will prefer to take low or high risks rather than moderate ones because they are more afraid of failing than they are interested in doing well! Our answer, in this invented dialogue, is to point to yet another hidden assumption in the Atkinson formulation: *Achievement is by its nature competitive, and achievement motivation is motivation to compete successfully with other persons.*

For this reason, we have described in detail the scoring procedure employed by achievement motivation researchers in using TAT stories to identify achievement-oriented persons. While the explicit definition of achievement imagery involves "competition with a standard of excellence," the scoring manual makes clear that it is very frequently represented by competition with others, express or implied. Thus, the achievement-oriented persons identified by this technique are often people who are interested in or drawn to competition with others. The use of the text-anxiety questionnaire as an indicator of fear of failure insures that the competitively oriented persons selected are not also ambivalent about or made anxious by competition.

We are suggesting here that Atkinson and his colleagues have quite unwittingly been caught up by the general competitive ethos of Western culture identified by Karen Horney [46] and other observers. They have made achievement equivalent to competition with others, just as the Protestant ethic upon which much of modern Western culture is based makes virtue a matter of accumulating more material goods than others accumulate. That is not to say that the achievement motivation investigators have gone wrong altogether or have studied the wrong thing; in truth, people in our culture generally "achieve" through competition, and the most successful persons are probably those who unambivalently enjoy competition and its fruits. We emphasize, however, the importance of making clear that the motivation to achieve, to accomplish, or to do productive work comes from a large number of sources and not only from the desire to compete successfully with others. We shall discuss this issue in detail in chapters 8 and 9.

We shall also argue in chapters 8 and 9 that the Atkinson model, by concentrating almost exclusively on the personality determinants of achievement motivation, creates difficulties for taking account of other important factors that lead people to work productively. The decision to assume that incentives to attempt tasks are tied only to the subjective probability of succeeding on those tasks, for example, quite ignores other factors that make tasks seem attractive or important to perform regardless of their apparent difficulty. If we think carefully about the model's prediction that failure-oriented persons try to avoid tasks that are likely to lead to achievement, the implication becomes evident that such persons do not accomplish or do work that we might call productive. We believe that this position is simply not tenable and will make clear later that the issue here is to identify the conditions under which such persons—and, for that matter, other persons—will expend energy in a persistent way to accomplish productive work.

We shall not delve further into a critique of the Atkinson model or the research conducted to support it. Readers interested in technical criticisms are referred both to Heckhausen's thoughtful work [39] for a sympathetic and thorough critique and to Entwhistle's paper [27] for a somewhat less sympathetic approach. Our own position is simply that the Atkinson position is not sufficiently broad in scope to be useful for our enterprise.

Women's Conflicts about Achievement

Recently it has become popular to explain the difficulties that many women confront in their attempts to achieve in traditionally male-dominated professional arenas by alluding to a motivational tendency on the part of women to fear success. According to this view, fear of success is presumed to be a characteristic of a sizable proportion of women—but not men—and is thought to result from the sex-role socialization experienced in our culture. Women learn that the requirements necessary for the feminine role are fundamentally inconsistent with the requirements necessary for successful achievement; the one presumably precludes the other. Strivings for success are generally believed to require the personal characteristics of aggressiveness and competitiveness, which are qualities considered to be masculine characteristics in this society. As a result, successful achievement is said to be associated with negative consequences for women, such as being disliked or rejected by men or being seen as unfeminine. Since women learn, through implicit and explicit socialization experiences, to anticipate such unwelcome social and/or personal consequences for achieving, they might understandably become motivated to avoid success and its negative consequences. In contrast, men are not led to expect negative consequences as a result of their successful achievements. They should therefore not be similarly motivated to avoid success. In fact, men are more likely to anticipate negative consequences as a result of failing to achieve and might reasonably be motivated primarily to achieve success and avoid failure.

The idea that many women may fear success as a result of their sex-role socialization has become popular in the last decade or so for a variety of reasons. Not the least among them has been an attempt to understand the roots of economic and political inequalities between men and women in this society. A concern with this issue has led many people to examine and question the socialization patterns and cultural norms and expectations that help to create the boundaries of acceptable behavior for men and women. Strong impetus for the argument of a feminine fear of success was provided by the dissertation study of Matina Horner in 1968 [42].

Horner was originally concerned with attempting to understand why research results on achievement motivation could not successfully be obtained with women. While Atkinson's model of achievement motivation had apparently received considerable support from data provided by samples of male subjects, findings for women had been highly inconsistent. Researchers had been unable to demonstrate that need achievement imagery produced by women in their TAT stories was predictably elicited by the same conditions as it was for men or that predictable performance differences were associated with women's resultant achievement motivation. Horner's innovative contribution to the tradition of achievement motivation theory and research was to suggest that in order for the model to be applicable to women, it must incorporate an additional factor: a motive to avoid success. Women's motive to avoid success (or fear of success) was thought to lead to anxiety that could not only interfere with the production of need achievement imagery in their TAT stories, but could also interfere with their performance levels in achievement situations. Horner speculated that this might then account for the failure of the model to explain data collected from women. Fear of success was described as a "... latent, stable personality disposition acquired early in life ... a disposition to become anxious about achieving success" [43, p. 159].

In order to test her ideas, Horner developed a projective test similar in some respects to the TAT measure of need achievement. A group of female college students was asked to write a story in response to the written cue, "After first term finals, Anne finds herself at the top of her medical school class." A group of male college students wrote stories to a cue that was identical except the protagonist was named John. The stories were scored for fear-of-success imagery by a simple present-absent system if they contained references to negative consequences because of the success (such as conflict, loss of femininity, and social rejection), denial of the situation, or bizarre or inappropriate responses. Subjects also participated in an experiment in which their performances in competitive and noncompetitive situations were studied. The implications of the line of research inaugurated by this initial work have been widely reported and have generally been accepted as indicating: (1) that fear of success is a personality disposition that is characteristic of women and not men and (2) that it adversely affects the performance and achievement strivings of women, particularly when they are competing against men.

While such ideas may be consistent with widely held cultural beliefs, the empirical evidence in support of them is weak. Reviews by ourselves and others of Horner's original study and the subsequent body of research literature that has accumulated [60,109,110,111,122] have repeatedly come to the same conclusions, which we briefly summarize below.

First, although Horner reported that the stories of 62 percent of the women in her sample contained fear-of-success imagery while less than 10 percent of the men's stories did, investigations since then have not consistently been able to duplicate these marked differences. Many studies have found only small differences in the incidence of fear-of-success imagery between males and females, while others have actually found a higher proportion of fear-of-success imagery in male than female samples. In a recent review, Tresemer [110] has concluded that overall no major differences exist between the sexes in the incidence of fear-of-success imagery. He compared data from fifty-six studies that had assessed fear-of-success imagery for both males and females and found that although women told a somewhat larger proportion of fear-of-success stories than men, the variability among the studies was also very large. He suggested, therefore, that the difference must be interpreted cautiously. Clearly, the accumulated data do not provide strong support for the contention that women in particular, but not men, are motivated to avoid success.

Second, in a detailed review, Zuckerman and Wheeler [122] have argued that the reliability of the projective measure used to identify persons who fear success is quite low. Adequate reliability is an important quality for all personality measures because reliability is an indication of a test's ability to identify consistently and stably people who possess the characteristic presumably measured by the test. Finally the validity of the projective measure of fear of success is highly questionable. Although data from Horner's original study is frequently cited as supporting the conclusion that women who fear success perform more poorly in competition with men, important shortcomings in this study make such a conclusion unwarranted. We believe that inappropriate comparisons and inappropriate statistical analyses were used to arrive at such conclusions.[3] When appropriate analyses are performed on those data, no differences are detectable in the performances of high fear-of-success women (identified by Horner's projective measure) when they work alone, in competition with a man, or in competition with another woman.

In addition to the methodological problems with this pioneering work, Tresemer [110] has argued that the research that has followed indicates that the production of fear-of-success imagery is unrelated to other personality or attitudinal correlates, even those that would be predicted on theoretical grounds to be related, such as gender-role identification and measures of anxiety. Neither has the measure been shown to predict performance. Most of the studies conducted using the projective measure of FOS have been concerned primarily with measuring fear-of-success imagery in different groups of people. The reviews by Zuckerman and Wheeler [122] and Tresemer [110,111] have both concluded that in those experimental studies in which measures of task performance were obtained, the relationship between the production of fear-of-success imagery and those performances has been inconsistent. The evidence for the predictive validity of the fear-of-success measure is at best inconclusive. Further, while a new scoring system has been developed by Horner and her colleagues to score stories for fear-of-success imagery [44], the new system does not solve the problems of the approach nor does it change our suggestions made below about the meaning of the conflict over the issue of feminine fear of success. Jackaway and Teevan [52] have argued that the new scoring system blurs the original theoretical and conceptual distinction between fear of failure and fear of success.

Why, then, in the face of mounting contradictory evidence, do people persist in clinging to the belief in a feminine fear of success? At one level the answer is quite simple. In the past decade growing numbers of people have embraced the tenets of what has loosely been referred to as the women's liberation movement. In the midst of this gradual social change, many women have recognized in their own experience the difficulties of trying to combine successful achievement with the culturally defined ideas of being a woman. Many even have recalled instances from their own youth of being warned that boys would not like them or they would never find a husband if they were "brains," and some have had to face the reality of such potential threats. Following the publication of Horner's work, "fear of success" became a catchy and convenient term with which to label the complex set of values, role expectations, conflicts, and difficulties that professionally oriented women may confront. Belief in a feminine fear of success resulting from sex-role socialization has provided a rallying point for many women to blame society for its pernicious socialization and for their low-status positions. At the same time, it has permitted those who may be in a position to redress such inequalities to blame women's personalities for their own plight and thus continue the economic status quo.

This politically motivated response to the research, however, has masked a more general phenomenon implicit in it—the phenomenon that sociologists and social psychologists have for some time called "role conflict." The nature of the research that has been done on the feminine fear of success to date has tended to obscure the interesting psychological issues involved in these conflicts rather than illuminating them. Most researchers have assumed that the TAT-like measure of fear-of-success developed by Horner is a reliable and valid instrument and have focused their research on attempting to investigate certain theoretical issues by comparing, for example, the proportion of stories containing fear-of-success imagery in different samples or by varying characteristics of the verbal cue presented to subjects. Such studies, by their very nature, unfortunately have not provided much information about the essence of the presumed conflict as it is experienced by women or the consequences it has for their lives.

Many women, particularly those who are highly motivated to succeed in areas that have traditionally been reserved for men in this society, do indeed experience difficulties and conflicts, and these may spring from a variety of sources. For example, in many instances there are genuine external-to-the-person barriers constraining women's achievement. These barriers operate on at least two levels. At the more overt level are the long-established and formally institutionalized rules and regulations of educational or occupational organizations that stem from entrenched traditions of discrimination and that effectively serve to exclude women from opportunities. Or barriers may exist at the more subtle covert level in daily interpersonal relations with persons who are carriers of culturally inspired "sexist" practices.

Many women may also experience psychological conflicts surrounding such achievement strivings; these conflicts arise from their attempts to implement values, goals, and aspirations that appear to be mutually exclusive or at least in conflict with one another. Many women may simply have difficulties assigning priorities to activities that fulfill different goals they consider equally important and desirable, when implementing the activities simultaneously is realistically impossible (due, for instance, to finite amounts of time, energy, or other resources). Finally, many women may experience difficulties in simultaneously meeting the requirements of different culturally defined roles and associated expectations for behavior. We suspect that the phenomenon that has captured people's imagination and interest under the banner of a feminine fear of success is more appropriately viewed as a perfectly conscious solution to a realistic role conflict—that is, a reluctance on the part of many women to violate important social norms, where they believe that violation of those norms may be genuinely costly to them. The normative requirements for the role "woman" and "professional achiever" (e.g., doctor, lawyer, scientist, and so forth) in this society are sometimes at odds. On the individual level, women may experience conflicts integrating the associated goals of "succeeding with men" and "succeeding professionally." We would argue, however, that such conflicts need not be unconscious (as is implied by the use of projective measures to identify them), nor do they necessarily form a stable personality disposition. In addition, such conflicts do not *necessarily* lead to actual performance interference or a lessening of achievement strivings. Although in some instances they may have such consequences, in other instances they may lead instead to goal-oriented problem solving.

Behavior in situations that make salient the conflicting requirements and demands of two or more roles will be determined primarily by the constellation of the person's attitudes, values, goals and aspirations as well as the person's perceptions of normative expectations, assessments of probable outcomes of given courses of action in the particular situation, and perceived implications of different actions for future situations. Labeling this phenomenon as "fear of success" has had an unfortunate consequence for the history of this research problem. It has focused people's attention on what is presumed to be an intrapsychic conflict linked to the person's stable personality structure. Conceiving of the phenomenon in terms of role conflict emerging when women find themselves in situations that make differing role demands coupled with the recognition of a genuine external political reality that may be discriminatory focuses the researcher's attention on a wide range of issues heretofore underemphasized in the literature on the feminine fear of success.

The assumption in much of the work on "feminine fear-of-success" is that it interferes with women's actual performances or their achievement strivings. This approach seems to us to be rather one-sided and incomplete. No doubt some women resolve the conflict between succeeding with men and achieving in professional arenas by lowering their achievement aspirations and even their accomplishments in order to build or preserve their relationships with men. Others, in lieu of actual performance inhibition, may hide or make light of their aspirations and accomplishments or may delay fulfilling their achievement goals until they have established stable and secure relationships with a spouse. However, equally common solutions for achievement-oriented women are to delay making interpersonal commitments to men so that those commitments do not interfere with their achievement activities, or to establish reference groups and membership groups in which the two activities do not conflict, or to work out solutions in which they are able to separate successfully (either temporally or spatially) the two areas so they are not confronted by conflicting role demands. At any rate, a variety of ways of resolving role-related and achievement-related conflicts appear to exist. Unfortunately, the research on feminine fear-of-success to date provides us with little information about them. Conceiving of the fear-of-success phenomenon in terms of the broader issue of role conflict suggests alternative avenues for future empirical research. These would include investigations of the panoply of achievement-related and role-related conflicts experienced by *both* women and men, the situational contexts in which such conflicts are made salient, and the consequences of such conflicts. In any event, it is clear to us that the phenomena to which we address our attention in this book are very different from the phenomena studied by Horner and her associates.[4]

Conclusions

Our fundamental problem—finding a set of ideas about the motivation to achieve or accomplish that can be connected with our work on fear of success—is not solved by the work on the achievement motive. The theory of achievement motivation of Atkinson and his coworkers is limited in two major ways and is therefore not useful to us. It restricts itself to studying a personality disposition and thus neglects the influence of situational and environmental factors, and it is too exclusively focused on sources of task motivation that have to do with competitive achievement and thus neglects situations in which people do productive work for other reasons. Clearly, then, we require a broader set of ideas about motivations to accomplish, and we move in that direction in chapter 8.

Notes

1. An interesting controversy has arisen over the problem that need achievement scoring for individual respondents tends to have very low reliability over time; the same person tested repeatedly can score very differently from one to another testing session. Entwhistle [27] has argued that the TAT measure, because of its low reliability, cannot be an adequate measure of stable differences in achievement motivation. In a recent paper, Atkinson, Bongort, and Price [7] have presented a creative reply to Entwhistle's argument that makes use of computer simulations to predict whether assignment to a rough need achievement category can be accomplished successfully by using highly unreliable test scores. We suspect the controversy will continue.

2. The possibility has occurred to us that respondents in the subgroup who score high in TAT achievement imagery and who also score high on test anxiety (and who might therefore be called conflicted about achievement) may be like the people we have identified as success-fearers.

3. Explaining why the data are not adequate for the conclusions that have been drawn from them requires describing in some detail the relevant aspects of Horner's experimental procedures. Each of the ninety female and eighty-eight

male subjects who participated in the study took part in two sessions held at different times. During the "initial assessment" session, students worked by themselves to complete a variety of personality assessment measures (including the verbal cue described in this chapter) and several performance tasks. Students worked individually in a large auditorium in which all the other students were simultaneously working individually on their copies of the materials. The instructions read to the subjects during the session indicate no attempt was made by the experimenter to orient subjects to their peers in a competitive fashion or in any way to call attention to the group setting or the presence of other people; indeed, they indicate that every attempt was made to ensure that the session was as neutral as possible. For the second session, each student was randomly assigned to one of three experimental conditions: (1) a noncompetitive condition in which students completed a different set of performance tasks while working alone in a room, (2) a mixed-sex competitive condition in which students were paired and performed the tasks while competing against their partner of the opposite sex, and (3) a same-sex competitive condition in which students performed the tasks while competing against another student of the same sex.

Although the appropriate analysis to assess the relative effects of competitive situations on the performance of women who fear success is the comparison of the performances of FOS-present and FOS-absent women in these three experimental conditions, this analysis was not reported. Rather the performances of the thirty women who worked alone in the second session (the noncompetitive experimental condition) were compared to their own performances when they worked in the group setting of the first session. The data from the group setting were assumed to reflect performance under a mixed-sex competitive situation and that situation was relabeled accordingly. Despite the appropriate post-hoc labels for the groups (noncompetitive from the second session versus mixed-sex competition from the first session), all that was really compared were the performances of women while working alone and while working in a group setting that happened to include men on the other side of the room.

In addition, the statistical treatment of the data can be questioned. Since students performed different tasks during the two sessions, their scores on each were converted to z-scores (an indication of how discrepant one person's score is from the mean of the entire group in standard deviation units). During the first group session, students had completed an anagrams task, and during the second session they had completed a task in which they constructed words from a longer word. In the analysis employed, a difference score between the subjects' z-scores were computed. Subjects who had previously written stories either containing or not containing fear-of-success imagery were then classified according to whether they had a positive or negative difference score. Horner reported that thirteen out of seventeen FOS-present women had a positive difference score (presumably indicating they worked better alone) and twelve of the thirteen FOS-absent women had a negative difference score (presumably indicating they worked better in competitive situations). Since a z-score is a *relative* and not *absolute* performance indicator, an individual person's performance level is hopelessly confounded with the performance levels of the other members of *the specific group on which the z-score is based.* In this manner, a positive or negative difference score can be obtained in many different ways; for example, by changes in the person's own performance level, by changes in the performance level of some or all other group members, or both. Therefore, it is impossible to draw unequivocal conclusions about the performance level of any specific person.

These data are usually cited to support the conclusion that competition against men interferes with the performance of women who fear success. The data and the statistical handling of them, however, fail to address the question they have been cited as answering. When the appropriate analyses are performed, there are in fact no differences among the performances of FOS-present women in the three conditions. We went back to the original data that Horner presents in her dissertation and computed a 2×3 analysis of variance on the performance data for the FOS-present and FOS-absent women in the three experimental conditions of the second session. The analysis revealed only one significant effect—the main effect for the FOS category. This effect indicated that FOS-present women, regardless of experimental condition, constructed more words from the letters of the master word than did FOS-absent women ($F = 9.77; df = 1, 84; p < .01$).

Tresemer [111] has conducted several additional reanalyses of the data from Horner's original dissertation [42], but he also used the somewhat unusual z-score transformations of the data in his reanalyses. The first several analyses which Tresemer conducted also failed, as ours did, to demonstrate the effect hypothesized by Horner. A final analysis, which was essentially the same as Horner's original analysis with only minor differences, led Tresemer to conclude that the predicted effect did exist. He then conducted further internal analyses and concluded that the eight FOS-present women who exhibited performance impairment in the large mixed-sex group in Horner's Session I differed from other FOS-present women in that they were lower in need-achievement. In any event, the additional analyses performed by Tresemer do not substantially alter our conclusions.

4. Helene Deutsch [22] and Karen Horney [47] have explored some of the psychodynamic determinants of the neurotic fear of success in feminine psychology. It is important to note that the Pappo measure of neurotic fear of success has been shown to be uncorrelated with responses to Horner's story cues in several studies (see, for example, the doctoral dissertation of Judith Beldner, New York University, 1975; and Curtis, Zanna, and Campbell, *American Educational Research Journal, 12,* 1975, pp. 287-97).

8 Other Sources of Accomplishment Motivation: Asking the Question Differently

McClelland's and Atkinson's theories of achievement motivation were based in part on a simpler and somewhat more modest set of notions about "level of aspiration" investigated by social psychologist Kurt Lewin and a number of his students and colleagues [65]. These investigators were concerned with situations in which a person can choose to undertake a task at any of several levels of difficulty; for example, easy, moderate, or difficult mathematics problems, or various pole heights in a high jump event. The investigators' problem was to predict the level of difficulty at which the person would choose to do the task at hand.

Level of Aspiration

The approach taken by Lewin and his colleagues will by now appear familiar to the reader who has read through the preceding chapter. These investigators suggested that when people approach a task that has various levels of difficulty, the attractiveness (or valence, V) of any particular level of difficulty will be affected by four factors: What they believe they can gain from succeeding at the task at that level (the valence of success, V_{su}), what they think will be lost by failing to accomplish the task at that level (the valence of failure, V_f), and their estimates of the likelihood that they will succeed or fail at that level (the subjective probability of success, $S.P._{su}$, and of failure, $S.P._f$). Thus, the valence or attractiveness of a difficulty level can be represented in the following form: $V = (V_{su} \times S.P._{su}) - (V_f \times S.P._f)$—that is, the valence of any difficulty level is a function of the positive valence of success at that level weighted by the subjective probability of success, minus the negative valence of failing at that level weighted by the subjective probability of failing. The idea is that the person contemplating the task at various levels of difficulty will choose to attempt the task at the level that has maximum valence: the person's choice, then, represents his level of aspiration. The subjective probability of succeeding and failing at any level is usually assumed to sum to one ($S.P._f = 1 - S.P._{su}$). This approach also recognizes that for many tasks in our culture the attractiveness of succeeding increases as the difficulty of the task (and therefore the subjective probability of failure) increases; succeeding at more difficult tasks is often viewed more positively than succeeding at less difficult ones.

Stating the problem in this way makes the task of the researcher who wishes to understand factors that influence and modify level of aspiration quite manageable. The problem becomes one of specifying the circumstances that influence the attractiveness and subjective probability of success and failure at various levels of difficulty. Various researchers have studied the influence of a large number of factors on the level of aspiration: the person's prior history of successes and failures at the task [41,54], the standards established by the groups to which the person belongs [2,40], the person's general level of self-confidence [41], and many others. Since the person's satisfaction with his performances depends on whether or not the level of aspiration has been reached, other consequences of level of aspiration can be studied. Furthermore, the level-of-aspiration formulation lends itself well to the study of cultural influences on performance and to the study of reactions to performance [65]. Thus, we can easily see why this simple and fertile set of notions was used by the achievement motivation theorists as one of the foundations of their formulations.

In describing the Atkinson version of achievement motivation theory in the preceding chapter, we pointed out that this theory adds two additional simplifying assumptions to the basic level-of-aspiration ideas. First, it assumes that the incentive value of success is based solely on its subjective probability. Thus, the attractiveness of a successful performance is based only on its difficulty (the more difficult, the more attractive), and the unattractiveness of a failing performance is based only on the extent to which the task is easy. The second simplifying assumption—which is implicitly though not explicitly made—is that the probabilities of success and failure in any instance are seen as equivalent by everyone. These assumptions have the effect of making individual differences in level of aspiration—choice of the level of difficulty at which a task will be attempted—depend completely on whether the person is more achievement motivated than fearful of failure or is more fearful of failure than achievement motivated. Since achievement motivation and fear of failure are stable personality traits, the theory in effect diminishes consideration of environmental influences on people's tendencies to approach or avoid tasks at one or another level of difficulty, and it turns attention away from the large number of situations in which the valence of or incentive for succeeding at a task is not tied solely to the difficulty of succeeding. Some examples of such situations may be useful. Many achievement situations involve learning. A person who is learning a new task is often less interested in attempting highly or even moderately difficult levels of the task than with performing reliably at some lower level; a beginner in darkroom work in photography will be as delighted to be able to produce consistently acceptable black and white prints as to produce a single good color print (which is usually believed to be more difficult). In addition, many people set out with great motivation and industry to learn new tasks they are certain of being able to learn; although the subjective probability of success is very high, motivation is very high also.

Furthermore, as we suggested in chapter 7, the assumed relationship between valence and subjective probability may well break down even in American culture when the person is performing in private, out of the view and evaluation of other people. The person may in fact get more pleasure out of the successful performance of a simple task than a more difficult one simply because the sheer fatigue costs of the more difficult performance may be great enough to reduce the person's pleasure in accomplishing the task. Building a cabinet that is intended to fulfill a certain function may be done in various ways, some of which are more challenging than others. If the product is intended to serve immediate functional requirements, building the cabinet in the simplest and least challenging way may produce the greatest pleasure and may therefore have the greatest valence or incentive value. These examples may seem trivial, but they should make clear that the Atkinson assumptions are likely to hold under some conditions but not others.

Let us now consider what might be gained if the Atkinson formulation were to abandon the restricting assumption that ties incentive to the probability of success, as well as what would not be gained. One consequence is that the researcher is led to examine more closely the situational determinants of choice of level of difficulty and persistence. A second consequence is that the investigator is led to consider a variety of incentives for choosing to attempt a task at a given level of difficulty—not just subjective probability of success. Both of these are important consequences, since they broaden the range of factors other than stable dispositions that may be investigated as antecedents of achievement behavior. To be fair to Atkinson and his coworkers, however, we must point out that their primary interest has been in the stable *personal* characteristics of people that lead them toward or away from productivity and that situational or environmental factors have been much less central to their concerns.

We have been implying repeatedly that one must indeed go beyond personality characteristics in the study of the motivation to achieve or accomplish, and it is time we made our position more explicit. In our view, the following questions are appropriate:

1. What are the environmental and situational sources of motivation to attempt and persist at productive work?
2. What characteristics of people interact with these sources of motivation to affect the degree to which a person will work productively?

The reader should note that these questions have implications that are very different from the implications of the Atkinson achievement motivation position. The Atkinson position is concerned with levels of individual aspiration, while the questions above are concerned with the performance of productive work in general. It is clear when the questions are asked this way that a person's level of aspiration tells much less than the whole story of his motivation to do productive work. Level of aspiration theory is intended to deal specifically with situations in which the person contemplates a task that can be done at various levels of difficulty. It predicts the degree of difficulty at which the person will undertake the task as well as his or her satisfaction or dissatisfaction following a performance. The questions we have posed are concerned with these issues, but they are also concerned with issues involving tasks that cannot be graded in terms of the extent to which they are personally challenging—including, for example, tasks that present more sheer drudgery than difficulty, tasks that are quite unfamiliar and must be learned, and tasks that may have no direct consequences for personal achievement. Productive work that does not have individual achievement as its goal or consequence is, after all, very often done. Our questions, furthermore, point us toward examining not only level of aspiration but also the degree of persistence, concentration, and effort expended on the task, the person's attitude toward the task and his or her pleasure in doing it, the flexibility or creativity with which the task is done, and other similar issues. We are interested, in other words, in developing an account of a larger number of motivational phenomena than is dealt with by level-of-aspiration theory and its derivatives, both in terms of the antecedent conditions of motivational states and in terms of their consequences for feelings and actions.[1]

Sources of Accomplishment Motivation

What motivates people to do productive work? Imagining a question that is more far-reaching in its social importance than this one is difficult. The question is sometimes asked and answered explicitly, as when people invent new ways of organizing farming communities and factories or when they justify favorite new or old ways of educating their children. More frequently, people simply predicate their everyday decisions on their implicit answers to the question, as when they decide on a piecework system for paying employees in their business or use the economic principles of an "incentive system" in attempting to train their children to become productive members of the society.

In everyday conversation, people often seem to assume that the motivation to do productive work comes from two general sources: from incentives offered for work (money, prestige, and the like, and the avoidance of unpleasant consequences) and from the character or personality of the person (some people are harder workers than others). From systematic psychology we have learned, in addition, that people work hard for reinforcements such as praise or approval as well as material rewards; that people often are impelled to complete the tasks they have begun [50,66,121]; that people with high resultant need for achievement are strongly motivated to compete against others or against objective standards of excellence [5], that people are more likely to persist at "interesting" tasks than "dull" ones [20]; that under certain conditions people work to help others [24,48], and that sometimes people work to attain new competence or mastery over tasks [38,117]. These sources of motivation to accomplish can be divided into the three general categories listed below:

1. Extrinsic "material" motives:
   the desire to obtain money and other commodities;
   the desire to avoid unpleasant consequences such as hunger, physical pain, or financial loss.
2. Extrinsic "social" motives:
   the desire to obtain praise, approval, acceptance, and affection;
   the desire to avoid disapproval, ridicule, and criticism;
   the desire to obtain status and prestige;
   the desire to compete successfully against others;
   the desire to avoid losing a competition;
   the desire to help others complete their tasks, obtain rewards, or avoid unpleasant consequences;
   the desire to cause others to be uncomfortable or distressed by one's accomplishments;
   the desire to perpetuate good interpersonal feelings that may follow upon a group's accomplishments.
3. Intrinsic motives:
   the desire to complete tasks that have been begun;
   the desire to attain competence or mastery;
   the desire to express one's self through work.

This list is not intended to be exhaustive. It is intended to show two things: first, that the task motivation problem is a large one; and second, that the material rewards that usually serve as explicit incentives for productivity in our society are only a small subset of what is available to motivate such work. The various extrinsic social goals for which people do work are discussed in detail in chapter 9. We discuss in the final section of this chapter one of the more important sources of intrinsic task motivation: the motivation to attain competence.

Intrinsic Task Motivation: The Concept of Competence

The motivation to become competent is an "intrinsic" source of motivation— that is, intrinsic in the sense that no rewards or punishments from sources external to the task are connected by the person with his or her performance. No incentives, in the usual sense, are offered; rather, the performers work at their tasks because the tasks excite and interest them. Some writers have located the source of intrinsic motivation in the task [20]: Some tasks, in their view, are intrinsically more interesting than others. We take the position that while tasks are interesting to individual people, the same tasks are not equally interesting to all persons or even to the same person at different times. Thus, asking the question somewhat differently seems more fruitful to us: What aspects of the relationship between a person and a task lead that person to become intensely interested in the task and to work very hard at it or lead a person to dislike the task and withdraw from performing it?

Nearly twenty years ago, Robert W. White [117] offered a profound critique of theories of motivation based on "tissue needs" such as hunger and thirst. These theories, White argued, are unable to account for many important responses that are exploratory in nature, as for example when infants attend and orient to new stimuli, reach out and grasp, begin to crawl, and so on. These activities seem to emerge quite spontaneously and are not a secondary result of the operation of "primary" drives. White developed the notion that many organisms are constructed in such a way that they strive to interact effectively with the environment in which they live—to become competent. He proposed that intensely pleasurable "feelings of efficacy" are experienced when a person perceives that he or she is developing competence. These feelings are highly rewarding and are sought out and lead the person to seek them elsewhere. Effectance or mastery motivation has also been a central assumption in the work of many other psychologists, such as Jean Piaget [90], George Kelly [57], Abraham Maslow [75], Lois Murphy [83], Richard de Charms [19], M. Brewster Smith [104], and Jerome Kagan [55]. We too have become fascinated with the potential of the concept of competence and have extended White's ideas into a more comprehensive theory of intrinsic task motivation and psychological stress [38]. We have based this section on our own theoretical ideas.

The basic idea underlying our view of competence motivation is a simple one: Certain *beliefs* that people come to hold about themselves in relation to the tasks they undertake have powerful emotional consequences that affect their motivational states, their estimates of what they can do, and the quality of their performances. Competence beliefs arouse positive feelings, increased self-confidence, and heightened task motivation that lead to enhanced task performance. Incompetence beliefs have the opposite consequences. They generate unpleasant feelings, reduced self-confidence, and reduced task motivation, and they tend to interfere with subsequent performances.

Consequences of Competence Beliefs

A person who concludes that he or she is gaining competence on a task is, in effect, saying "I can do this, which I could not do before." This simple assertion implies several ideas: the person has a definition of the task; the person has adopted or accepted a standard against which the performance is measured; and the person has tested the new skill against his or her prior repertory of skills. To put it more formally: *A competence belief will be adopted by a person performing a task (whose parameters are defined by the performer) when (1) his or her performance on the task meets or exceeds standards of performance that he or she has accepted, provided (2) he or she has adopted a set to evaluate his or her competence; (3) he or she has reason to believe the task performance is reproducible and is under his or her control; and (4) he or she believes the skills involved in the performance have not been a part of his or her prior repertory of skills.* Not all instances of competence beliefs involve tasks in the usual external-to-the-person sense. People may also conclude that they are developing competence vis-à-vis their own responses to situations; for example, controlling stagefright during public speaking, overcoming blocks against regular studying, getting over social awkwardness, and so on.

Competence beliefs can produce self-sustaining productive motivational cycles. First, they induce pleasurable emotional arousal, which may be experienced as satisfaction, pride, joy, excitement, elation, and so on. These positive feelings produce an increase in the person's liking for the situation and the task in which the feelings were generated. They also produce a tendency for the person to evaluate his or her past and present task performances favorably and a tendency to be optimistic about the quality of future performances on this and closely related tasks. These feelings and judgments are likely to lead the person to continue to work hard to master new levels of the task or to master new tasks in order to perpetuate the pleasurable feelings. Thus, the person is motivated to continue to broaden the scope of his or her competence. The adoption of a competence belief promotes a chaneling of functioning that is task directed and may be manifested as greater persistence, attention, or effort. These factors, in turn, increase the likelihood that the person will indeed acquire new knowledge and skills, which may generate additional competence beliefs and their attendant consequences.

The consequences of a competence belief are stronger to the extent that the new competence has implications for the person's ability to perform other tasks, to the extent that the new ability is seen as important by the person, and to the extent that the person is certain about the new competence. These consequences are also stronger to the extent that the competence belief occupies the person's attention—that is, the extent to which he or she thinks about it rather than thinking about other things. Once the competence belief becomes fully integrated into the person's repertory of competencies, however, further evidence of the competence will no longer have motivational consequences.

We shall attempt to illustrate what we have said thus far with a hypothetical example: a story about a young man who learns to sew. Let us first set the stage. The person in our story has, like most men, grown up believing that sewing is usually done by women and that it is a rather mysterious activity. He has many times watched women sew with a sewing machine. After considerable reflection and with a total disregard of rationality, he has concluded that sewing machines simply cannot work—sewing a seam is quite impossible without passing the needle completely through one side of the material and back again from the other side. During college, however, our young man has become a passionate backpacker and has become increasingly interested in designing, for his own use, ideal back-packing equipment. One day he decides he wants to build a tent he has designed. In order to do so, he must try to learn to sew. The stage is set.

The young man is now seated before his mother's sewing machine with the door to the sewing room carefully closed; he is poring over the machine's instruction book. He prepares the machine for sewing by winding a bobbin and threading the machine, meticulously following the instruction book. After two failures he threads the machine successfully and is ready to begin to sew a line of stitches on a scrap of nylon tenting material. His first several attempts end in frustration: tangled thread, stitches that pull out easily, needle holes in the material with no thread, and so on. He makes adjustments of various kinds on the machine and finally discovers that a particular adjustment eliminates these problems. At this stage he begins to work at sewing a straight line of stitches with the machine. Gradually, his wavy lines begin to straighten out, and he finds that he can guide the material under the presser foot in such a way as to produce a reasonably straight line of stitching. All this work has been preliminary activity, as our young man sees it. He now puts his scrap of practice material aside and carefully inspects the stitching on his best commercial tent. Since he has mastered stitching in a straight line, his next task is to try to produce a flat felled seam that looks approximately like the seams in his tent. After a considerable amount of adjusting of the machine and a number of attempts, his practice seams begin to look like the model, and he finds himself becoming able to produce such seams at will.

At this point, the young man has developed a competence belief. He is trying to learn something he has never been able to do before and is therefore likely to have adopted a competence-evaluation set. He has set a standard for his performance and met that standard; further, he believes that he can reproduce the performance. Our theory says that the person will now begin to feel highly excited and elated. He will find the entire sewing task pleasing and enjoyable and will tend to like the machine, the new tent, and other things that may be associated with the task. He will be pleased about what sewing he has done up to the present and may inspect his product repeatedly and with considerable pride. He will be optimistic about being able to do his next sewing task well and about his ability to learn whatever he might need to learn to do a good job on his tent. Thus, he will be highly motivated to continue to work on the task—to perfect what he already knows and to learn more.

The intensity of our young man's feelings about his new competence will be greater if he sees his tent-making task as important. They will also be stronger if he believes that his new competence will help him to perform other tasks he could not have done before, such as repairing his favorite cold weather clothing or manufacturing a new sleeping bag. Anything that increases the extent to which he attends to his new skill will intensify the feelings, and anything that focuses his attention away from the competence belief will tend to reduce the intensity of those feelings, as well as the task motivation associated with them. Since external sources of rewards for a good performance may focus the performer's attention on the hoped-for reward rather than on the competence, they can interfere with the motivational consequences of the competence belief. Thus, incentives such as prizes, winning a competition, and so forth can be detractors from competence motivation.

Consequences of Incompetence Beliefs

Incompetence beliefs frequently arise when persons have evidence that they cannot meet the demands of a situation for their performances. The elements of incompetence beliefs include a recognition by the person that he or she will incur costs if he or she is unable to meet the performance standards that appear to be required by the situation. Thus, an incompetence belief will be adopted when the following four conditions are met:

1. The person perceives that a certain level of task performance is demanded of him or her.
2. The level of performance demanded is not substantially higher than the standards of performance the person might ordinarily set, so that the person can accept the standards as his or her own.
3. The person believes that he or she will incur costs if this level of performance is not achieved.
4. The evidence indicates that the person is or will be unable to meet the level of performance required.

The consequences of incompetence beliefs are roughly the opposite of the consequences of competence beliefs. They produce in the person unpleasant emotional tension experienced as anxiety, anger, shame, or other forms of emotional distress. These feelings lead the person to dislike the situation and the task in which the belief was generated, to underevaluate the quality of his or her present and past task performances, and to anticipate with pessimism the quality and consequences of future performances. The emotional tension engendered by the incompetence belief tends to produce a degree of disorganization of cognitive and motor functioning that can actually disrupt the person's performance on tasks requiring close attention and intact skills. Taken together, these factors increase the likelihood that the person will receive information that is perceived as confirming the original incompetence belief. By the same token, they also increase the likelihood that other incompetence beliefs will be entertained by the person. The potential for a self-confirming and self-perpetuating cycle is quite clear: incompetence beliefs generate further incompetence beliefs.

The consequences of incompetence beliefs are more intense to the extent that the costs associated with the incompetence are perceived by the person to be high, to the extent that the person is certain of his or her incompetence, to the extent that the incompetence is perceived as implying other possible incompetencies, and to the extent that the person focuses his or her attention on the belief. Thus, incompetence beliefs reduce the motivation to do productive work. They induce, instead, a psychological state that leads to withdrawal from tasks and disruption of functioning.

The consequences of incompetence beliefs mentioned above are similar to the consequences that in the scholarly literature have been associated with psychological stress. We argue [38] that thinking of incompetence beliefs as the immediate cause of *all* psychological stress reactions is useful for a number of reasons. Most investigators of psychological stress have assumed that stress reactions are due to threatening forces external to the person, such forces as loud noises [35], crowding [30], surgery [53], illness [113], combat [36], and so on. Our point of view suggests that whether a person will have a stress reaction in a given set of circumstances depends upon the person's own interpretation of those circumstances. If the person believes he or she can manage in the circumstances and does so, the result may be a competence belief rather than psychological stress, and the person may actually enjoy the adverse circumstances as a challenge and an opportunity to extend his or her own ability to handle such situations. The person who believes that he or she cannot manage—and that being unable to manage will be costly—is likely to experience stress reactions, with their unpleasant short-term and perhaps also longer-term consequences. Our position, then, is that a great many situations that are usually thought of as benign, such as the classroom, the cocktail party, the "date," and the conjugal bed, contain the potential for the generation of incompetence beliefs and therefore may generate psychological stress reactions.

We have mentioned incompetence beliefs in the context of discussing sources of positive task motivation because we are convinced that incompetence beliefs have strongly inhibitory effects on the desire to do productive work no matter what its source may be. For example, our view of competence motivation proposes that the psychological consequences of competence beliefs and incompetence beliefs are incompatible with one another. The existence of a belief of one category will tend to inhibit the formation of a belief of the other category and will attenuate or eliminate the consequences associated with a belief of the other category if such a belief is already being entertained. We assume also that the consequences of incompetence beliefs are more potent and durable than the consequences of competence beliefs. This concept helps to explain the common observation that persons who appear to be under stress are not as likely as others to become involved in the joys of learning new skills. The notion that competence beliefs may inhibit and attenuate the consequences of incompetence beliefs also suggests some possible methods for reducing and preventing common psychological stress reactions.

Antecedents of Competence and Incompetence Beliefs

In our view, people come to the belief that they are becoming competent (or incompetent as the case may be) to perform a task as a result of processing information about their performances. Three categories of information can serve as evidence for establishing competence-related beliefs: (1) information the person receives directly from his or her work on a task; (2) information the person receives from comparing his or her performances with the performances of others whose ability levels the person knows or can estimate; and (3) information the person receives from the evaluations of his or her performances by credible other persons. As we pointed out earlier, a competence belief is adopted by a person when, among other things, the person's performance meets or exceeds a standard the person has set or accepted. These standards may vary from simple and primitive, as when the mere appearance of a model is approximately matched, to complex and sophisticated, as when superfluous or ineffective movements are eliminated from the *process* of producing an already perfected product. Such standards for evaluating competence may be acquired from any of the three sources of competence information. The process of making inferences about competence from each of these sources of information has unique features and unique problems that require extensive analysis. Interested readers are referred to our earlier paper [38] for a detailed statement of the theory.

Incompetence beliefs are, as we have suggested, easier to acquire than competence beliefs. In the case of incompetence beliefs, the standards of performance against which persons measure their own performances are usually defined by the situation (as when a boy must jump a certain distance in order to avoid the ridicule of his peers). The person must only decide whether the level of performance required by the situation could reasonably be applied to someone like himself or herself. While the processes are somewhat different than they are for competence beliefs, incompetence beliefs are also acquired in situations in which people work alone with tasks, situations in which they compare their performances with those of others, and situations in which another person evaluates their performances.

Conclusions

Issues of competence and incompetence are probably of great importance to people in a variety of behavior settings, such as schools of all kinds, hospitals and mental institutions, geriatric facilities, and all varieties of work-related and non-work-related organizations. Many severe human problems, encountered in unemployment, retirement, bereavement, physical incapacitation, emigration—as well as less severe ones such as pregnancy, divorce, role changes, geographic relocation, and so forth—might be ameliorated if we had a clear and usable understanding of the conditions under which competence and incompetence phenomena are manifested and modified. For our present purposes, however, competence and incompetence beliefs are particularly important as sources of motivation to approach and persist at tasks, motivation to avoid and withdraw from them, and as predictors of affective responses to tasks. These ideas allow us to specify the conditions under which tasks will be intrinsically motivating to people—that is, when no other sources of reward or punishment need be present or available to induce productive work.

We have examined these intrinsic motivation issues in considerable detail in order to illustrate the great scope and complexity of the issues involved in people's motivation for accomplishment. The phenomena we have discussed in this section, moreover, are concerned primarily with the intrapsychic consequences of the private relationship between the person and his or her task. Much productivity motivation arises under much less private conditions. In the chapter that follows we deal with the various interpersonal or social sources of accomplishment motivation, and the social contexts in which they occur. In chapters 9 and 10 we also discuss the relationship between these various accomplishment motives and the fear of success.

Note

1. The broader field theory framework of Kurt Lewin [21,61,62,63,64], mentioned briefly in chapter 1, provides a general conceptual structure within which these broader issues can be fit very well. Since field theory ideas also handle adequately various fear-of-success phenomena, we are persuaded that an eminently useful formal theory of productivity or accomplishment motivation can be constructed within a field theoretic perspective. Regrettably, we must leave this interesting and important task to other investigators or until a future time.

9

Cooperation, Competition, and Caring: The Relationship of Social Structure and Productivity

In the previous chapter we began to examine some of the sources of motivation to accomplish or do productive work. We suggested that the bases of productivity motivation are more numerous than investigators of achievement motivation have recognized. In this chapter we continue our examination by analyzing in some detail the sources of productivity motivation that emanate from the social contexts within which people work, achieve, and accomplish various goals.

As we shall see, this analysis also helps to extend our understanding of the behavior of success-fearing persons. The discussion in chapter 1 led us to the conclusion that competition within the family—that is, competition surrounding separation-individuation conflicts and Oedipal conflicts and competition in the form of sibling rivalry—is a focal event in the childhood origins of this personality disposition. Furthermore, we suggested that a heightened sensitivity to competition remains a principal characteristic of success-fearers throughout their lives. The research presented in part II has shown that from this framework we can predict the conditions under which success-fearers are particularly likely to sabotage their performances. Our work has made clear to us that persons who fear success do not sabotage their performances to the same degree in all achievement situations. The contexts in which people do productive work vary widely in our culture. A reasonable assumption is that some of those situations are more evocative, and some less evocative, of the early childhood circumstances that led initially to the development of fear of success. The success-fearer's typical responses to success and failure are likely to be especially pronounced to the extent that contemporary achievement contexts elicit those early conflicts. The analysis in this chapter thus enables us to make further predictions about when success-fearers will sabotage their performances and when they will be less likely to do so according to the social context within which they perform.

In this chapter, then, we first discuss the relational characteristics that distinguish different types of social structures in which people are organized to do productive work and analyze some of the general consequences of these structures for the group dynamics that emerge, for the individual member's self-concept and self-esteem, and for productivity motivation.[1] We then turn to a more detailed analysis of three specific types of groups. After laying this foundation, we return to the central topic of this book and suggest how these social contexts affect success-fearing persons.

Social Structures

People frequently work with other people to accomplish tasks. In the context of a family, among parents and children, in the context of educational institutions among administrators, teachers, and students, in employment contexts among upper management, middle management, and other employees, and in many other contexts, people are organized either formally or informally for the purpose of accomplishing their goals. We shall refer to these systems of people organized to work on tasks simply as task groups, since they exist in many forms with a wide variety of tasks to accomplish and can be small or large, simple or complex. Regardless of the size and complexity of the task group, three important characteristics can be identified to define the structure of these social units. These characteristics have to do with: (1) the way one member's goal-directed activities affect the progress of other members toward their goals; (2) the extent to which members' feelings are affected by the gains and losses of the other members; and (3) the extent to which the reward distribution criteria foster invidious comparisons among members. These characteristics are not entirely independent of one another, but they are nevertheless different enough to make considering them separately useful to our purposes.

Relational Characteristics of Groups

The first characteristic of social structures or task groups, *goal interdependence*, defines the relationship among group members in terms of reaching their goals and obtaining the rewards available to them.[2] In *positive* goal interdependence, the more one member obtains, the more the other members obtain, or, alternatively, the closer one member comes to achieving his goal, the closer the other members will come to achieving goals that they have, as when a crew of painters paint a house. Groups in which positive goal interdependence exists among the members are often referred to as cooperative groups. In *negative* goal interdependence, the more one member obtains, the less can be obtained by others, or the more closely one member approaches his goal, the more difficulty other members will have in reaching their goals. As an example of a negatively interdependent group, consider a college course in which the instructor announces that only one student in the class—the best one, according to the instructor's standards—will receive an "A" grade for the course, and only one student, the second best, will receive a grade of "B." The closer one student comes to obtaining the grade of "A," the less the likelihood that the others can also obtain it. Groups in which negative goal interdependence exists among the members are frequently called competitive groups. The work of social psychologists such as Morton Deutsch [23,24,25,26] and Muzafer Sherif and his associates [100,101] on cooperative and competitive groups has contributed greatly to our understanding of the types of group process that result in groups that have positive and negative goal interdependence among their members.

The second characteristic, *goal identification with others' outcomes*, refers to situations in which members of the group care enough about what happens to other members that their own pleasure is strongly determined by the consequences to those others. In *positive* goal identification, a person derives joy from the accomplishments and rewards of other members and is distressed by their failures and losses. These feelings often occur in "caring" relationships, in which some members have the role of caring for or socializing others, and in friendships. In *negative* goal identification, a person derives pleasure from the others' failures and losses and is distressed by the others' gains and successes. Rivalrous relationships have this characteristic.

The final characteristic of groups has to do with the *nature of the reward distribution principles* that members adopt to regulate the division of gains and rewards earned by the group to individual group members. There are many principles or criteria that can be used to divide the rewards; for example, distribution according to seniority, according to degree of contribution, according to need, according to the principle of equality, according to a random process, and so on. These criteria differ in the extent to which they encourage group members to make *invidious comparisons* with one another—that is, to evaluate other members and their activities along a good-bad dimension or a dimension of relative worthiness. This psychological characteristic of reward distribution principles is the one which concerns us here. Invidious comparisons foster the idea that some members of the group and their activities are more valuable than others and thus lead to the denigration of some members and their activities by other members and by themselves.

These three characteristics are listed across the top of the chart in table 9-1. Six distinguishable groups result from combining these characteristics: (1) cooperative-solidarity groups—positively interdependent groups in which the reward distribution principles do not instigate invidious comparisons; (2) cooperative-equity groups—positively interdependent groups in which the reward distribution principles do lead to invidious comparisons among members; (3) caring groups—groups in which members are positively invested in or goal identified with one another's successes and gains and distressed by one another's losses; and the negative counterparts of these three kinds of groups, (4) competitive groups without invidious comparisons; (5) competitive groups with invidious comparisons induced; and (6) rivalry groups.

These characteristics, we shall argue, have consequences for many things that occur in groups. They affect the interpersonal behaviors of members, members' interpretations of the behavior of others, members' feelings about one another, members' values and goal orientations, and members' self-concepts and self-esteem. They also have consequences for the kinds of productivity or task motivation that are likely to exist in the group. The specific consequences of

Table 9-1
Consequences of Six Relational Structures in Task Groups

	Cooperation: Positive Interdependence		
	Low Invidious Comparisons (Cooperative-Solidarity)	High Invidious Comparisons (Cooperative-Equity)	Positive Goal Identification (Caring)
Behaviors:			
Help-hinder	High helping	Low helping to low hindering	High helping; needs are addressed
Share-withhold information, resources; division of labor	High sharing of resources and information; high degree of division of labor	Reluctant sharing to withholding of resources and information; high degree of division of labor	High sharing of resources and information; high degree of division of labor
Accept-reject influence, suggestions, requests	High acceptance of influence and suggestions	Moderate, ambivalent acceptance of influence and suggestions	High acceptance of influence; high responsiveness to requests
High-low communication	High communication: open, honest, effective, persuasive, spontaneous, and undefensive	Moderate communication: primarily task-oriented, guarded and defensive	High communication: constructive and empathetic
Perceptions of Others:			
Common-conflicting goals and interests	Common goals and interests	Common goals and some conflicting interests; recognition of power and outcome differences	Shared interest and commitment to each other's goal-attainment; focus on the striving member
Positive-negative motives and intentions	Trustworthy, friendly and helpful	Ambiguous and variable	Trustworthy, friendly, helpful, and respectful
Similarities-differences emphasized	Mutual similarities emphasized; realistic assessment of other's strengths and weaknesses; skill complementarity valued	Status and ability differences emphasized	Similarities emphasized and shared; recognition and acceptance of differential power, expertise, and roles
Emotional Reactions to the Other:	High liking; high trust; high esteem	Low liking; reserved trust; variable esteem	High liking; high trust; high esteem; high identification and empathy
What Becomes Valued and Important:	Solidarity; good feelings; interests of other members; wide range of task-relevant activities; group tasks and products	Status in group; fairness of outcome distribution; external standards for performance; task orientation	Progress of the other; solidarity, friendliness, wide range of task-related activities
Self-Concept and Self-Esteem:	Self-concept has many dimensions; high self-esteem; narrow range of esteem in group; stable self-esteem	Somewhat multidimensional self-concept; wide range of self-esteem in group; high status members have high self-esteem; the low status have lower esteem	Moderately multidimensional self-concept; high, stable self-esteem
Sources of Productivity Motivation Other than Material Rewards:	Completion of tasks and subtasks; desire to maintain solidarity; desire to help others, and not to "let down" others; enjoy-	Completion of tasks; desire to improve or maintain status	Desire to increase the other's pleasure and to relieve the other's distress; reluctance to let down the other; competence motivation

Competition: Negative Interdependence

	Low Invidious Comparisons	High Invidious Comparisons	Negative Goal Identification (Rivalry)
Behaviors:			
Help-hinder	Low hindering	High hindering	High hindering, often unobtrusive
Share-withhold information, resources; division of labor	Withholding of resources and information; minor sabotage; no division of labor	Withholding of resources; false information-giving and sabotage; no division of labor	Withholding of resources; engaging in veiled obstruction and sabotage; no division of labor
Accept-reject influence, suggestions, requests	Some rejection of influence, suggestions and requests	High rejection of influence, suggestions and requests	High rejection of influence, suggestions and requests
High-low communication	Low communication, guarded	Low communication, deceptive	Moderate to low communication: egocentric, destructive, critical, ridiculing
Perceptions of Others:			
Common-conflicting goals and interests	Conflicting goals and interests within a limited domain	Conflicting goals and interests over an extensive domain	Conflicting interests over extensive domain; commitment to each other's defeat
Positive-negative motives and intentions	Not trustworthy; not friendly	Untrustworthy, hostile	Untrustworthy, hostile and destructive
Similarities-differences emphasized	Differences somewhat emphasized	Differences exaggerated, similarities minimized	Differences exaggerated; similarities virtually denied
Emotional Reactions to the Other:	Neutral to some disliking; no trust; esteem varies	Strong disliking; moderate to strong suspicion; esteem varies	Strong disliking; strong suspicion; strong contempt
What Becomes Valued and Important:	Winning; relative performance; not losing; specific task activities	Winning; relative performance; not losing; solidarity is disvalued; specific task activities	Failure, defeat, and distress of other
Self-Concept and Self-Esteem:	Self-concept has few dimensions; self-esteem somewhat unstable and affected by winning and losing; moderate range of esteem in group	Self-concept has very few dimensions; self-esteem unstable and strongly affected by winning and losing; wide range of esteem in group	Self-concept affected by perception of rival; self-esteem is defensive and precarious
Sources of Productivity Motivation Other Than Material Rewards:	Desire to win, desire not to lose; excitement of competing; desire for prestige	Strong desire to win; strong desire not to lose; excitement of competing; desire to increase status	Desire to cause other the pain of one's own success

these characteristics are outlined in table 9-1 for each of the six groups that illustrate them and will be discussed in greater detail below for several of the groups. In order to provide an overview of what will later be presented in detail, we first briefly sketch how the relational characteristics have various social and personal consequences.

General Consequences of the Relational Characteristics

When people first begin to work together, predictable actions emerge as a direct consequence of the group structure and the members' perceptions of their relationship with one another. These ways of interacting are likely to be self-perpetuating as members act and react to one another. They begin a process which gradually affects not only the group's dynamics and the relations among members, but also how members come to think and feel about themselves as well as members' motivation to do productive work. In discussing cooperatively and competitively interdependent groups, we assume that the individual members accurately perceive the nature of their goal interdependence.

Group Process. People's perceptions of the relationships among them influence how they act and behave in the group—both toward other group members and toward their goal-directed activities. For example, in groups having positive goal interdependence (cooperative groups), persons perceive that the effective goal-directed actions of each member have positive consequences for their own goals and those of other members. Therefore, functional behavior calls for members to help each other and to share their resources with one another. When negative goal interdependence (competition) obtains between group members, quite different behaviors emerge. Because all persons cannot simultaneously reach their goals, there is likely to be little helping or sharing of resources and information. Rather, the members perceive their competitive relationship with one another and recognize that the other members' progress toward the goal is a danger to their own goal attainment. Thus they may attempt to hinder or obstruct the other members if the opportunity arises, thereby creating an advantage for themselves.

The way persons act within a given social context—whether they help or hinder other persons' activities, whether they accept or reject influence, the extent to which they share resources and information, and the quality and quantity of their communications with others in the group—will influence other members' perceptions of and beliefs about them, how other members interpret their actions, and the kinds of motives, intentions, values, and traits members attribute to each other. These inferences are likely to affect both members' expectations about other members' future behaviors and their feelings—liking, disliking, trust, suspicion, admiration, respect, hostility, and so on—towards the other members. These in turn help to determine the subsequent actions and reactions of group members. Because each person in the group has the capacity to think, feel, initiate acts, and respond to others' actions and, moreover, because each is aware that others also think, feel, initiate actions, and respond to others' actions, a complex process of social interaction is established. All this simply makes explicit the point that the behavior of any person within a group is in part dependent upon what other group members say and do and in part dependent on the person's perception of what they are thinking and intending.

Table 9-1 summarizes the group process that can be expected in each of the six categories of groups. As the table shows, the relationships among members of positively interdependent groups (cooperative groups) and caring groups in which positive goal identification exists are very different from the group process that emerges in competitively interdependent groups or in rivalry groups, in which negative goal identification exists. Caring groups are very similar to cooperative groups in which invidious comparisons are not instigated. In these groups, members help each other, share resources and information, accept influence from other members, and communicate with one another in a relatively open and honest manner. Members correctly perceive that they have common goals and interests and attribute positive motives and intentions to the others. They view others as trustworthy and helpful and are trustworthy and helpful themselves. Similarities among people are likely to be emphasized and some differences are viewed as positive qualities that can actually or potentially promote goal attainment. The table also points out that many of these beneficial consequences of cooperative groups are weakened when invidious comparisons are made among members.

The relationships among members in competitive groups and in groups in which rivalry exists among members are also similar. When invidious comparisons are not promoted in competitive groups, the consequences are somewhat less pronounced than when invidious comparisons are extensively fostered. Groups in which rivalry exists among members look like extreme caricatures of competitive groups.

The group process that emerges in competitive groups and rivalry groups contrasts sharply with that of cooperative or caring groups. Here there is little helping or sharing of resources, and there may even be overt attempts at hindering or obstructing other persons' activities. Communication among members is guarded and often deceptive. Members realistically perceive that they have conflicting interests and are thus untrusting or suspicious of other's actions directed at themselves and attribute negative motives and intentions to others. Issues of winning and not losing become focal for participants and concern with status positions in the group color many of the activities of group members.

In all types of groups, the group process that emerges will ultimately influence the probability that members will actually accomplish their goals. The group process will also influence what comes to be valued by group members—

that is, the kinds of rewards or outcomes the members believe are important, the kinds of activities they consider worthwhile, the performance standards they consider relevant, and so on. These activities, in conjunction with the distributional criteria used by the group for the division of rewards will in turn determine the specific rewards that individual members receive.

Self-Concept and Self-Esteem. The self-concept and self-esteem of the individual group member—the dimensions that are important in defining the member's self-concept and the level and stability of his or her self-esteem along these dimensions—will be affected by membership in these different groups. We distinguish between self-concept and self-esteem because they refer to different aspects of the way people view themselves, and also because membership in the various group structures in some cases affects self-concept in one way and self-esteem in another. *Self-concept*, then, refers to the particular set of traits or characteristics a person uses to define himself or herself. Self-concepts differ not only in their specific content ("athletic" vs. "musical") but also in the number of dimensions they contain; some people define themselves narrowly, using only a few characteristics, while others use many different characteristics when they think about themselves. As we shall see, some groups lead their members to take a narrow view of themselves while others encourage members to view themselves multidimensionally. In contrast, *self-esteem* refers to people's overall evaluation of themselves. In our view, self-esteem results from the person's implicit evaluation of each of the dimensions or traits in his or her self-concept, a process in which the traits that are considered more important receive greater weight. It is worthwhile to distinguish between two properties of a person's self-esteem: its *level* (whether it is positive or high, medium, or low) and its *stability* (whether it remains stable over time or fluctuates between high and low).

Group members' self-concepts and their feelings of worthiness—their self-esteem—are determined not only by their own ideas about what characteristics are important and where they stand on those characteristics, but also by their perceptions of the ways other people perceive and react to them. The essential idea here (which originated in the work of George Herbert Mead [79]) is that people's self-concepts are to a large extent determined by their perceptions of what characteristics important other people use to classify them. Similarly, people's self-esteem depends largely upon their perceptions of how they and their characteristics are evaluated by important others. In other words, we learn how to conceive of ourselves and we determine our self-esteem by seeing ourselves through the eyes of others; we make inferences about how others perceive and esteem us from what they tell us directly as well as from their behavior and reactions toward us.

We must point out at this time that here and elsewhere in this chapter when we refer to self-concept and self-esteem, we are referring to a person's situationally determined view of him or herself. While many people, including a number of psychologists [17,120], prefer to conceptualize self-concept and self-esteem as relatively stable and enduring personality dispositions based on accumulated experiences in a variety of situations, we believe a more fruitful approach is to examine the particular situational determinants of the ways people both conceive of and evaluate themselves. We do not intend to deny the possibility that some persons, due to the consistency of their previous experiences, may view themselves similarly regardless of the situations in which they find themselves. We do suggest, however, that the way most persons regard themselves is modifiable and varies somewhat from one situational context to another. Thus, we prefer to view self-concept and self-esteem not as permanent ways of viewing and evaluating oneself regardless of the situation, but rather as particular ways of thinking and feeling about oneself in a given situation.

The dimensions that persons use to define their self-concepts and how they evaluate themselves along those dimensions are strongly affected by the type of group in which they work. When invidious comparisons are made among members, the self-esteem of many group members is likely to be adversely affected. Particularly when invidious comparisons occur in the context of competitive groups, *relative* task performance becomes an important concern, and the quality of performances or products is "good" if (and perhaps only if) it is better than that of others. The performance-related characteristics of members thus become the paramount criteria of personal evaluation as well as the primary basis of social esteem in the group. The self-concepts of persons who work in competitive groups tend therefore to be defined rather narrowly while they are in the work context and confined primarily to dimensions directly related to task performance. Self-esteem is closely correlated with relative standing in the group in terms of performance; those who perform relatively well have higher self-esteem than those who perform relatively poorly. To the extent that individual members' relative performance in the group is at all variable, the potential exists for the development of unstable self-esteem. Perhaps we should note that competitions can be conducted without involving such invidiousness, for example, by basing the outcome on factors like luck or chance or on the effort expended by competitors. Thus, for example, a competition in which neighborhood children try to collect the most paper for a recycling effort has very different consequences than a competition to decide which children will be designated the smartest or best students in the class.

When invidious comparisons are not part of the group's dynamics, as in some types of cooperative groups and among caring or positively goal-identified persons, self-esteem consequences are quite different. In such groups, because members generally esteem and value one another, the members are more likely to esteem and value themselves. The distribution of self-esteem levels, furthermore, is usually fairly even, with no major disparities among members. If we, as group members, are aware that the other members know our weaknesses as well as our strengths and that the others still believe we are valuable, we are inclined to accept ourselves, to value ourselves highly, and nevertheless to desire to improve our skills. Criticism and self-derogation are not, after all, the only sources of desire to improve. Furthermore, since members are esteemed—and esteem themselves—on the basis of a relatively wide range of personal qualities and skills, a given member's self-esteem is not closely tied to any given performance or product. Within this breadth of esteem exists protection against great discouragement as a consequence of some failure, and that helps to maintain the stability of self-esteem.

Productivity Motivation. People often assume that persons will be motivated to do productive work when they have incentives to do so. The term *incentive* in this context is almost always taken to mean either money, the commodities that money will buy, or some other marketable resource. Occasionally, the term incentive is stretched to include such "commodities" as social approval or social esteem. While we accept the assumption of many reinforcement theorists that people work to obtain things and conditions they value and to avoid conditions they wish to prevent, this principle by itself is not sufficiently detailed for our purposes here. We make the further assumption that the extent to which people will work hard, persistently, and innovately depends on more than the nature of the things and conditions they may wish to obtain or avoid. Our discussion of productivity motivation within the various kinds of groups thus emphasizes other sources of motivation.

In cooperative groups, for example, task motivation comes from a variety of sources. Members work hard not only because of the material and prestige rewards that may be available from the completed work, but also because they (a) like the others and desire to help them; (b) enjoy the interaction and the "we-feeling" in the group and wish to perpetuate and increase that enjoyment, part of which derives from successful task completion by the group; (c) enjoy the admiration of other members of the group that comes of tasks well done; and (d) permit themselves (and are encouraged by others) to enlarge their realms of skill and competence, which they find intrinsically pleasurable and exciting.

In contrast, the primary sources of task motivation in competitive groups are (a) the material and prestige rewards of good performance, and (b) the pleasures of winning over capable others in a competition—and the pain of losing. The latter two sources of motivation are likely to be quite potent. Poor relative performance is accompanied for most people by discouragement and loss of interest in the task, while good relative performance is a source of sharp elation and subsequent performance enhancement.

Having briefly overviewed the consequences of membership in various kinds of groups, we now turn to a more detailed analysis of three specific group structures: (1) negatively interdependent groups in which invidious comparisons are extensively promoted, as an example of competitive groups in their more extreme forms; (2) positively interdependent groups in which invidious comparisons are not fostered, as exemplified in their ideal form by what we have called "cooperative-solidarity" groups; and (3) groups in which positive goal identification exists among the members. As an example of this latter group we have chosen to analyze caring groups in which some members have the responsibility of caring for or socializing other members. We have selected these three groups for close scrutiny because the consequences of the relational characteristics are most clear-cut in these three ideal forms. Similar analyses could be done for the other types of groups listed in table 9-1. Because the arguments for the other group types are analogous to those contained in the following discussion, the reader interested in the detailed analysis of the group types not discussed should be able to reconstruct them from the outline in table 9-1.

Our analysis of these groups derives from the work of Morton Deutsch and others on cooperation and competition cited earlier, and from our own theoretical extensions of Deutsch's ideas about the psychological consequences of membership in cooperative and competitive groups. The consequences of group membership that have been the concern of Deutsch and his colleagues are summarized in the first eight rows in table 9-1. These ideas, which have received a great deal of empirical support, have to do with group members' behaviors toward one another, perceptions of one another, and emotional reactions to one another. The portion of the analysis that is based on our own ideas is summarized in the last three rows of table 9-1. Our extensions are concerned primarily with the consequences of memberships in various kinds of groups for the members' values, their self-concepts, the level and stability of their self-esteem, and for the sources of their desire to work productively in the group. These notions are new, and we are just beginning research on them. They must, therefore, be considered tentative.

Competitive Groups

All of us have experienced competitive groups and relationships. Indeed, competition is often thought to be an integral part of the "American way of life." The phenomenon of competition is pervasive, and the label *competitive* is widely used to describe everything from individual people to gigantic corporations to economic systems. Most people probably assume, therefore, that they are intimately familiar with the workings of competitive groups, and probably most also assume that they understand the consequences of competition for productivity. Partially because of the ubiquitous nature of competition, however, we necessarily want to define our terms with some care so that we may all share common ground and to make clear our analysis of the interpersonal consequences of membership in competitive task groups as well as the consequences of such groups for the self-esteem and productivity of individual members. Since competition is a focal issue for success-fearers, competitive groups easily trigger their neurotic conflicts and consequently their typical responses to success and failure. The type of competitive group that we analyze in detail in this section is outlined in table 9-1: groups in which negative goal interdependence exists among the members and in which invidious comparisons are promoted among members.

The negative interdependence of members of competitive task groups leads them to take the point of view, with perfect rationality, that sharing their task-relevant resources or information with other members will help the others and hurt themselves. There is likely to be little sharing of resources or information in competitive task groups, therefore. Indeed, in fiercely competitive groups there may be attempts at espionage—obtaining information from others that the others would not willingly provide—and even sabotage of the efforts of the others to hinder their progress toward the goal. After all, a group member can win if the others lose through their own ineptness or mistakes or even though "bad luck." Task-directed activities, then, have the flavor of "every man for himself." The interaction among members about task accomplishments and productivity that does occur is likely to be subtly or openly obstructionist and oriented to hindering the other's progress and thus attempting to create additional advantages for oneself.

The negative interdependence in these groups also leads to duplication of function and effort among the members. Members do not feel that the actions of other members can substitute for their own actions in pursuit of their goals—they must do everything for themselves. By the same token, members' relations with one another are often superficial and guarded or strained. Lack of trust and even active suspicion is characteristic of the members' feelings toward one another, and untrustworthy and devious behaviors are not surprising. Members may also come to believe that they are quite different from the other members, since they tend to emphasize not their similarities in abilities, values, and opinions, but their differences. Furthermore, when the distributional criteria foster invidious comparisons, these real or imagined differences come to be evaluated on a good-bad dimension, so that each member feels he is "good" in these ways, while the others are "bad."

These characteristics of competitive task groups may sound exaggeratedly negative or even unfamiliar to some readers. The reader should keep in mind that we are describing highly competitive groups in which invidious comparisons are made. Many of the real-life groups in which we all participate and that we call competitive are in fact complex mixtures of the various categories of groups discussed in this chapter. For example, some readers may think of competitive games (in which the opponents like, respect, and enjoy one another) as counterexamples of what we are asserting. In most competitive games or sports, the participants amicably and cooperatively agree to compete for a short period under a cooperatively determined set of rules; the shared goal of the participants may be the mutual enjoyment of the game or sport. In such groups, invidious comparisons are usually absent.

Competitively organized groups are likely to construct or adopt certain values and principles that support and justify the system and its functioning. First, they tend to assume that resources and rewards—indeed, all that is valuable to them—are in short supply. This assumption may or may not reflect the reality in which the group is functioning. Because resources are believed to be scarce, principles of justice are adopted that allow members to be confident that the resources are being distributed fairly and to those who most deserve them. In competitive groups guided by the economic principle of equity, for example, deservingness is defined by the member's relative position in the productivity hierarchy: the more a person produces, the more rewards that person deserves to receive. Moreover, because members' inputs of resources, ability, and effort are presumed to determine their rewards, the members are considered to be personally responsible for the share of the rewards they receive.

Since status in the group is also defined in accordance with the share of rewards that is assigned to members, a corollary principle is often adopted: the higher a member's status in the group, the greater the share of outcomes the person deserves to receive. What also follows is that the higher the status a member enjoys, the more capable, productive, valuable, and worthwhile that member is considered. Of course, there is often, in reality, some slippage in the system. Ability, productivity, and status are not always perfectly correlated: people are frequently accorded status by virtue of some accidental or irrelevant characteristic, and people of genuinely high ability are not always afforded full opportunities to be productive. Nonetheless, members develop a stake in the belief that objective, rational criteria provide the foundation for members' positions and rewards in the group and that therefore people earn what they deserve and deserve what they have earned. These assumptions, in concert with the other characteristics of competitive task groups, have important psychological consequences for the members of the group at the individual level.

Self-Esteem. In competitive groups, not only are there a limited number of rewards that will be distributed, but there is also a parallel status structure, which has a limited number of desirable or "winning" positions and therefore a number of lesser, undesirable "losing" positions. In such groups, everything is relative; nothing is absolute. Ironically, a winner can win on the basis of a product or performance that is unsatisfactory by comparison to an absolute standard. Similarly, a product or performance that is more than acceptable by absolute standards can be considered a bad product because an even better or more acceptable product or performance exists. This notion that no performance or product has absolute merit or value rather quickly leads to a comparison among people along the same lines—that is, people are assigned worth or value only in comparison with one another, and a member is "good" not because he or she is able to do something but because he or she is "better." The quality of a performance or product according to objective standards subtly loses importance as an evaluation criterion, and this objective quality can deteriorate unnoticed. The comparison among people along a higher-lower, better-worse dimension has direct implications for the way people evaluate themselves as well as others. Thus, to succeed in the competition is to be worthwhile in one's own eyes and in the eyes of others and to fail in the competition is to lose worth in one's own and other's eyes, regardless of what one is able to do.

The self-concepts of members in the competitive group, then, are largely defined according to the activities that are at the heart of the competition and the status positions members occupy. As a consequence, the self-esteem of the members is likely to be determined by their outcomes in the various tests and contests. Generally, however, the fact of winning or achieving in competitive groups is not permanently determined; members must constantly defend their positions in subsequent contests and competitions. Since self-esteem depends to a large extent upon the evaluations resulting from one's competitive achievements and one's status and since continued performances are required to maintain one's level in the competitive group, self-esteem is likely to be rather unstable—that is, fluctuating with changes in one's hopes and fears, one's success or failure in repeated competitions, and with changes in one's status.

Considering the entire membership in the competitive group, we see there is likely to be a rather wide variation in self-esteem from person to person. Since such competitive groups are status-oriented and classify individual members along success-failure and winner-loser dimensions, these classifications determine to a large extent how others evaluate and respond to individual members. To the extent that these evaluations by others are incorporated into members' images of themselves, the distribution of self-esteem is likely to parallel the distribution of rewards and statuses: Persons who are consistently successful are likely to have relatively high self-esteem, those who consistently fail are likely to have relatively low self-esteem, and those who sometimes succeed and sometimes fail are likely to have relatively unstable self-esteem that rises and falls with their successes and failures. We should note that relative to members in the other kinds of task groups, the majority of members in competitive groups may be less confident in their self-evaluations. Because winners must continually defend their positions against others who wish to occupy the high status positions, the possibility always exists that they may lose their position in future contests, and the losers often hold out the hope that they will become winners in the future. The potentially fleeting nature of successes and failures, then, leads people to be relatively unsure of how to evaluate themselves. The continuing process of comparison and evaluation of oneself relative to others may ultimately lead the individual contestants, even the successful ones, to feel quite isolated and alone in the group and to feel defensive or uncertain in their self-esteems.

Productivity Motivation. People frequently seem to assume that in competitive groups the material (and status) rewards accruing to high-quality performances motivate members to invest their attentions and energies in performing and producing, presumably deriving therefrom the personal benefits of a job well done—that is, a kind of intrinsic task reward. Then, if they have performed well, they also receive the extrinsic rewards offered for successful competition. In a great many competitive groups, however, there are probably few intrinsic task rewards enjoyed by highly involved members. Because winning or doing better than others is one of the major yardsticks for evaluation in competitive groups, it becomes an important instigating force in the members' productivity. "Winning" engulfs the field, as it were; indeed, it is most frequently the dominant motivational goal, overshadowing interest in the process of learning or producing, and even overshadowing interest in the product that is produced apart from its value in the competition. Satisfaction is derived not so much from the job well done or the new skills and abilities acquired (unless they will be of certain benefit in future competitions), but in faring well in the immediate comparison with other people.

The motivation underlying the productivity of members of competitive groups is potent and multifaceted, with both carrot-and-stick characteristics. On the one hand, persons strive to win or do better than others—to succeed in the competition—in order to obtain whatever material rewards are available and to acquire high status in the group and the positive evaluations and esteem of outsiders. Indeed, the winner of a competition often experiences rather intense pleasure in the form of pride, joy, and release from the tension that is usually involved in the competitive process. Winning also brings with it the expectation that one will be admired and sought out by others and frequently that one may eventually enjoy additional material or symbolic rewards as a consequence of the winning. Winners also experience a sharp increase in self-esteem—that is, an increase in their conviction that they are persons of value who deserve good things.

At the same time, members of competitive task groups are also motivated by strong desires to avoid losing the competition, with the costs associated with losing: feelings of disappointment, frustration, uncertainty, and reduction in self-esteem. These feelings may also include incompetence beliefs, which bring with them a reduction in task motivation and a reduction in the quality of subsequent performances. Further, losing means the loss or nonacquisition of economic as well as prestige rewards. The closer one has come to winning a competition, the less intense are the negative feelings associated with seeing oneself as a loser. Thus, persons involved in competitive task groups work hard not only to win but also to come as close to winning (and to get as far away from losing) as possible. There are, of course, many avenues to such competitive success other than relative skill at the task: cheating, harming the other, skullduggery, and so on.

While incompetence beliefs and their associated stress reactions seem easy to come by in competitive groups, the productive motivational cycle associated with competence beliefs from the task is less easily available. The major focus of the competitive group is on powerful rewards and costs that detract attention from one's evaluation of competence at the task at hand. Doing better than others is critical, and members' concern is oriented to success and failure rather than to products or processes. Despite these powerful detracting conditions, some people may nevertheless focus on skill acquisition as the route to competitive success and may enjoy competence beliefs as a result. Others may enjoy competence motivation from a redefinition of the task; they may see themselves as good at defeating other people, manipulating situations to be on top, and so on.

Participation in competitive task groups, then, involves working to win or defeat others in search of the sharp delights of success and working to avoid the pervasively unpleasant costs of losing or being defeated. We are probably correct to view the individual incentive value of competition as very intense and very potent—probably more potent for a great many people than other sources of productivity motivation.

Cooperative-Solidarity Groups

We can easily think of examples of task groups that are organized in ways that fit the defining characteristics of cooperative-solidarity groups: groups in which the members are positively goal interdependent and in which invidious comparisons are not made. In common language, we often refer to such cooperative projects as "team efforts" or "collaborative enterprises." Such team efforts may simply involve internal cooperation among the members to complete their tasks and reach their goals, as in the cases of a ballet troupe or a scientific research team. Alternatively, the team members may cooperate among themselves in order to do better than another team or teams, as in the case of high school sports teams. In any event, the internal structure of such enterprises is cooperative in nature. In our discussion we shall assume that whether the group is struggling against other groups, a hostile environment, or a difficult and important task, the members of the group are vitally interested in completing the task successfully. We further assume that membership in the cooperative-solidarity task group is perfectly voluntary—that is, the members have chosen or decided to be in the group. Involuntary membership may have somewhat different consequences.

Members of cooperative-solidarity groups are likely to define their rewards more broadly than are members of the competitive groups discussed above. While "economic" rewards are likely to be valued and sought after because the group's continued existence may rest on their procurement, other rewards—such as interpersonal affection and esteem among group members, feelings of security and belonging, and the like—are also likely to be highly valued and worked for by the task group. The fostering and maintenance of interpersonal solidarity among the members is seen by members as important for the continued existence of the group. The members of the group individually benefit from such interpersonal solidarity and value it as a legitimate goal to be pursued and a reward to be reaped.

The term *cooperation* as used here must not be misunderstood as "altruism," where people are assumed to help each other out of sheer sympathy or kindness, nor is it intended to connote a "welfare-state" equality where the group and its members receive outcomes and benefits regardless of what they produce. Rather, cooperative-solidarity groups are groups in which each member's work helps other group members because it contributes to the quality of the joint product. The economic rewards the group receives are predicated on the level of productivity of group members and the quality of the product that emerges. Thus, for each group member to contribute to the group at his or her highest capability is in each person's best interests. The good interpersonal relations that tend to arise are viewed not as unnecessary frills, but as important and integral aspects of the group that contribute to its productivity.

Because members of the group are positively interdependent with regard to the accomplishment of their group-defined task, resources within the group, such as specific skills or information, are openly shared with others in the group, and especially with those members who most need them or whose own part of the overall task could most benefit by them. In many instances division of labor is possible so that members are able to perform the tasks and functions for which they are uniquely suited and at which they can be most productive. When members are unable to carry out their responsibilities for whatever reason, other members may substitute for them. People are likely to help rather than hinder each other's productivity and contributions to the group goal and are likely to attempt to influence and be willing to be influenced by other members in directions that are harmonious with the group's goals. Because members are mutually helpful towards each other in accomplishing their common goals, friendly interpersonal relations among members are likely to arise and be maintained. Members come to like and respect each other; openness and honesty characterize their communication with each other, and they are both trusting and trustworthy. Openness and trust have the consequence of continuing the free give-and-take and sharing of ideas and resources, with each member having an interest in the maximization of others' skills and resources as well as his or her own. This process contributes both to the strengthening of interpersonal bonds among the members and also to the creative productivity of the group as a whole. Once engaged, the process is likely to be cyclical and self-reinforcing.

In addition, a system of principles and values is frequently endorsed by the members of the group to guide and justify the group structure and its interpersonal processes. In cooperative-solidarity groups, equality and mutual respect predominate as fundamental values shared by the group members. While the group recognizes that members may contribute different resources and inputs to the group product, most contributions that are indeed helpful are recognized as valuable and worthwhile to the group enterprise. In cooperative-solidarity groups, "different" does not mean "better" or "worse." Furthermore, since cooperative-solidarity task groups generally do not assume that resource scarcity is a necessary fact of group life, they are likely to focus on ways of generating more resources when scarcity does arise and to make use of whatever capabilities the members of the group have.

The actions and investments of individual members of cooperative groups are helpful and useful not only to the individual members but to the group as a whole. For that reason, members of such groups not only like and care for one another, but also attend to and often approve of one another's opinions, actions, and activities. Thus, members attach value to a relatively wide variety of skills and resources that other group members may have even when some of those skills and resources do not contribute directly to the group's task accomplishment. This emphasis stands in marked contrast to the typical situation in competitive groups, in which the value emphasis is overwhelmingly on those skills and resources that contribute directly to measurable production.

Self-Esteem. Since in cooperative-solidarity task groups a large variety of members' skills and resources are highly valued, we might anticipate that members notice much about themselves. Thus, for example, the member whose organizational skills, sense of humor, and nurturant tendencies are appreciated by other members will see all three of those aspects of himself or herself as important. Persons in cooperative groups, then, tend to receive more information about themselves from other members, and this information is likely to be multidimensional as well as mostly positive. Here we include characteristics that are related to members' contributions to the group process and to group solidarity, such as kindness, the ability to help and provide constructive criticism, and the ability to communicate realistically-based esteem and liking and create feelings of belonging. The high levels of interaction, sharing, trust, and openness that characterize the cooperative process provide part of the context in which friendly feelings of mutual liking develop and are promoted. Additionally, this atmosphere gives members relatively secure opportunities to be themselves or at least to behave spontaneously in a manner that allows each person's individual style and abilities to develop, to be known, and to be accepted. Secure and positive *acceptance* rather than competitive evaluation is probably an accurate description of the evaluative consequences of cooperative interaction.

A phenomenon we can call a "we" feeling [48] emerges in cooperative groups. The "we" feeling describes not only the sentiment of a mutual positive identification among group members, but the real existence of an important entity to which each member contributes and in which each takes part. Members have not only a personal identity but a group-related identity as well, which adds another dimension to their conceptions of themselves. The self-concepts of members of cooperative groups, then, incorporate both individual ("I") characteristics and group ("we") characteristics.

Because there is likely to be a division of tasks fitting individual abilities and because people are likely to help each other if trouble arises, the cooperative group member is likely to perform acceptably well on his portion of the task. This individual performance and evaluation, is, however, only a part of the task performance and performance evaluation; another important part derives from the progress of the group as a whole on its task. Because each member contributes to the group product and shares ownership in it, each is able to count among his or her assets the group-level productivity and, frequently, the skills of the group as a whole.

The member of a cooperative-solidarity group, then, is likely to develop a differentiated or multidimensional conception both of himself and of other members. At least two broad dimensions have been identified that contribute to the self-concepts of members of cooperative groups: those related to task performance and those related to interpersonal-relations abilities. Within each of these broad categories, people can attend to a wide range of skills and personal attributes in forming their self-concepts.

If members of cooperative groups do use more skills, characteristics, and activities in defining their self-concepts, then we can also reasonably suggest that their self-esteem will be relatively stable or consistent over time. While some self-evaluations may vary with changes in individual or group-level task performance (temporary successes or failures), other feelings of self-worth—for example, those deriving from interpersonal dimensions—are likely to be more consistent. In addition, since more attributes are counted as important in defining the self-concept, momentary failures and negative evaluations along one or a few dimensions are not likely to have the net result of altering appreciably the member's overall self-esteem. Furthermore, we would expect to find that the level of self-esteem in these groups is fairly similar among the members since the economic rewards are distributed equally and there is relatively little basis for discrimination among people and little motivation to make such discriminations.

Productivity Motivation. We have argued that cooperative-solidarity task groups frequently generate interpersonal affection, trust, warmth, and mutual esteem among their members, and that they also tend to generate in their members relatively high, evenly distributed, and stable levels of self-esteem. These are pleasurable feelings indeed; most people enjoy being accepted and valued by others and like very much believing that they are worthwhile, useful individuals. Members of such groups will desire to perpetuate and intensify such feelings. Provided the group is strongly task-oriented and derives its solidarity in part from working on the task, working effectively will be considered an efficacious way of maintaining and adding to the interpersonal resources of the group—its pride in accomplishment, sense of shared fates, and so on. Thus group members can be expected to be highly motivated to work on the task, and to invest time, energy, and other resources in the service of the group's goals.

Research evidence bearing upon the relationship between task group solidarity and productivity has not been clear. Investigators have shown that task group solidarity leads to high job satisfaction [99,112], but their attempts to show that task group solidarity leads to greater group productivity have met with only partial success. While some studies have found that task groups composed predominantly of people who have positive feelings towards one another are more productive than groups in which most members do not [13, 51,88,112], others have failed to demonstrate that relationship [49,89]. These studies are rather difficult to compare with one another, since both the nature of the interpersonal environments they deal with and their measures of productivity vary widely. We would probably be fair to say of task groups having a high degree of solidarity that, as some of the research has shown [11], if the group norm is to work hard (as work is defined by the larger organization), the members work particularly hard, and if the group norm is to avoid working hard, they avoid work very successfully also. We note that this does not necessarily mean that they are unproductive in their own terms. Recently conducted surveys of worker satisfaction [114] have tended to show that highly satisfied workers are more productive. Some of these studies have suggested that high productivity leads to high satisfaction [103]; others have suggested that satisfaction and productivity can cause one another [107].

Despite the ambiguities in this literature, we are reasonably confident in the assertion that under the conditions we have stated, the feelings created by cooperative-solidarity groups will tend to act as productivity motivators for the members. There is good evidence, in any case, that cooperatively organized task groups have greater task motivation and enjoy their work more than competitively organized groups; they also have been shown to surpass competitive groups, under specifiable conditions, in the quality and quantity of work their members produce [23,37,82,108,119].

The range of tasks and activities members of cooperative-solidarity groups will undertake is likely to be quite broad and is likely to include activities that might not be counted as "productive" in the strict economic sense of the term. For instance, in a cooperative-solidarity group whose task goal is to write a book, a member might not only write, but also make lunch for the others, locate a reference, share his pleasure in how the product is progressing, edit another member's first draft, help another to plan a chapter or to get his thoughts straight, clean up and order the group's work space, or even provide needed distraction from the task. The same member might at another time acquire skill in the use of a technique that could later be useful to the group's efforts. Each of these activities is likely to be positively valued and seen as productive by the other members.

The tasks done by cooperative-solidarity groups are often larger than can be accomplished by individual members working alone, and the individual members share not only the economic rewards earned by the group and the affectional rewards generated in the process, but also a personal pride in the accomplishments of the group: the person comes to feel he or she can do what the group can do. This feeling can generate a competence-evaluation set in a benign context. If the group is not merely struggling to survive or to avoid serious costs, members are frequently encouraged and given opportunities to develop new skills and abilities that may at some subsequent time contribute to their own and the group's productivity. While they are learning new skills, members are permitted to set lenient and flexible performance standards for themselves on those tasks. Thus, competence beliefs and the productive motivational states associated with them are likely to be generated in members.

If the task group divides its labor in such a way as to permit the assignment of members to those tasks that best fit their capabilities and interests, the potential for all members to maximize their satisfaction with their performances is enhanced. This satisfaction tends to prevent the formation of incompetence beliefs and the unproductive states associated with them even in times of difficulty for the group, when the costs associated with substandard performances are seen as high. Furthermore, the internal social consensus available to members of cooperative-solidarity groups help them to maintain some confidence in the value of their performances even in the face of negative evaluations by persons outside the group. Thus, members may be able to withstand external pressures and costs, thereby maintaining their self-esteem and productive motivation in circumstances where an individual person might be ridden with self-doubt, confusion, and overdefensiveness or depression.

Cooperative-solidarity groups tend to be friendly and benign environments in which to work. A temporarily unproductive, ineffective, or destructive member is, however, a detriment to the other members' progress and welfare. Such members tend not to remain ignored by other group members; they are usually persuaded and/or helped (rather than coerced) to return to a productive state. The social pressure exerted to encourage or lead members to be productive is subtle but nevertheless strong, and members usually learn to want to avoid incurring the displeasure of their fellow cooperators, about whom they usually have good feelings, and upon whom they are dependent. Thus, cooperative motivation joins together self-interest with the desire to promote the interests of trusted and well-liked other persons; it also links the desire to be productive with a concomitant desire not to "let down" important others who contribute to one's own interests and welfare. We should point out that an unproductive or destructive member who refuses to change is likely to be rejected by the group. Rejection from a cooperative group is particularly painful because of its implications about one's personal characteristics as well as task-related abilities.

Caring Groups

An example of a group defined by positive goal identification (see table 9-1) is the caring relationship. The defining quality of this group, as with all groups characterized by positive goal identification, is that one member derives pleasure from the successes of the others and is distressed by the others' failures.

We should note at the outset of this section that because caring relationships often stimulate unresolved problems from early childhood, these relationships frequently become the focus of neurotic interactions: The "parents" become competitive with the "children" over the children's activities, or the children begin to feel hemmed in and unable to find their own individual ways of working, or they are overdependent and simultaneously resentful; the "children" thus play out in their adult lives the conflicts of childhood. These potential relational pathologies can be serious and must be identified early and handled with care. Competitive relationships are easier to build and maintain than cooperative relationships, caring relationships, and friendships—as every marriage partner and parent can attest. Unfortunately, we have relatively little empirical evidence bearing upon the care and feeding of such relationships. What is known is only that they tend to be somewhat fragile, and they require a good deal of attention and effort for their maintenance. With this caution, we can proceed to an analysis of caring groups.

Caring relationships are nearly as common in everyday life as are parents and children, teachers and students, physicians and patients, or therapists and clients. Although the mere establishment of such role relationships between or among persons is not *sufficient* to define them as caring relationships (and, hence, not all parent-child or teacher-student relationships qualify, strictly speaking, as caring groups), the existence of these role relationships is an inevitable component of the caring system. Caring groups are similar in many respects to cooperative-solidarity groups, particularly in the kinds of interpersonal processes that arise. Their many unique features, however, and the general inattention accorded such systems by social scientists, make analyzing them separately useful for our purposes.

We should point out that the goals set by members of caring groups are usually defined somewhat differently than the goals of the other types of groups. The groups we have previously discussed are generally involved in the task of producing some kind of tangible product or commodity; these may take a wide variety of forms such as a vaccine for a viral disease, a letter grade in a school course, or multicolored widgets in three convenient sizes. Their goal may be said to be product oriented. In contrast, the goals set by caring groups are generally more process oriented: socializing and personal growth in the parent-child relationship, healing or curing in the doctor-patient relationship, teaching and learning in the teacher-student relationship, and so on. Although certain specifiable behaviors or even products may be taken as indications that the task is being accomplished successfully, production is usually not viewed as the end in itself. In addition, the time perspective for accomplishing the task is frequently longer than that set by product-oriented task groups. Socialization, learning, healing, and personal growth do not often occur overnight or even in a week or a month. As a result, caring groups are generally more enduring than some other task-oriented groups.

Whether or not the goal of a caring group is reached depends upon the mutual resources and efforts of the members. Because the relationship of the members of the caring group is in part defined by the social roles that they occupy (e.g., teachers, students, parents, children, and so forth) each must carry out his or her particular role in order for the group to succeed. Although they may help each other, neither side of the membership can substitute for the other by fulfilling the other's role. The teachers must teach, and the students must learn. Although teachers may modify and tailor their teaching in order to facilitate the students' learning, teachers cannot do the students' part of the job—learning. Thus, all persons in the caring group are dependent upon the others to fulfill their own roles; the members are truly interdependent, albeit somewhat differently than in the goal interdependent groups described earlier.

Persons who occupy the care-giver role (parents, teachers, doctors) do so in part by virtue of their presumed greater resources or expertise relevant to the task. They either impart this expertise to the others or use it for the others' welfare and benefit. Persons who occupy the complementary role—the care-receivers—do so in part because of their dependence upon the resources, knowledge, and expertise of the care-givers for growth, healing, or welfare. While the caring group may appear to be one in which the care-givers give and the care-receivers receive, this is not the case. The members are quite interdependent; neither party is passive, and both receive rewards from the relationship. The care-receivers' effort, work, and contributions are necessary for successfully accomplishing the goals of the group. Consider, for example, the consequences of emphysematous patients' refusing to quit smoking, psychiatric patients' inability or refusing to attend sessions, or students' refusing to complete their lessons. Such examples reveal a common occurrence in caring groups: while all parties to the relationships usually recognize that the care-receivers are dependent, frequently the case is that only the care-givers are aware that they are in fact interdependent with the other members.

The explicit goal of most caring groups is the welfare or growth of the care-receivers. In truth, caring relationships are those in which the goal of enhancing the welfare of the care-receivers is done primarily for their benefit and not for the personal enhancement or enrichment of the care-givers. While there are certainly personal rewards (and there may even be economic rewards) for the care-givers, these are subordinate to the welfare of the care-receivers. The care-givers feel a commitment and responsibility to such relationships and to the welfare of the care-receivers for their own sake, and they respect the care-receivers as individuals in their own right. In this regard, then, the caring group cannot be identified simply by the observation that a person helps another, as in many contractual arrangements where a person pays another for services the other provides.

Quite often caring relationships occur within the context of commercial contractual relationships, in which people pay money to receive goods or services. A consumer-oriented buyer-seller view of caring relationships does not take account of the importance of the cared-for "consumer's" active participation in the production of the "product." Unfortunately, people sometimes confuse caring relationships with simple buyer-seller relationships and appear to believe that if they pay, they should receive; they act as if physical health, learning, and even mental health can and should be delivered by an active care-giver to a passive consumer. This contractual view of caring relationships can occur on either side of the relationship; when it occurs, it usually distorts, devalues and sometimes defeats the goals of the caring relationship. The would-be care-giver who views the relationship as contractual and him or herself as a seller may see his obligation as merely delivering the usual product—a lecture, a fifty-minute therapy session—without regard for its helpfulness to the particular purchaser or to the interdependence between himself or herself and the other. The care-receiver who views the caring relationship as simply contractual and himself or herself as the buyer also fails to acknowledge the interdependent nature of the relationship; he or she equates services with commodities and processes with products. Thus, the interdependence of caring group relationships runs deeper, and the relationship between the members is more intense than most contractual relationships.

Caring, as we use it in this chapter, also indicates more than giving immediate help. It involves giving guidance and assistance which is calculated to result, over the long-term, in the welfare and growth of the care-receivers, even though, as many care-givers know, their assistance is not always experienced as immediately helpful. Clearly, then, in caring groups, giving and receiving are intricately related; so too are the rewards that members receive from the group. Some of the rewards are individual and private to each member, and some are mutual and shared; both categories lie in the processes of the relationship. For the care-givers, there are the rewards and satisfactions of giving and helping and witnessing the effects of their efforts in the other members. For the other members, the rewards include the security of being cared for, the satisfaction of important needs, the excitement of growth or regained health or competence, and the fruits of the growth or learning processes undergone in the relationship. In a caring group, the members do not always experience the same event similarly. Frequently learning, growth, and healing involve temporary physical or psychological discomfort for the care-receiving members; when this pain or anxiety is a growth sign, the care-givers may be pleased, and the care-receivers angry or frustrated. Similarly, small improvements may cause great joy in the care-receivers and only a routine nod of approval from the care-givers. These are the private moments that sometimes are not shared, though each side may try to understand the other. The sharing, however, will include events and milestones both have agreed upon, perhaps after negotiation, as indicating progress.

For both sides of the membership, there may also be the rewards resulting from participation in the caring group; for example, affectional ties, mutual esteem, feelings of solidarity, and feelings of belonging. In some special instances, there are also the profound rewards of being identified with a person or group of persons in the expression and reenactment of valued activities or traditions—that is, of being a link in a chain through which valued practices are transmitted and maintained. In certain specialized caring groups, the care-givers may also be rewarded by being in frequent contact with something they love, such as art, music, or science, through transmitting it to others.

Many caring groups provide other rewards as well. Often the care-givers have professional positions and the major duties of their occupations involve providing and giving care or help to others. The persons who are cared for or helped either directly or indirectly pay for this care, thus providing monetary rewards for the care-givers. In addition to monetary rewards, members of some caring groups may also acquire prestige and acclaim in the broader social context.

Interpersonal and Personal Consequences of Caring Groups

Caring groups are predicated on the needs of the care-receivers. The principle of justice endorsed, which determines the allocation of resources and rewards, is one of deservingness based upon need, which usually means that group resources (which generally originate with the care-givers) are allotted to the use of the care-receivers. This unequal allocation is supported by the care-givers' feelings of responsibility for the welfare of the others and their desire to do all that is possible to assist the care-receivers in the learning or growing process. Members who are goal identified with the others thus willingly provide help and resources to them. Since they give evidence of their investments in the others' successes, the others are inclined to accept influence from them and to communicate openly with them. Mutual feelings of affection, esteem, respect, and admiration generally develop between the members of a caring group and reinforce and perpetuate each side's desires and efforts to accomplish successfully the goal of the group. The goal is reached when the care-receivers are no longer needy, when they are independent, and/or when they have adequately mastered the new skill or growth goals. These explicit outcomes—the new welfare, the new skills, or the growth—then belong to the care-receiving members of the group.

Self-Esteem. Care-givers come to the caring group with the resources they hope will assist the care-receiving members. Among these resources are stable and positive self-esteem, training or experience, openness to new learning, and a commitment to the growth or welfare of the care-receivers. Thus, many of the care-givers' personal needs, including self-esteem needs, must be met elsewhere.

In the course of the caring relationship, the care-receivers, in their interactions with the care-givers, are likely to maintain or acquire self-acceptance, self-respect, and a realistic self-conception with respect to the task of the group. Depending upon what has transpired in the group, they may acquire a more positive sense of self-worth, such as gaining new skills and competencies. The self-concepts of members are likely to be multidimensional; they are esteemed for a variety of qualities they have that the others are aware of. As in the positively interdependent relationships, then, high and stable self-esteem will be the usual state of affairs, particularly for those members with whose goals the others are identified.

If we assume that the care-givers are competent and have invested in the welfare of the care-receivers and that reasonable motivation exists on the part of the care-receivers, the success or failure of the group depends upon how close the members have come to meeting standards they have set for themselves. Sometimes caring relationships succeed in reducing needs and producing growth, and sometimes they do not. More often the result is more ambiguous than clear "success" or clear "failure"; such an indeterminate outcome is likely to occur where standards have been vague or unrealistic or when the care-receivers undergo appreciable improvement though less than was hoped for. When the caring group is not reaching its goal—when the illness is not improving or the student is not learning—then the members may examine the situation and the standards of evaluation that are not being met and make appropriate changes.

The success of any caring group is limited by whatever degree of growth, change, or improvement the members can produce by using the resources they have available to them. Frequently, what both sides of the membership might desire is not realistically possible. Since the caring group and its goals are important to all members, its apparent inefficacy may be extremely disappointing and threatening to each member. Sometimes under these conditions, the members try to explain the failure to reach their goal by blaming themselves or by blaming the others. In different ways the self-blaming and the other-blaming approaches to explaining failures have negative consequences for the productivity motivation and the self-esteem of the persons whose efforts have failed. If the members take the route of mutual blaming, then they maintain at best a defensively high self-esteem—that is, each person attempts to maintain his or her esteem at the cost of the other and defends himself or herself from the real or imagined accusations of the others. The genuine loss, frustration and sadness is not shared and is then turned destructively against the relationship. The self-blaming alternative is equally unproductive. The care-giver who feels guilt over the failure is likely to suffer distress over his or her presumed incompetence as a care-giver and over feelings of having failed the others. The care-receiver's guilt is likely to be expressed in feelings of undeservingness—that is, he or she did not deserve the treatment and resources that were made available. The care-receiver also feels incompetent, having not only failed at the task but also having failed the others. These negative consequences, though understandable, are in contradiction to the implicit agreement made in the caring group as it began—that is, the care-givers would try to help and hoped to be able to, and the care-receivers deserved the help. In fact, neither side of the membership owes any specific outcome to the other.

Productivity Motivation. Care-giving members of caring groups are committed and motivated to accomplish the goals of the group and to expend considerable effort on their tasks. Care-givers, because of their experience with the process undertaken, are likely to base their goals and standards for the care-receivers' progress and accomplishment on realistic expectations that take account of the care-receivers' apparent capabilities and potentials. While the care-givers may have a relatively clear idea of the ultimate goal, their standards for subgoals are likely to be rather flexible and subject to modification as the process continues, and they and care-receivers meet with successes and setbacks. Their major investment is in the caring process itself more than in the product of the group, and the major source of their motivation comes from their desire to see the others do well and to avoid bad outcomes for them.

In contrast, the goals and standards of the care-receivers are likely to be based predominantly on their needs and desires. Their ideas of what should be accomplished in a short period of time may be, at least initially, rather grandiose, particularly if they have had little or no previous experience with the task. In the early stages of the relationship their standards may be inflexible and thus lead them to be dissatisfied with any progress short of the idealized goal. "I want everything and I want it now" may reflect the attitude of many care-receivers when they enter a caring relationship. As a consequence they may very well suffer bouts of incompetence-induced states adversely affecting their task motivation and productivity. With greater experience with the process and increased understanding of how the process operates, they may come to reevaluate the goals and standards they set for themselves to bring them increasingly in line with realistic projections for progress. One of the important functions the care-giver fulfills is helping the care-receiver understand the nature of the task and helping him or her to set obtainable subgoals, thus insuring that the care-receiver will experience the beneficial consequences of self-induced feelings of competence throughout the process.

Indeed, competence motivation is likely to be a central motivator for the care-receivers in the caring group, along with their desire not to let the care-givers down. If the care-receivers can learn to set and adjust their standards throughout the process to reflect obtainable subgoals, they will experience the psychological consequences of competence beliefs: positive feelings of elation, pride, or satisfaction; a desire to extend new skills and accomplishments; and increased task motivation, renewed effort, and perseverance. This competence-induced productivity cycle may be somewhat undermined, however, when the members of the caring group are not free to establish their own standards for the task and what is to be accomplished in the relationship. Sometimes the members of the caring group must meet externally imposed standards representing the expectations or demands placed on them by situational requirements or by persons peripheral to the caring relationship itself; for example, the parents of a music student, the wife of a psychotherapy patient, a colleague of a beginning professor. The imposition of such external demands and standards, if they exceed those the members of the caring group themselves would normally establish, may create the conditions that will foster incompetence beliefs by one or both parties in the relationship and thus undermine their productivity. The successful completion of the task may encourage the original care-receiver to expand those skills and abilities that were initially obtained in the caring relationship.

Other Relational Structures

In day-to-day observations, we are likely to see many kinds of task groups that are not precisely like any of the groups we have discussed above. Three categories of groups appear in table 9-1 that we have only briefly noted: (1) negatively interdependent groups in which invidious comparisons are not promoted and which have consequences similar to the competitive group discussed above but in attenuated form; (2) groups in which negative goal identification exists among members and which are characterized by exaggerated processes of the competitive groups; and (3) positively interdependent groups in which invidious comparisons are made and in which the processes of cooperative-solidarity groups occur in attenuated form. Table 9-1 is not, of course, an exhaustive list of all the possible ways of structuring task groups. Another type of group that does not appear in the chart but that occurs with some frequency is the mixed cooperative-competitive group.

Such mixed cooperative-competitive groups have in them both positive goal interdependence *and* negative goal interdependence. The group members are positively (cooperatively) interdependent over the accomplishment of the group task and the group goal or goals and are negatively (competitively) interdependent over the accomplishment of other goals the members may seek. A professional basketball team, for example, illustrates a mixed cooperative-competitive group. The members have a common group goal—winning the game or the championship—and each member of the team is positively interdependent with each other member of the team for the accomplishment of this goal. The members are also likely to have goals for which they are negatively interdependent with each other—that is, being the "star" of the team, scoring the most points, and so forth. Faring well in the competition over these latter goals is likely to become especially salient to members if important rewards (such as money or fame) are based on their relative performances. Frequently, for example, the star player can command a greater salary or more fringe benefits than other players. The salience of the negative interdependence and the linking of important rewards to relative performances is likely to create some conflict or tension in the individual player. Imagine, for instance, a basketball player who is carrying the ball but is some distance from the hoop; he calculates that he has a 60-40 chance of scoring if he shoots, but recognizes that a teammate closer to the net may have an 80-20 chance of scoring. Does he try to work for their cooperative goal of winning the game by passing the ball to his teammate, or does he work for his competitive goal of being the highest scoring player and shoot?

Mixed cooperative-competitive groups are probably rather unstable, in that they are likely to evolve either into groups that are dominated primarily by the competitive negative goal interdependence or by the cooperative positive goal interdependence. Maintaining the stability of a group demands a common definition of the situation by participating members—that is, a consistent way of being able to anticipate and respond to the behavior of other members of the group as well as a strategy for deciding on one's own moves and their likely consequences for oneself and the other members. In coming to a mutually shared definition of the situation, then, a mixed cooperative-competitive group is likely to resolve its latent instability by emphasizing and making salient for the members either their positive interdependence or emphasizing and making salient the negative interdependence. Whichever direction the group moves, the members are thus able to be coordinated in their expectations and behaviors.

The kinds of interpersonal rewards that accrue to members of mixed cooperative-competitive groups, and the productivity motivation which is engaged and self-esteem consequences that result, depend to a large extent on the direction in which the instability is resolved. A resolution in either a cooperative or a competitive direction is likely to result in interpersonal relations and consequences that are similar to the cooperative and competitive groups described earlier, albeit perhaps in a somewhat attenuated form. The cooperative resolution is weakened by the temptations and opportunities the structure offers to compete and also by the status system engendered by an unequal distribution of rewards. The competitive resolution is weakened by the structural necessity that the group meet its group goal in order for anyone on the team to enjoy the outcomes resulting from accomplishing that goal.

A number of factors are likely to influence whether a mixed cooperative-competitive group becomes more like a cooperative group or more like a competitive group: the degree of status mobility in the group; the importance of the group to its members; the relative magnitude of the potential rewards from competing compared with the potential rewards from cooperating; and the extent to which the attainment of the group goal is in jeopardy. When the potential for status mobility within the group is high, when the group is not valued very highly by the members, when the anticipated competitive rewards outweigh the anticipated cooperative rewards, and when the group's success or repeated success is insured, the group is likely to become more similar to competitive groups. Alternatively, when there is little opportunity for status mobility within the group or when status distinctions are unimportant or deemphasized, when the continued existence of the group and continued membership in the group are very important to group members, when the anticipated cooperative rewards outweigh the anticipated competitive rewards, and when attainment of the group-level goal is important to the members but may be in jeopardy, the mixed group is likely to move in the direction of a cooperative task group.

Another way of organizing groups to accomplish tasks which is probably quite common is noninterdependence; while the people may work on the same task and may have the same goal for their individual tasks, they are independent of each other with respect to meeting their goals. When the members of noninterdependent groups work in close physical proximity and are able to observe each other's progress and rewards, however, the group can become unstable in the sense that members do not remain truly independent. Such groups tend also to move either toward competition or toward cooperation.

Social Structures and Fear of Success

We return now to the central topic of this book: the fear of success. The digression that has filled virtually all of part III has been necessary to provide us with an understanding of where the fear of success might fit into the important and broader issue of people's motivation to do productive work. The question we raised in the beginning of chapter 7—How may the fear of success be connected with this larger complex of motives and activities?—can now be answered.

In view of the theoretical perspective we have taken about the origins of fear of success, the answer to the question appears almost obvious. The fear of success, we asserted, originates primarily around various issues of competition that arise in early childhood. The child has competitive impulses toward the same-sex parent connected with the Oedipal situation and develops anxieties and guilt feelings about those impulses. The parent or parents may actually contribute in some way to making the child's Oedipal conflicts seem more real and to making them more difficult to resolve.

Alternatively, the child may be in a competitive conflict with one or the other parent over his attempts to achieve independence. Whatever the source of the conflict, the child's family is seen by the child as competitive in important ways, and he learns the importance of winning and at the same time not winning the competition. The competitive atmosphere creates strong ambivalence and anxiety about any important success and a tendency to avoid both success and failure. We have theorized also that the complex emotional charge with which competition is invested leads the child to become—and the adult to remain—highly vigilant about competition—that is, sensitive to possible competition even when it is not obviously present. We would thus expect success-fearing persons to become particularly anxious in situations in which they believe they are in competition with others and that those situations would lead them to expend their energy defending against the fantasied dangers of competition and would instigate their fear-of-success reactions. Competitive task groups, then, would be expected to arouse, maintain, or exacerbate success-fearers' anxieties about successful performance and would interfere with their motivation to accomplish and their productivity.

The analysis just presented may not seem warranted to some readers due to the indirectness of the evidence for it reported in part II of the book. Thus, reviewing that evidence briefly may be useful before presenting the additional evidence we have obtained. Two pieces of evidence from part II can be brought to bear. First, each of the three questionnaire measures of the fear of success contains several items that indicate a preoccupation with possible competitive aspects of ambiguous situations. Responses to those questions have been consistently correlated over thousands of respondents with responses to the remaining items in the fear-of-success scales and thus would appear to be a part of the entire fear-of-success syndrome. Second, the study by Cohen reported in chapter 3 shows that success-fearing persons are made anxious by successful competition with others and that they are particularly likely to sabotage their successful performances when they are in competition with people of the same sex. While these results are provocative and consistent with what we have been suggesting, they say nothing very direct about the early family interaction patterns of success-fearers. Certainly we would want to have more direct evidence for the assumption that the families of origin of success-fearing persons are in fact more competitive than the families of persons who do not fear success.

A study we have recently conducted does provide us with such evidence. This study, which is described in greater detail in the discussion in chapter 10 of the etiology of fear of success, was conducted with elementary school age children and one of their parents. Half of these children were high scorers on the children's fear-of-success scale and half were low scorers. They were seen one at a time in an experimental session with either their mother or their father present. The children performed a word construction task during the session, and the parents were told that they could do or say whatever they wished (whatever they felt comfortable saying or doing) while the child worked on the task; the interaction between the parent and the child was carefully observed throughout. After the task was completed, the children and the parents were separated, and completed two questionnaires about the session and about general issues. Two of the results of the study will be mentioned here; others will be discussed in chapter 10.

The success-fearing children in this study performed less well on the task than the non-success-fearing children; *however, this was the case only when the same-sex parent was present.* We note that this finding repeats Cohen's earlier finding, mentioned above, that for success-fearers, performance in competition with a same-sex person led to more self-sabotage behavior than performance in competition with an opposite-sex person. We may infer from this result that for success-fearing children, the possibility of competition with the same-sex parent is disturbing and leads to a reduction in the child's performance level. Even this result, however, tells us nothing about the actual competitiveness of the success-fearer's family; it says something only about the child's responses to his or her perceptions of the parent.

The responses of the parents to several questions they answered at the end of the session, however, provide us with some clues about the actual state of affairs in these families.[3] Parents of success-fearing children, more than parents of children who do not fear succcess, said that knowing "how smart my child is compared to other children his (her) age" was important to them. The greater interest on the part of these parents in comparing their children's abilities with those of others is in itself an indicator of a competitive attitude. The parents of success-fearing children also agreed, more than other parents, that parents ". . . should always try to identify a child's mistakes because it is more difficult for a child to know when he is wrong than for him to know when he is right." On the other hand, they also believe, more than the parents of children who do not fear success, that their child ". . . knows when I am pleased about his performance, even if I don't tell him." We might infer from the foregoing responses that these parents are merely intensely ambitious for their children. While this could be true, their ambition is not unconflicted: They, far more than the parents of other children, agree that they ". . . have mixed feelings about how successful I want my child to be in life." The picture is one of ambivalence, emotional investment in performance and success, and at least subtle competitiveness. Additional results of the study, reported in the next chapter, make the picture even clearer; the parents of success-fearing children in the study were quite intrusive in their behavior toward their children.

Given this support for our position, we may now speculate further about the conditions under which the productivity motivation of success-fearing persons will be engaged and the conditions under which it will be interfered with. If we take seriously, as we are inclined to do, the notion that success-fearers tend to interpret neutral situations as having competitive elements, we would be reasonable to suggest that not only competitive task groups but also mixed cooperative and competitive task groups and even cooperative task groups that foster invidious comparisons may be responded to by success-fearers as being potentially competitive and therefore potentially dangerous. Success in such groups would be, for success-fearers, anxiety arousing and something to be avoided. In cooperative-solidarity task groups, on the other hand, the instigations to competition are minimal; these groups are less likely to arouse the performance anxiety of success-fearers. Furthermore, the positive interdependence and friendly feelings of cooperative-solidarity groups probably allow success-fearers to take comfort in the knowledge that their efforts and successes are for the good of liked others as well as for themselves. These same friendly interactions probably reassure success-fearers that their successes are not viewed by other group members as competitive and hostile. We would go so far as to suggest that many success-fearers are likely to view cooperative-solidarity task groups as unique, highly desirable work environments that release them from the conflicts and inhibitions they so frequently experience about performance and productivity and that provide them with valuable and important rewards.

Like cooperative task groups, caring task groups are characterized by a form of positive interdependence among their members. As we have pointed out above, however, this positive interdependence may not always be apparent, particularly to the care-receivers. Nevertheless, such groups may well arouse productivity motivation in success-fearing persons who occupy caring roles. The task of the caring group is, after all, the growth or welfare of the care-receivers and not the aggrandizement of the care-givers; the success-fearing care-giver may remain comfortably in the background even when he or she clearly succeeds. In general, then, we see caring task groups as generally unlikely to arouse productivity-inhibiting motivation in success-fearing persons and as equally likely to arouse productivity motivation in success-fearers as in others. On the other hand, we have pointed out that a requirement for effective care-givers, particularly in task groups concerned with growth and development, is that the care-givers meet their self-esteem needs outside the task group. Since success-fearers probably have unstable self-esteem and since their own conflicts about competition may be communicated to others who are dependent on them (see chapter 10), we cannot be certain of the consequences for the care-receivers of having success-fearers act in the role of care-givers. While we would recommend caution and some attention to this problem, we feel that no definitive statement can now be made about this issue.

Notes

1. An interesting analysis of issues relating to the productivity of decision-making groups has been undertaken in a volume by Collins and Guetzkow [16] who have made several statements similar to the ones we make in this chapter.

Although these authors have emphasized factors that relate specifically to interpersonal behavior in conferences organized for decision making, their review of the psychological literature through 1963 on social factors influencing productivity is recommended to the reader interested in the more general question. A more recent review of this literature (through 1971) is available in a volume by Steiner [105] who has made useful suggestions regarding the productivity of certain task group organizations as related to the characteristics of the tasks such groups may undertake.

2. Some authors [56,93] have made an interesting and useful distinction between goals interdependence (our concern in this chapter) and means interdependence in task groups. Means interdependence has to do with whether and how the members are dependent on one another for the tools and resources necessary for them to reach their goals or complete their tasks. Members can be means independent (each member has all the tools and resources required for the completion of his or her task or tasks), or they can be positively or negatively interdependent with regard to the means required to reach their goals. In the case of positive means interdependence, members perform complementary tasks and need each others' products for their own task completion. In negative means interdependence, there is a scarcity of the tools and resources required by members to complete their tasks such that if some members have access to resources they need, others are denied access to those necessary resources. While our own analysis could be elaborated by using this distinction, we do not require this elaboration for our present purposes.

3. The questions were designed by Sandra Headen as preliminary to her doctoral dissertation, now in progress, about the childhood origins of the fear of success.

Part IV:
Implications for Theory,
Research, and Practice

Introduction to Part IV

In the final chapters of the book we return to a direct focus on the fear of success. Chapter 10 addresses both the origins of fear of success and its treatment. The twin questions of development and maintenance of fear of success are approached first; our discussion of development builds on the results of a preliminary study of parent-child interaction during the child's performance of a task. Two general strategies of treating persons who suffer from fear of success are then considered in chapter 10. Chapter 11 presents a summary of our thinking and our findings to date. Here we consider various possible alternative interpretations of the results of our research and discuss the assumptions we have made in interpreting those results, with particular emphasis on those assumptions that have not yet been tested. Finally we make explicit the important questions about fear of success that remain to be answered, as a way of taking stock of how far we have come in our attempts to solve the puzzle of fear of success and how far we have yet to go.

10 Origins and Treatment of Fear of Success

This chapter is devoted to an examination of two questions that have considerable practical importance: the origins of fear of success and the strategies that have been developed to treat persons who lives are affected by it. While the etiology of fear of success has not been neglected in the preceding pages, it has been approached in a very general way. For example, our theoretical perspective informs us that *something* takes place in the families of success-fearing children that is different from what happens in other families, but we have very little information about what it is that happens. This chapter looks more closely at this issue. Following the discussion of how family interaction contributes to the etiology of fear of success, we discuss briefly the role of other social institutions in its maintenance or intensification. Finally, we turn to the question of treatment, with primary emphasis on behavior therapy and insight therapy as general strategies for helping success-fearing persons.

Origins of Fear of Success

The measures of fear of success used in the research we have reported in preceding chapters were based on a number of assumptions regarding its origins. Our general assumptions have been that fear of success is at least partially unconscious, that it originates in childhood, and that its central dynamics revolve about competition. More specifically, we have assumed: (1) that fear of success is instigated or intensified during the Oedipal period by the child's rivalrous fantasies about the parent of the same sex; and (2) that the conflicts and fears that arise in most children during this period are perpetuated and made more difficult to resolve when parents act so as to make the child's Oedipal fantasies seem real. These assumptions are, of course, quite abstract. We are not informed, either by theory or research, about concrete events in families that actually bring about fear of success. In chapter 9 we alluded briefly to a study we have recently conducted that was intended to shed light on these more concrete events. We shall describe this study in somewhat greater detail here and then build on its findings in our discussion of the etiology of fear of success.[a]

---

[a]The authors are grateful to Karen Kurlander and Nellie Vanzetti, who served as experimenters in this study, and to Kathy Ault, Yohel Camayd, Cathy Flaherty, Sandra Headen, Eliza Hewat, and Deborah Rubin, who alternately served as observers and interviewed parents.

185

A Preliminary Study of Parent-Child Interaction
and Fear of Success

Over eleven hundred fourth-, fifth-, and sixth-grade children in a socioeconomically and ethnically heterogeneous New England suburban community were
given the children's fear-of-success scale. From this larger sample, forty-three
high scorers and forty-three low scorers on the scale, about half males and half
females, participated in the study with one of their parents, chosen in advance
and at random. Thus, the participants in the study were male and female
children who were identified as either success-fearers or non-success-fearers by
the scale and who were accompanied in the experiment either by the same-sex
parent or the opposite-sex parent. The persons who served as experimenters and
observers in the study did not know the fear-of-success category of the children
who participated.

The children participated individually and were asked to perform several
timed word-construction tasks in which they were to construct as many smaller
words as possible out of large words such as "chrysanthemum" and "automobile." The letters in each large word, printed on small wooden blocks, could
be used anew in the construction of each smaller word. The parent was
instructed to behave normally and naturally—that is, to say and do what he or
she wished. Both parent and child were told that any word the parent
constructed would not "count" in the child's score. In order to prevent the
parent from being overly self-conscious about being watched, both participants
were told at the beginning of the session that the researchers were primarily
interested in studying children's "styles" of working and that the parent would
be asked later to confirm whether the child had worked during the session as he
or she normally worked on tasks. In actuality, the two observers in the room
coded the behavior of the child and the parent and attended to virtually
everything each one said and did during the session.

The study was designed not only to provide answers to general questions,
but also to serve an exploratory function. We were, of course, interested in
finding out whether the success-fearers' same-sex parents behave differently
toward them than their opposite-sex parents. Furthermore, we were interested in
finding out whether the actual performances of the success-fearing children
would be affected by the presence of their same-sex and opposite-sex parents
and interested in how these parents felt about their children's performances.
Beyond these general questions, however, we were vitally interested in exploring
the specifics of the parents' behavior. Would the parents of success-fearing
children be bossy, pushy, critical, interfering, silent, rejecting, encouraging,
seductive? Would they behave in an overtly competitive manner toward their
children? Would they behave ambiguously, thereby allowing their children's
fantasies about them to have free rein? Certainly, many possibilities existed, and
many were highly plausible under the theory. Assuming that the behaviors

parents engaged in during the sessions would reflect at least in part the way they normally behave toward their children regarding their children's performances, we hoped to obtain some useful clues about actual parent-child interactions associated with the development of fear of success.

At this writing, our analysis of the results of this study has not been completed. We have therefore chosen to report the results informally, restricting our discussion to major findings. However, the differences discussed have been subjected to statistical tests and are statistically stable.

As we mentioned in chapter 9, the children identified as success-fearers tended to perform more poorly than the children identified as non-success-fearers. This poorer performance was especially clear in the case of success-fearing children who worked in the presence of their same-sex parents; these children produced, on the average, about 10 percent fewer correctly spelled words than the remaining children. Thus, we may infer that the presence of the parent—particularly the same-sex parent—inhibited the performance of the success-fearing children.

The actual behavior of the parents in the study is quite instructive. Parents of success-fearing children both said more to their children and participated more actively in the task than did parents of non-success-fearing children: on the average, they made about 70 percent more comments to their children and were more than three times as active in the child's task than the parents of non-success-fearing children. What was the content of these comments and the nature of the parents' participation in the child's task? Parents of success-fearing children made substantially more critical comments to the children—comments that were coded as criticisms, corrections, and scolding—than did parents of non-success-fearing children. No appreciable difference existed, on the other hand, between the number of praising or encouraging comments made by parents of success-fearers and parents of children who do not fear success. The parents of success-fearing children, furthermore, gave their children more hints, commands, and instructions than the parents of non-success-fearing children. We should note that these differences in critical comments and hints and instructions were equally apparent for opposite-sex parents as for same-sex parents.

In coding parents' participation in the child's task, we distinguished between instances in which the parent reached out to make a word but did not actually complete the word and instances in which the parent actually made words; the reader will recall that the parents were told that words made by them would not be counted in the child's score. Parents of success-fearing children reached to make words (without completing them) much more frequently than parents of non-success-fearing children. They also actually completed substantially more words than the parents of non-success-fearing children—nearly three times as many, on the average. Again, we note that these findings were as strong for opposite-sex parents as for same-sex parents.

The pattern of results just described is complex and appears somewhat puzzling as well. Let us see what can be made of it. First, we know from the results that the parents of success-fearing children do indeed behave differently toward their children over performance issues than the parents of children who do not fear success; we are not dealing entirely with a figment of the child's imagination. Second, we know that these parents are more active rather than more passive and quiet than the parents of non-success-fearing children in regard to the children's performances. Third, we know that both same-sex and opposite-sex parents of success-fearing children engage in this high level of activity. This finding may appear puzzling in light of the result mentioned above that the success-fearing children in our study performed particularly poorly in the presence of their same-sex parent. If the opposite-sex parent was as likely as the same-sex parent to intrude actively into the success-fearing child's work, why were the actual performances of these children impaired only by the presence of the same-sex parent? We shall return to this interesting puzzle following the discussion of the remainder of the results of the study.

What could the behavior of the parent of a success-fearing child be communicating to the child? If we can answer this question while remaining faithful to the results of the study, we will be closer to understanding the implications of the results for the development of fear of success. First, we know that these parents were very active during the session: They said a great deal about the task and gave a great many hints and instructions. We may surmise that at a minimum such activity indicates to the child that the parent is vitally interested in his performance and that the parent considers such task performances to be important. Second, we know that the parents of success-fearing children were more likely to criticize, scold, and point out the child's mistakes than the parents of non-success-fearing children. These critical comments communicate that the parent believes that the child's performing well and without errors—avoiding failure—is also important. Thus, doing well is both important and presumably good in these families, while making mistakes and doing poorly is something to be avoided.

The latent meaning of the parents' direct participation in their children's tasks is more difficult to ascertain. Very few parents were overtly competitive with their children; in only two cases (both involving success-fearing children) did the parent actually move the child's hand away while the child was attempting to work, so that the parent instead of the child could construct words with the wooden blocks. In most cases, the parents who constructed words did so during times when the child's word construction had slowed materially or stopped, so that the parent's intrusions could be interpreted by the outside observer as prompting, suggesting, or other help, or as offers to share the task with the child in a comradely and cooperative way. From another perspective, however, much of the participation on the part of parents can be seen as interference with the child's work. When the child had stopped actively making words and seemed stuck, he or she was probably thinking of additional ways in which words could be made with the letters available. Thus, the parent's verbal or nonverbal hints probably interfered with the child's thinking or decision making and effectively made it seem that the parent's thoughts about the task were to be considered richer, more useful, or more important than those of the child. Particularly because of the time limit set for each word, the child was probably strongly impelled to accept and build on the parent's suggestions. If the parent attempted to make words at the same time the child was doing so, the message conveyed is clearly competitive: "*I* want to do this; don't get in the way." If, on the other hand, the parent frequently made words or parts of words when the child appeared "stuck," the parent may have communicated that he or she, in contrast, was not "stuck"; a comparison is implied. Furthermore, given the time limit, any time the parent spent in constructing words tended to shorten the time that was available for the child to do so and thus to decrease the child's ability to add to his or her score. More importantly perhaps, the parent's activity with the task made it more difficult for the child to feel that his performance on the task had resulted from his own efforts.

Let us try to imagine the situation from the point of view of the child of this age. He is at an elementary school—clearly his own arena of performance— being watched by a group of university researchers and by one of his parents. The researchers want to see how he works and presumably to see how well he can do this school-related task. Suppose now that the parent frequently offers help in the form of hints, suggestions, reminders, or completed words. If the child ignores the parent's train of thought (which may be very difficult to do), he is losing an avenue of word production he might not have found on his own. If he builds on the parent's suggestion or word, he is made uncertain about where this part of his performance came from: Did he do it himself, or did the parent really do it? He may also be uncertain about what the researcher thinks about his ability to do the task. In either event the child may feel somewhat cheated or thwarted by the parent's help—not entirely without justification. He may also have emotional reactions that are difficult to deal with, particularly in the circumstances, such as anger, humiliation, competitive impulses, and so on. We are, then, arguing that the parent's *actions* (rather than the intentions behind those actions) could have led the success-fearing child to feel that the parent was not altogether comfortable with the child's attempts to do well on his own. Since in all likelihood the child very much wants to act independently and to reap the fruits of independent action, the parent's message is, in effect, a competitive one. The parent may or may not experience the interference as competitive; in fact, the parent's explicitly experienced motives may be helpful, friendly, and cooperative. The child's implicit interpretation, however, is likely to involve the idea that "mother or dad doesn't really want me to do this, or to have this."

The results of the study just described suggest that certain interaction patterns in the families of success-fearing children create *ambivalence* in the child about his task performances. The parent scolds the child for mistakes and responds to the possibility of a poor performance with criticism or derision, and the child learns that doing something poorly, or failing, is a bad thing. The parent instructs the child and offers a number of hints and suggestions, and the child learns that doing well is important—that is, succeeding is a good, desirable, and hopeful thing. The parent interferes with the child's efforts to perform tasks on his own, and the child learns that his attempts to achieve independence in this way are intruded upon and perhaps frowned upon by the parent. If the child experiences angry and competitive impulses in response to the parent's behavior, the situation may begin to feel dangerous to him. He may experience his attempts to acquire independence through good performance as creating an angry struggle between himself and the parent, either over the issue of his independence, or, more directly, over the issue of who can do the tasks better. If the parent is not actually feeling angry or competitive, the child may confuse his feelings with those of the parent. Alternatively, the child's subtle manifestations of anger and resistance may themselves create anger or feelings of competition in the parent, which in turn are perceived by the child. In either event, the result is the same: the child "learns" that doing a task well on his own is dangerous. The various ingredients of ambivalence about successful performance are created. The two notions—that performing well is good and important and that such performances are dangerous—appear, at first glance, to be incompatible and mutually exclusive. The ambivalence can be resolved, however, if the positive thoughts and feelings about success—the hopes—are experienced only when success is relatively distant, psychologically speaking, and the negative thoughts and feelings—the anxieties—are experienced when success is nearby and clearly attainable. Thus, what the child ultimately "learns" is not only the various thoughts, feelings, and responses involved in the conflict, but also the conditions and situations in which he experiences and responds to the feelings. He can keep the feelings conveniently separate in this way. The inconsistency remains covert; being covert, it is perfectly tolerable.

We return now to the puzzling finding mentioned earlier that while both same-sex and opposite-sex parents of success-fearing children intruded actively into the children's work, the children's performances appear to have been affected only by the presence of the same-sex parent. This result must be examined closely, and is best seen in conjunction with a parallel result that appears equally puzzling. This parallel result has to do with the behavior of parents who were themselves success-fearers, and with the responses of success-fearing children to them. Parents in the study were asked to fill out the Cohen fear-of-success scale after the session with the child was over. As might be expected, success-fearing children were more likely than non-success-fearing children to be accompanied by a parent who was also a success-fearer. The relationship was not very strong, however (the contingency coefficient was .40), and some of the success-fearing children brought with them parents who were low scorers on the fear-of-success scale.

Thus we could ask two important questions: First, was it especially likely that the parent who was intrusive during the child's performance was also a high scorer on the fear-of-success scale? Second, were the children's performances disrupted more when they worked in the presence of a success-fearing parent than when they worked in the presence of a non-success-fearing parent? The answer to both questions was a clear "no." The behavior of the parent toward the child was predicted only by the *child's* score on the fear-of-success scale. Non-success-fearing parents were as likely to behave in an intrusive way during the session as the success-fearing parents. Furthermore, the child's actual performance on the task was predicted only by whether the accompanying parent was of the same sex or the opposite sex; the parent's fear-of-success score was unrelated to the child's performance on the task. The parallel nature of this result with the one described earlier is now clear: the parents of success-fearing children were likely to be actively intrusive whether they were same-sex or opposite-sex parents, and whether they themselves were success-fearers or not. Furthermore, the success-fearing child's task performance was made worse by the presence of the same-sex parent whether that parent was intrusive or not, and whether the parent was a success-fearer or not.

This pattern of results suggests two things to us. First, it suggests that parents work together to mold the achievement attitudes and achievement conflicts of their children. Second, it suggests that the children themselves play an important part in the picture. We might describe the situation as one in which the family operates as a *system* to create fear of success in the child. Let us consider how this might work, beginning with the roles the parents play and then dealing with the child's own contribution. We know that there was a moderate correlation between the fear-of-success scale score of the child and that of the parent. Since the parent who accompanied each child in our study was selected at random, we may assume a moderate likelihood that at least one of the two parents of any given success-fearing child will also have fear-of-success conflicts. We may also presume that a person who is strongly conflicted about performing, succeeding, and competing is likely to marry someone whose attitudes about these matters are, at the very least, not in conflict with his or her own attitudes. This idea is supported by a result we obtained in an earlier pilot study, in which the fear-of-success scale scores of the parents of a group of twenty-four children were moderately positively correlated with one another ($r = .41$). This finding clearly implies that success-fearing persons marry other success-fearing persons more frequently than would be expected by chance alone, and bolsters the assertion that success-fearing persons tend to choose spouses whose ideas about achieving and competing are compatible with their own. It is only a small step from this idea to the notion that such persons implicitly cooperate with the spouse to transmit their attitudes to their children; without necessarily being aware of it, they support one another's basic views in their child-rearing practices.

We are suggesting, then, that the messages about performance and achievement that are transmitted to the success-fearing child by his parents are, in effect, assented to by both parents. Either parent may serve as the primary communicator of these messages to the child, or in some cases both parents may be active participants, taking the "teaching" role whenever the situation calls for it. This suggestion contradicts the theoretical position we took in chapter 3 in our description of the thinking underlying Cohen's research. We assumed in that discussion that the intensification of the Oedipal conflict in the child was accomplished by the same-sex parent's subtle or overt competitiveness with the child. The present results suggest that such instigations to conflicts about competition may come from the actions of either parent.

What is the child's contribution to this family system? In our study, the performance of the success-fearing child was impaired only by the presence of the same-sex parent. This result clearly implicates the child's own Oedipal fantasies in the origin and manifestations of fear of success. Thus, while the same-sex parent does not have to be an active participant in creating fear-of-success conflicts in the child, the child's fantasies about the same-sex parent are nevertheless involved in the picture. These anxieties, once they are intensified by the actions of one or both parents, are manifested most clearly and strongly with the same-sex parent and, as is shown by the results of Cohen's study, with other persons of the same sex. It is worth emphasizing, furthermore, that in all likelihood Oedipal fantasies by themselves, without parental intervention, do not have fear-of-success consequences. Childhood fantasies combine with parental feelings and behaviors, expressed by one or both parents, to accomplish the task.

The research just described points very clearly to the notion that the family, perhaps in some cases including siblings as well as parents, operates as a system to create or intensify performance conflicts in the child. There is no suggestion, however, that family members are conscious of what they are doing, of the consequences of their actions, or even of the concerted nature of their actions. The various ways in which family members interact to produce the effects we have observed are not illuminated by our study. That issue requires further research, including research conducted in the natural settings in which these families interact.

Maintenance of Fear of Success in Other Settings

We have been arguing in favor of the view that the family helps to create fear of success in the child by serving as a conduit through which the conflicts of the culture at large regarding competition and success are transmitted. Those parents who generate the fear-of-success conflict in the child do so because they are themselves affected by a part or all of it in one way or another. Not so surprisingly, then, many of our other important social institutions—including those charged with the socialization of our older children—also express the culture's conflicts about success and competition. The schools, of course, are a very clear example, as we have already pointed out. To excel as a pupil in primary and secondary school, or as a student in college or even graduate or professional school, is to stand out, to perform better than the "run of the mill," or, ideally, to be the best performer. The push toward competition, while often subtle, is nevertheless very powerful. Thus, the child with fear-of-success problems initiated in the family finds the same messages being delivered by events in the school: succeeding is very good; failing is very bad; and people who succeed are envied and made targets. Many of us may remember, for example, that the outstanding students in primary and secondary school were often singled out by other children and subjected to name calling, ridicule, or social isolation, sometimes openly and sometimes more subtly and in combination with signs of admiration. Teachers also convey multiple messages about success to children: Succeeding is very fine, but one must not do so by being openly and boldly competitive with other children; "getting along" with others is also important, we find. The major reward structure of the schools is predicated on competition, however, rather than on interpersonal skill or even individual task performance. The various pieces of the message are perfectly evident, particularly to those who are already sensitive to them.

The world of work, of course, is a carrier of the same set of messages. In a great many commercial, industrial, educational, and even governmental institutions, workers advance in rank and salary by competing successfully with other workers. Success is highly valued and esteemed, and success is usually measured in relative terms. Failure is anathema, and workers who fail are generally not held in high esteem by others. At the same time, being cooperative and helpful—to be a good "team player"—is often deemed important in these institutions. The point is not that these conflicting messages are impossible to resolve or deal with, but that they are kept alive and salient by many of our social institutions. People who are sensitized to these issues in their families of origin and become neurotically conflicted about them are frequently reminded of them in school and at work and are thus more likely to play them out in their own nuclear families and to transmit the conflict in turn to their children. The problem is rather clearly a cultural as well as a psychological one.

We have suggested in chapter 9 that clearly and strongly cooperative environments may help children and adults with fear-of-success problems to perform well without the unpleasant conflicts that are generated in them by competitive or individualistic environments. We turn now to the issue of therapy for success fearers; a desirable therapeutic goal would be helping these persons reduce the intensity of their conflicts, not only under highly cooperative conditions but under other circumstances as well. As we have pointed out, these other circumstances are, by and large, more common.

Treatment of Fear of Success

Because fear of success is a psychological problem that interferes with performance in school and work, we might correctly assume that psychotherapists have become aware of it and developed ways of treating persons who fear success. Generally speaking, there are two very different approaches to the treatment of fear-of-success problems that differ markedly from each other: behavior therapy and insight therapy. There are in fact many different points of view within each broad category regarding the nature and treatment of psychological dysfunctions. Although we do not intend to discuss the nuances of the various schools of thought and practice in each category, we briefly discuss the general outlines of each treatment process below.

Behavior Therapy

Behavior therapy has developed as a technique of assisting people to change their reactions and behaviors to certain specifiable categories of stimuli: people, places, things, situations. There are two general kinds of behavior changes: (1) changes in the direction of avoiding often harmful stimuli that were formerly approached, such as changing smoking, drinking, or eating patterns; and (2) changes in the direction of approaching potentially positive or neutral stimuli that had formerly been avoided as exemplified in various phobias about such stimuli as snakes, crowds, people, and, as we shall see, success. The theoretical foundations of behavior therapy and the procedures followed by the behavior therapist are based primarily on the principles of classical conditioning and instrumental conditioning. While patients in behavior therapy may gain insight into the reasons for their behavior, the primary focus of the therapy is on the contemporary experiences and behaviors of the patient and not on early childhood experiences. In other words, ideas such as unconscious motives and repression are regarded as unnecessary and irrelevant by a behavior therapist in the explanation and treatment of fear of success or any other phobia. Behavior therapists theorize that any well-entrenched approach or avoidance behavior has been learned and maintained according to principles of conditioning and reinforcement and can therefore be unlearned or changed through the use of similar principles, particularly counterconditioning and the reinforcement of alternative responses.

Let us be more specific by describing the course of behavior therapy for persons with fear of success, our central interest here.[b] In coming to behavior therapy, the patient in many instances knows what behaviors he wants to change; for example, cigarette smoking, extreme shyness, and so forth. In the

[b]The authors are indebted to Dr. Leo Reyna, one of the founders of behavior therapy, who provided much of the information upon which this section is based.

case of fear of success, the patient is likely to define his problem somewhat more vaguely in the beginning; for instance, he may complain that he procrastinates, doesn't follow through on projects, or perhaps even that he has trouble succeeding or being assertive. Whatever problems and symptoms bring him to the behavior therapist, two activities begin immediately. First the patient responds to a multi-item phobia questionnaire on which he indicates the kinds of situations that make him feel anxious, fearful, upset, and disturbed and therefore lead to avoidance or withdrawal behaviors. The responses to this questionnaire, in conjunction with interviews with the patient, provide a kind of diagnosis and clarification of the phobias or problem areas upon which the treatment will be focused. Fear of success will emerge as a more precisely defined problem than it appeared to be in the patient's initial definitions.

In the second step, the behavior therapist actually begins the treatment procedure by teaching the patient how to achieve total physical relaxation. This process has many steps and takes both time and practice to learn fully. It is also the basic therapeutic weapon against the powerful forces of the phobia, since total relaxation on the one hand, and anxiety or fear on the other are incompatible responses; a person cannot be anxious and totally relaxed simultaneously. Although learned in the consulting room, the practice of total relaxation is continued as homework.

In the counterconditioning phase of treatment the patient, in a state of total relaxation, imagines that he is in an anxiety-producing situation invented by the therapist and himself and relevant to the phobia. In fact, a large number of such situations, graded hierarchically by the patient from zero (indicating minimal anxiety) to 100 (indicating maximally severe anxiety), have been devised. The situations the patient imagines during relaxation are as real and concrete as possible, and several different situations are specified for each level of anxiety. Beginning with the situations that are rated as low in the extent to which they produce anxiety, the patient imagines each of them in the relaxed state until he is no longer made anxious by them; he then gradually moves up to imagining—and relaxing in—increasingly anxiety-arousing situations.

In the meantime the patient continues to practice relaxation at home and also starts to keep detailed records of the actual life situations that make him anxious. He makes a rating of the degree of anxiety experienced in each situation, what was done in the situation, and indicates what situations were avoided. These records are kept for two primary purposes. First, over time, the records of what situations make the patient anxious or those he avoids entirely provide the patient with evidence of improvement as the anxiety and avoidance patterns change. In addition, as the initial fears and avoidance behaviors begin to disappear, patients often discover new anxieties connected with the phobia that they had not known about previously because they had avoided even approaching those fear-producing situations. For instance, a student with a success phobia may have avoided answering any questions in a classroom. Once he has overcome his fear of answering questions, he may encounter anxiety when someone compliments him on an answer, an anxiety he could not have known about until he could first actually answer a question. These new situations are then added to the list of situations that are imagined during relaxation.

As the therapy progresses, the patient is asked to record situations that precede and co-occur with his anxiety states and to pay special attention to the things he does and feels that contribute to his problem. For instance, a success-fearing student may notice that he does his homework in a state of exhaustion and often begins with the hardest assignments, which is a work style that exacerbates his problem. Or the person may notice that he speaks to people in such a way as to make them irritated or angry and himself anxious. These behavior patterns can be changed.

The goal of counterconditioning is to rid the patient of the disabling physical and emotional responses which he has learned to connect with certain situations or stimulus events, such as success and competition. Presumably success-fearing patients have the goal of being able to engage successfully in competitive and other enterprises. If the patient's fear of success had not led to serious skill deficits, the counterconditioning may be sufficient to enable him to reach his goals—that is, once the fear is gone, the other skills and behaviors necessary to succeed will emerge, if they were learned in spite of the phobia. If, however, the success-phobia effectively blocked the development of these other skills, then the therapist will provide assistance in learning new skills. For example, once the success-phobia has been counterconditioned many success-fearers show deficits in being able to be appropriately assertive, particularly in the face of criticism. A period of assertiveness training is introduced for these persons. This process occurs both in the consulting room and as homework and is accomplished through role playing and role reversal, in which therapist and patient take turns at playing the role of patient and significant others with whom the patient has difficulty in being assertive. For instance, they may role play interchanges between the patient and his boss, the patient and his spouse, the patient and his parent, and so on; the therapist at one time plays the role of the patient and at another, the role of boss, spouse, parent, or other. In the course of these role playing and role reversal exercises, the patient learns how to be appropriately assertive from the therapist and also acquires an understanding (from playing the role of boss, and so forth) of how others feel about and respond to appropriate assertiveness. As the therapy progresses further, patients bring in lists of any new events or situations that upset them, including anxieties about things they anticipate might happen (fantasies) and about which they are fearful. The fantasies and the events that are still upsetting can be counterconditioned. Interestingly, a large percentage of the things people fear and worry about are fantasies—that is, things that haven't happened and in fact seldom do happen, but nevertheless lead the patient to avoid important arenas of living.

Behavior therapy for fear of success is usually accomplished in fifteen to sixty sessions; the duration of the therapy depends mostly upon how much new skill learning the patients must do after the success phobia has been counter-conditioned. The therapy sessions in the consulting room are usually fifty minutes in duration and occur once a week; daily homework and recordkeeping are required.

Insight Therapy

Insight therapy is based on and has developed from the theories of clinical psychologists and psychoanalysts who stress the idea of unconscious motivation of behavior and the influence of early childhood experience on later develop-ment. The approach of insight therapists is to assist patients in rediscovering their repressed and forgotten childhood conflicts, fantasies, and beliefs and to understand how patterns of behavior and thought that were established early in life still operate in the present. Insight therapists who treat patients who fear success do not usually single out that particular inhibition for special treatment; rather, they address the totality of each patient's problems and life experiences.

The session-to-session process of psychotherapy is little understood by persons who have never experienced it. Unfortunately, the increasingly wide availability of self-help books and even the theories of clinicians have tended to obscure rather than illuminate what actually goes on in therapy sessions. Clinical theories have been written primarily to organize and conceptualize the descrip-tions and explanations of psychological dysfunctions for other clinicians. Technical terms like "defense mechanism," "Oedipus complex," and "repres-sion" are no more a part of most therapists' direct interaction with their patients than is the technical terminology pertaining to diagnostic procedures a usual part of surgeons' interaction with patients who may have cancer.

Rather, these technical terms are intended only to assist the therapist in his attempts to understand and ultimately to help a particular patient. Telling one patient that he fears success as a result of his repressed Oedipal conflict is probably no more helpful than telling another that he is mentally ill or that he suffers from an inferiority complex. Instead, the therapist uses common everyday language to assist the patient gradually to remember and reexperience the events, thoughts, feelings, and fantasies that relate to his problem and to connect these formative experiences with contemporary events and patterns of perception and behavior. The task of therapist and patient in insight therapy is subtle and involves a gradual understanding and awareness of the relationship between past and present and of the relationship of feelings, thoughts, and fantasies to behavior. The idea that people may have unconscious motives that affect their behavior is introduced delicately—by specific examples from the patient's life—and gradually, rather than by confrontation that may lead to anxiety, disbelief, and resistance.

The two major tools that the insight therapist employs are himself in his relationship with the patient, and the patient's increasing ability to report whatever comes into his mind at the time he thinks of it. In the technical vocabulary of psychoanalysis, these tools are called "transference relationship" and "free association," respectively, and the patient's inability to say or even know what comes into his mind is called "resistance." While the patient talks about what he feels and thinks, the therapist, in an accepting and nonevaluative fashion, listens to and observes the patient, himself (his own feelings and reactions), and the relationship. As the therapist gains increasing confidence in his observations and understanding of the patient, he begins to comment on these observations to the patient. These comments are made in the normal vocabulary of social intercourse. For instance, a therapist, noticing that a patient very frequently says "I should" and very seldom says "I want," may begin to think in theoretical terms that the patient has an overbearing conscience and that he suppresses his motives for gaining pleasure and gratification. Since the process of gaining insight proceeds slowly, the therapist doesn't suggest these ideas at once, but may start with "You seem to use the word 'should' a lot," and saves for much later, "What do you *want* in that relationship?"

In the early part of the treatment, the patient is likely to see in the therapist certain characteristics, traits, and reactions that the therapist does not actually have but that the patient, as a result of his early experiences, expects many people to have. For instance, he may see the therapist as judgmental, rejecting, evaluative, and domineering. In addition, because the patient is likely to feel anxious and perhaps threatened, he has difficulty saying what is on his mind and may instead censor and rehearse what he says so that his statements will be acceptable to his image of the therapist. Gradually, through the therapist's comments and interventions and through the patient's increasing awareness of what he is feeling and thinking, progress takes place. The patient's free expression, his more realistic perception of the therapist as a helper and not a judge, and the therapist's comments and observations lead to insight into the relation between past and present and eventually to changes in feelings, perceptions, and behaviors.

The above discussion applies to most forms of insight therapy, and is not specific only to therapy for success-fearers. It is not easy to describe specifically what insight therapy for success-fearing patients is like. The therapist usually does not confront the problem directly, but rather indirectly through the dissipation of many of the patient's inhibitions. A well-known occurrence in insight therapy is that symptoms such as sexual impotence, performance anxiety, and shyness disappear in the course of working on other issues such as the expression of anger or the desire to remain a child. Similarly, therapeutic work that leads to increased feelings of self-worth, increased spontaneity, and a reduction in fear, anger, and competitiveness toward other people may result in a patient's increased ability both to succeed and to enjoy it.

Because success-fearers have a group of interrelated traits that have developed out of similar early experiences, some common problems are likely to emerge in the relationship between a success-fearing client and therapist. As a backdrop to the special problems of success-fearers in therapy, let us review briefly the characteristics they are likely to bring to the therapeutic relationship.

While the success-fearers were growing up, they perceived themselves to be in an atmosphere of hostile competition in which they constantly anticipated attack by superior others; these attacks were likely to take the form of competition, criticism, interference, domineering overcontrol, and the holding up of exaggerated standards of success. In such an atmosphere, the success-fearers were likely to feel intense anger toward their rivals and evaluators and the desire to destroy or defeat them in order to gain self-esteem, the esteem of others, and perhaps love. These growing persons were afraid of the intensity of their aggressive impulses and of the punishment or destruction they might bring; thus these impulses were repressed and controlled by conscience, which threatens great guilt if the impulses are consciously entertained. This inhibition of aggression success-fearers developed early in life continues into adulthood and, as most clinical writers agree, extends to include overtly expressed ambition and self-assertion. Success-fearers see assertion of their rights and desires as inconveniencing, hurting, or depriving others, and these perceptions create feelings of anxiety and guilt in the success-fearers. Finally, success-fearers also have chronic feelings of inadequacy, lack of self-confidence, and unstable self-esteem. All of these perceptions and feelings, then, are brought to the therapy task and to the interpersonal relationship involved in insight therapy. Under whatever polite or compliant facade success-fearers may present, they are likely to see the therapist and the task of getting better in much the same way as they usually see other difficult tasks and other people in authority. Not surprisingly, they fear success and failure as much in therapy as in other aspects of their lives [115].

In the early part of the therapy, success-fearing patients are likely to demonstrate that they are suspicious, guilty, self-derogating, inhibited, controlled and controlling, now and then ambitious, and apparently compliant. In this way, these patients project their usual perceptions of people onto the relationship with the therapist. They see the therapist as critical, controlling, evaluative, contemptuous or competitive, and perhaps rejecting; these feelings are probably intensified by the power, status, and expertise of the therapist's role.

By concentrating on these characteristics and attitudes of success-fearers, we can now describe some of the problems the insight therapist and success-fearing patient are likely to encounter in their work together. Psychotherapy, like most human endeavors, is an untidy affair. It focuses on each of its problems a little at a time in a chaotic fashion that defies systematic description; importantly, however, the process does have its own system, and progress in any area is useful to progress in other areas. The most fundamental problems faced by the therapist and the success-fearer in the therapeutic relationship are: (1) the problem of transforming the success-fearer's perceptions and reactions to the therapist from perceptions of an untrustworthy and critical judge to perceptions of a trustworthy, accepting helper-cooperator; (2) the problem of reducing the extent of the patient's negative self-evaluation and increasing the number of sources from which positive self-evaluation can emerge; and (3) the problem of reducing the patient's tendencies to control and inhibit his legitimate desires and the building of appropriate self-assertiveness, self-expression, and other sources of pleasure and spontaneity.

The first problem, that of the relationship with the therapist, is likely to require a great deal of patience on the part of the therapist and success-fearer alike. Since the success-fearer avoids and withdraws from conflict and competition, time will be needed for the view of the therapist as critic and judge to be made explicit and thus to be open to testing and gradual transformation by the everyday events in the therapeutic relationship.

The second major problem involves modification of the success-fearer's superego. In the terms of psychoanalytic theory, the superego is the evaluative agency of the personality—that is, the internal judge and jury of right and wrong. It has two parts: the conscience, which is primarily responsive to subjectively understood wrongdoing or internal prohibitions, and the ego-ideal, which is the internalized source of positive judgments, good feelings, and pride in the self. A large part of the operation of these self-evaluative processes is unconscious, though the consequences of guilt and pride are consciously experienced. Since the success-fearer's development has been overweighted in the direction of conscience, he has a large number of internal prohibitions that provoke intense feelings of guilt and of worthlessness. Further, the repressed impulses to aggression, competition, and self-assertion are provoked by everyday social events like competitive encounters, evaluation, and requirements or external demands. Although the success-fearer is unlikely to be consciously aware of the process, everyday events involving competition and evaluation trigger old desires to defend oneself and to defeat others; these unconscious aggressive impulses lead to action on the part of the conscience and thus to experiences of anxiety, guilt and self-derogation. The problem is enhanced by the paucity of activities and accomplishments from which the success-fearer has learned to get positive evaluations and good feelings. In these terms, not only is the conscience harsh and oversized but the ego-ideal, the source of good feelings about oneself, is profoundly impoverished.

The second major task of the therapy, then, is revealing and reducing the conscience and, if necessary, building and extending the sources of positive self-regard to include the simple, ordinary sources of pleasure and self-esteem that most people who do not fear success have and use. The major point appears subtle at first glance; the origin and maintenance of the success-fearer's unstable self-esteem and guilt is a problem of the unconscious self-evaluative processes—

the operation of the conscience and ego-ideal—more than it is a result of the realistic assessment of his virtues, vices, accomplishments, and failures. If the conscience is overbearing and the ego-ideal begrudging, the success-fearer cannot possibly notice, value, and respond favorably to realistically good things about himself and others; at the same time, of course, the person is highly vigilant to the many possibilities available for negative self-evaluation and negative evaluation of others.

Finally, with increasing trust and acceptance of the self and others comes increased sensitivity to and interest in the giving, getting, and doing involved in ordinary human relationships. With this reduction of inhibition, the success-fearer may become overassertive, or may continue to be tentative about his needs, desires, wishes, and goals. By this time, however, the improved relationship with the therapist, and the effects of that improvement on the success-fearer's relationships with other people in his life, provide supportive sources of experimentation for appropriate self-assertiveness. The therapy, then, continues in the success-fearing patient's life, because he has learned to look at his own reactions and to act, in a sense, as his own therapist.

Very little can be said about the duration of insight therapy for patients with fear of success problems. In the discussion above on behavior therapy, a range of fifteen to sixty weekly sessions was given. Estimates of that kind are seldom made by insight therapists for a number of reasons. First, as has been mentioned, the goals of insight therapy are usually broader and less well-specified, and they can change from time to time as the therapy progresses. A particular patient, for example, might begin therapy with the goal of reducing his self-defeating behavior or improving his relationships with authority figures. This patient may come to realize during the therapy that there are other important issues for him to deal with. He may, for example, become aware that he remembers very few details of his life before the age of sixteen, and he may wish to recapture some of these memories in order to gain a feeling of continuity between his past and his present life. This explicit broadening of goals also broadens the scope of the therapy and could extend its duration. Second, the extent to which the fear-of-success problems of individual patients are closely tied to other problems varies greatly. In some patients, for example, some degree of chronic depression accompanies the manifestations of fear of success, and this problem must be dealt with in the therapy. Third, the ease with which a useful working relationship is established between patient and therapist also varies. Therapists as well as patients differ from one another, and any given pair may establish rapport quickly or more slowly. Fourth, the course of any given therapy has its own logic, and the order in which problems are taken up and resolved cannot be predetermined or forced. The point at which a particular patient will be ready to understand a particular issue in his life is not easy to predict in advance. For these reasons, then, insight therapy takes a variable amount of time; it may be completed in less than one year in some cases and may continue for four years or longer in other cases.

While insight therapy usually refers to the situation in which one therapist sees one patient, group therapy and family therapy are common variations of insight therapy in which one or perhaps two therapists (a male and a female) see a group or a family of patients together. Occasionally a patient may attend group or family therapy as well as individual therapy.

In group therapy, a new resource is available to the patient and the therapist: the patient's responses to and interactions with other members of the group, which is usually composed of both men and women. The presence of these others, who from time to time compete for the attention of the therapist and for one another's attention, can very quickly stimulate the success-fearer's conflicts about competition. If these conflicts are manifest in the patient's behavior so that they are visible to the therapist, they can often be put to good use in the therapy. On the other hand, the intensified conflicts over competition may lead the patient to withdraw from the therapy as well; much depends on the characteristics of the patient, and the other group members, and on the sensitivity and skills of the therapist.

Family therapy focuses on the family unit as the client. Here the patient and the therapist have other members of the family available as additional resources for the therapeutic task. The primary focus in family therapy is on the interactions among family members and the ways in which family members interpret and respond to one another's behaviors. Since certain family dynamics can contribute to and intensify fear-of-success conflicts, family therapy can be a very useful approach for the success-fearers in a family by helping the whole family gain insight into those dynamics and their consequences. As should be clear, however, since family therapy is directed primarily at interpersonal processes in the family itself, a given member's feelings and actions outside the family context are dealt with somewhat less directly and less frequently than is the case in individual insight therapy.

All of these forms of insight therapy can be effective, but unfortunately we have no easy way of determining which form is likely to be best for a particular person with a particular problem at a particular time in his or her life.

Conclusions

Despite extensive differences in theoretical perspective and technique, practitioners of behavior therapy and insight therapy agree that psychotherapy is a process in which a great deal of reeducation takes place. Persons undergoing therapy learn new ways of interpreting their own and others' feelings and behaviors, and they learn to substitute appropriate and useful patterns of responding and behavior for dysfunctional patterns that were learned much earlier but have outlived whatever usefulness they might have once had. From the perspective of the psychotherapist of either persuasion who treats success-fearing patients, knowing what such patients are likely to have learned early in life that contributes to the problem is helpful, since, in a sense, the therapy must undo what earlier was done. The ability to anticipate the reactions of patients to important events and people in their present lives is also useful to the therapist, as is the ability to anticipate and understand the patients' reactions to events in the therapy itself. Clearly, then, research on the nature and origins of fear-of-success problems and on the conditions that trigger, intensify, or mitigate the various responses related to fear of success has practical implications for psychotherapy.

Since interpersonal events in the family appear to be crucial in the development of fear of success, the kind of research effort we have begun here can be of use not only to psychotherapists, but to parents as well, particularly in the prevention of fear-of-success problems. People who design and administer educational and work environments may also profit from research on success-fearing persons and the conditions that affect them. These practical issues require that we take stock of where we are in the process of learning about fear of success and where we must go. What have we learned? What ambiguities remain in what we have learned thus far? What assumptions have we made that require further examination? What are the important questions that remain open and invite investigation? We turn to these questions in chapter 11.

11

Looking Back and Looking Ahead

In this final chapter we review the central notions that have guided our research, the evidence provided by the research, and the conclusions to which we have been led by the evidence. We also examine the questions that remain open and the issues that are still unresolved. These unanswered questions take different forms depending upon who asks them. For our colleagues in the scientific community, the primary questions may have to do with technical issues of theory, measurement, and the interpretation of evidence. They may wish to examine alternative explanations of the results of the research or to raise questions about our measures or the plausibility of some of the assumptions upon which our position rests. Other interested readers may wish to raise questions about how our point of view accounts for observations they have made of themselves and others. For example, do some people just fear failure and not success? What about the person who calmly and rationally refuses a promotion or a desirable romantic partner—is such a person a success-fearer? Finally, there are the questions generated by our own work: the next steps. For example, do cooperative work environments really alleviate fear of success? How do success-fearing persons manage to succeed? What about fear of success in other countries? In countries where competitive success is less strongly emphasized than in the United States, do fear-of-success problems exist in the same way and with similar frequency? All three categories of unresolved questions are important and deserve careful thought and attention.

Recapitulation and Summary

We began our analysis of the fear of success from a personality-clinical point of view embedded within the general framework of psychodynamic psychology. We suggested that certain people—both males and females—are made anxious by an imminent success and tend to manage this anxiety by withdrawing from the success in one or more ways: they may actually sabotage the success, disavow responsibility for it, or rob themselves of its satisfactions. Taking the point of view of the psychoanalytic psychologists, we suggested that certain early experiences of success-fearing persons lead them to experience success as dangerous and frightening and thus make succcesses difficult to tolerate. These persons, according to the psychoanalytic theorists, unconsciously interpret a success to mean that they are doing things that one or both of their parents

205

considered threatening or unacceptable, such as moving toward independence, being competitive with the parent, and so on. To oversimplify the metaphor, success-fearers "see" their competitive, self-promoting, and/or independence strivings as dangerous, threatening, and anxiety-arousing; they connect success with such impulses and find ways to withdraw from the anxiety induced by success. The scales we developed to identify success-fearers and the studies we conducted to validate the scales and to explore the parameters of fear of success were anchored in this psychodynamic-personality approach.

Another notion we adopted from dynamic psychology was that success-fearing persons are ambivalent about success—that is, they are as much drawn toward it at a distance as they are eventually made anxious by it in close proximity. This idea received considerable support in our research. It also served to reinforce our early conviction that ideas about the fear of success would become more useful if they could be linked to a more general network of ideas and information about the motivation to succeed and accomplish. Accordingly, we examined existing ideas about achievement motivation and found them based in part on the implicit assumption that most motivation to achieve is competitive in nature. We had, after some reflection, little difficulty in conceiving of sources of motivation to do productive work that were *not* competitive in nature and thus were able to move toward a theory of achievement or productivity motivation based on a broader set of ideas about human motivation to work. Our conviction that the Atkinson-McClelland research on achievement motivation rests, in effect, in our culture's silent assumption that virtually all success is competitive made it even more clear to us that in our culture, ideas about success and competition are generally confused with one another and they are heavily charged with emotional meaning. That many people in this culture are conflicted about these issues becomes, from this perspective, very easy to understand.

Our theoretical point of view, as it has evolved, suggests that issues surrounding competition are focal in the problems of success-fearers. Indeed, our theoretical ideas, which we presented in chapter 1, are in many ways similar to the analysis of fear of success offered by Karen Horney [46]; in Horney's view, fear of success is but one manifestation of a more general neurotic fear of competition. Unlike Horney's work, however, which suggests that the neurotic fear of competition is manifested either as a fear of success or as a fear of failure, our theory and research suggest that the same persons will, under appropriate conditions, manifest the fear of success and the fear of failure. Fear of success and fear of failure are, then, two motivational tendencies of the subgroup of persons we have identified as success-fearers: the motive to avoid failure is engaged whenever failure seems close and helps to ward off the humiliation of failure; the motive to avoid success is engaged when success is close at hand and helps to ward off the anxiety accompanying the recognition of imminent success. The study presented in chapter 4 adds weight to this argument. The self-reports of subjects in that study showed that both successful and failing performances aroused anxiety in success-fearers. The anxiety, however, appears to have different consequences depending on whether it is aroused by failure or by success. Anxiety aroused when failure occurs acts as a facilitating anxiety that energizes both effort and competitive motivation to avoid failure and leads to better performance on a task following the failure. The anxiety accompanying successful performances is quite different in its consequences. This anxiety has debilitating effects; in our various experiments it has led to performance deterioration.

Persons who fear success also have a strong motive to achieve success, which enables them to strive, from a comfortable distance, for the successes they consciously desire. For these persons, however, succeeding implies hurting and defeating others who are thought to take a very dim view of being thwarted or displaced. Success is therefore associated, at an unconscious level, with a host of possible negative consequences: being envied or hated by others, being retaliated against by them, or losing their affection. Since success-fearers ultimately prefer neither to win nor to lose, their performances are often characterized by vacillation somewhere between the poles of the success-failure continuum; they attempt to remain comfortably distant from failure and alternately approach and avoid the successes to which they consciously aspire. The survey data presented in chapter 6 indicating indecisiveness, lack of satisfaction with decisions, and procrastination can be seen as reflecting this vacillation. The experiment reported in chapter 4, in which success-fearers were shown to have high task motivation after they had sabotaged a success, also demonstrates vacillation toward and away from success.

Thus, while some persons who have neurotic problems surrounding achievement may find relief from their problems by withdrawing completely from competitive arenas, people who fear success cannot resolve their conflicts by retreating altogether from achievement situations. The success-fearer inhabits a difficult, frustrating territory bordered by humiliating failure at one end and by compelling but also frightening success at the other; he or she is in frequent tension amidst this triumvirate of motives and does not easily find respite from them. We do not mean to say that persons with fear-of-success problems are failures in the eyes of others. Success-fearers often do succeed despite their out-of-awareness motivation to recoil from success. When they succeed, however, they appear (both to themselves and others) to have done so inadvertently and through no concerted effort of their own. Thus, they avoid appearing openly competitive and prefer to show that their strivings are ineffectual and almost offhand and that their skills and abilities are in no way outstanding. When they appear to an outside observer to have succeeded, they are unlikely to believe they are successful or to feel very good about their outcome. Thus, even when they do succeed, they manage to sabotage the satisfying consequences of what they have achieved.

We may now briefly summarize the evidence our research has thus far generated about the thoughts, feelings, and behaviors of success-fearing persons:

1. The neurotic fear of success is a characteristic that afflicts some men and some women in our culture.

2. The fear of success can be identified in children of elementary school age—both boys and girls—as well as adolescents and adults.

3. No appreciable differences exist in the frequency of fear of success or its manifestations among men and women. Fear of success has occurred with approximately equal prevalence among the men and women we have studied, and success-fearers of both sexes have demonstrated similar thoughts, feelings, and behaviors in the situations we have studied.

4. Following successful performances, success-fearers show a decrement in performance quality; following acceptable but not outstanding performances, they show an increment in performance quality. Persons who do not fear success demonstrate improved performances after either an initial successful performance or an initial acceptable performance.

5. This pattern of performance decrement is observable both when success-fearers believe they have had an immediate success and when they believe they have gradually improved their mastery of a task. In the latter situation, a performance decrement does not occur until evidence of mastery is obtained; until that point success-fearers, like those who do not fear success, show gradual improvement in their actual performances.

6. The performance decrements of success-fearers following success are accompanied by self-reported anxiety and concentration impairment.

7. Following failure at a task, success-fearers perform better. In contrast, persons who do not fear success perform more poorly following a failure experience.

8. The performance impairments shown by success-fearers following success are demonstrated both when they work on cognitive-intellectual tasks (such as those involving reading comprehension and memory skills) and when they work on more socially oriented tasks (such as those involving communication and interpersonal persuasion). Whatever the nature of the performance, if it is seen by the success-fearer as a success, it is a candidate for self-sabotage.

9. Success-fearers demonstrate greater performance impairments when success is achieved in competition with a person of the same sex than when it is gained in competition with someone of the opposite sex. In contrast, the performances of persons who do not fear success are not affected by the sex of the competitor.

10. Success-fearers' self-reports indicate anxiety and concern over issues of competition and evaluation even when competition is not overtly present. Concerns about aggression and rejection are both implicated in the success-fearers' anxiety about competition.

11. Following success and performance sabotage, success-fearers show enhanced performances on another unrelated task, which supports the idea that self-sabotage of success serves a function for these persons, releasing them to work hard toward a new success.
12. The ways success-fearers deal with their conflicts about success, including vacillation and indecisiveness, procrastination, and repudiation of competence, can be observed not only in experimental situations but also in success-fearers' responses to naturally occurring events in their lives.
13. Both the same-sex and the opposite-sex parents of success-fearing children are more likely than other parents to be evaluative, critical, controlling, and otherwise intrusive in their interactions with their children over task performances. Furthermore, the parents of success-fearing children are more likely than other parents to report concern about their children's abilities and ambivalence about their children's future successes.
14. The task performances of success-fearing children appear to be adversely affected by the presence of the parent of the same sex.
15. A moderate positive correlation exists between the fear-of-success scores of children and their parents and between the fear-of-success scores of mothers and fathers. Nevertheless, the behavior of the parents of success-fearing children toward the children appears unrelated to the parent's own score on the fear-of-success scale.

The list is a long one; we have learned a good deal about the success-fearing personality. In addition, the theory that has guided our research program has received substantial support from the results of the research. A great many issues remain unresolved, however, and many questions must still be answered. We turn to those issues and questions in the next section of the chapter.

Unresolved Issues

Various categories of unresolved issues and knotty questions are considered in this section. Two untested assumptions we have made in our work are considered first: that the fear of success is in part unconscious, and that it is best thought of as a neurotic problem. We turn then to a consideration of alternative explanations that could be advanced to account for one or more results of our research efforts. This discussion leads us to examine issues regarding the construction and adequacy of our measures of fear of success. Finally, we discuss important questions that we have not yet answered in our research.

Two Underlying Assumptions

Two of the assumptions that underlie our theoretical position are that fear of success is an unconscious problem and that it is neurotic in nature. We should make explicit our reasons for accepting these assumptions since we have no direct evidence to support them. In asserting that fear of success is unconscious, we mean that people who fear success are usually not aware of both sides of their strong ambivalence about success. They may be aware that they want to succeed, that they do not want to fail, and perhaps even that they become anxious when they are winning games or contests. They are not aware, however, that they also want *not to succeed* and that they regularly and actively do things in order to sabotage or destroy their successes. How do we come to accept this position if the persons themselves might not endorse it? Furthermore, why do we see fear of success as a neurotic characteristic?

Is Fear of Success Unconscious? Several ideas and observations convinced us that we could assume that success-fearers' desire to sabotage their successes is unconscious. First, this assumption is at the core of the psychodynamic positions upon which we have based both our theories of fear of success and the scales we devised to identify success-fearers. Generally, the psychoanalytic theories say that while repressed conflicts demand expression and exert influence on behavior, their influence must not be recognized by the conscious mind. In the case of fear of success, an early but forgotten conflict about competition or independence attaches itself to a contemporary substitute such as a particular success. The success thereby becomes a vehicle for the expression of the repressed conflict, including the motive to avoid the success. Through the displacement of the early conflict to the contemporary success and through the systematic use of psychological defense mechanisms, success-fearers are able both to express the early conflict and at the same time to be consciously unaware of its existence. From a contemporary point of view, success-fearers really don't want to sabotage their successes and are in fact the victims of forces they reject and cannot control; they are driven by conflicts they no longer remember. What they "really" want to stop is their own unwise desires to compete with formidable others in their old conflicts—not their contemporary successes.

A second reason that we adopted the assumption is that in social psychology, personality theory, and clinical psychology, there exists a well-accepted principle that people usually find ambivalence, inconsistent motives, and inconsistent attitudes difficult to maintain in consciousness for any length of time without resolving the inconsistency in some way—either by denying one side of the ambivalence or inconsistency or by changing the attitudes to make them appear consistent. In psychodynamic psychology, there exists the belief that a conflict between self-enhancing and self-defeating motives is intensely threatening and anxiety arousing because of the threat to the well-being of the self. Such inconsistencies are particularly likely to be resolved by suppressing awareness of the self-defeating element. In other words, most people find it not only unpleasant, but very difficult to experience their own desires to defeat their efforts and activities if they also desire the reverse.

Third, our experience in talking with people who fit our description of success-fearers is that they generally deny the desire to sabotage their successes as well as any voluntary participation in the events that interfere with the attainment of their successes. They do, however, frequently have explanations for their behavior and its consequences, often by ascribing it either to ego-alien traits and states like chronic indecisiveness and fatigue or to accidental and unfortunate events, forces, or people beyond their control.

Our fourth reason for assuming that the motivated self-sabotage in success-fearers is unconscious is that we believe that people who consciously wish to destroy their successes would behave differently. Either they would recognize that the desire was not rational and would not carry it out, or they would be less anxious and more premeditated and direct in their sabotage. They would not be so circuitous, for example, as subtly to induce other people to help them carry out their wishes to be rejected or to use their tendency to procrastinate as a way of avoiding successes.

In line with these arguments, we might usefully mention that those few people who do eventually recognize in themselves a fear of success usually do so in an abstract, cognitive fashion rather than by a direct awareness of their motives to sabotage their outcomes. What usually happens in these instances is that these persons recognize in themselves the defenses we describe and also recognize, in their history of attempts to succeed, behaviors that interfered with the achievement of successes. They may then infer they had motives or desires to wreck their efforts to succeed. This partial insight is an intellectualization, a theoretical explanation. These persons fail actually to experience their motives. This sort of "self-knowledge" that one fears success, then, is not by itself a cure for the problem. It is often only an hypothesis that success-fearers use in an effort to explain their behaviors and feelings. The deeper insight sought in psychotherapy involves direct experience and recognition of their motives in the contexts in which they occur.

Persons who consciously wreck their efforts at succeeding are in a different category than the success-fearers [e.g., 77,80]. Such persons might more appropriately be called self-defeaters. According to Warner's excellent description [116], self-defeaters usually feel that someone else, perhaps a parent, will suffer more from their failure than they themselves will. For this reason they are willing to endure the defeat for the pleasure they derive in causing pain or getting revenge.

Is Fear of Success Neurotic? We call fear of success neurotic as well as unconscious because within the contemporary context of the success-fearers' lives, it is wasteful, painful, irrational, and unnecessary. The reader should remember, however, that in terms of the unconscious dynamics of success-fearers, it is perfectly sensible. By avoiding the success and whatever it symbolizes, they are able to avoid some of the anxiety, pain, and guilt that the attainment of the success would have stimulated in them. While these reactions to success can be considered reasonable within the framework of the success-fearer's unconscious assumptions and commitments, however, it is neurotic because these unconscious assumptions are no longer realistic or appropriate to the person's contemporary reality. Thus, once we accept the notion that the conflicts of the success-fearing person are at least partially unconscious and the notion that pain and dysfunction are byproducts of the conflicts, we have defined them as neurotic.

Alternative Explanations of the Results of Our Research

As we have given talks and had discussions with colleagues and graduate students about the work reported in this book, some of them have offered interpretations of our results that are different from ours. Since many readers may wish to think about such issues, we discuss here the kinds of alternative explanations that have emerged most commonly, with special attention given to those that appear most plausible.

One family of alternative interpretations has to do with what our fear-of-success questionnaires may be measuring instead of fear of success. Some people have suggested that the questionnaires identify people who are low in self-esteem or high in general anxiety, or generally neurotic, or fearful of being different, or, as we have discussed in chapters 2, 4, and 5, fearful of failing. Several of these characteristics have been related by us to fear of success either theoretically, empirically, or both. Those who have suggested one or another of them as substitute concepts have done so on grounds of simplicity or parsimony. Why invent a complex concept that is composed of several characteristics when a simpler one will do the job? Why invent a new idea when one can explain the same things with an older, better-established one, particularly, one that does not offend common sense? These, of course, are critical questions. What we must really ask is this: Do any of these concepts render the notion fear of success irrelevant, subordinate, or wrongheaded as a way of explaining differences in the behaviors and feelings of people who score high and low on our scales?

For one or another of these ideas to replace our notion of fear of success, it would have to be embedded in a theoretical network that could explain satisfactorily all the data we have reported. We are not aware of a theory of general anxiety, self-esteem, fear-of-being-different, and so forth that could be made to account for the various features of ambivalence and vacillation we have observed in the people we call success-fearers. What has been called general neuroticism by some investigators takes different forms in different people (e.g., hysteria, obsessive-compulsive neurosis, and so forth); the same can be said about general anxiety and low self-esteem. Low self-esteem, general anxiety, or a general tendency to be neurotic would all be unable to account, for example, for the resilience that success-fearing persons show in the face of failure. In fact, each of these alternatives would be more likely to predict that anxious, neurotic, or low-esteem persons would respond to failure with depression, withdrawal, or worsened performance. Similarly, people who are "afraid of being different" would likely be reluctant to make themselves stand out by procrastinating, delivering unpredictable performances, and frequently changing their task interests.

Thus, while many of these other variables are related to fear of success in some way, none of them provides a satisfactory explanation for all the data. Knowing that particular persons are low in self-esteem would not lead us to predict that they procrastinate and are indecisive, seek success and then recoil from it, snap back from failure, and report high anxiety when doing either well or poorly, but not in the face of less extreme evaluations. Not only would low self-esteem lead to a different set of predictions, but it is also highly likely that many people with low self-esteem would not show these characteristics at all; surely many people with chronically low self-esteem would not be willing to expend energy in a search for success. Likewise, not all people who are low in self-esteem are high in anxiety, and not all highly anxious people would be identified by the usual measures as low in self-esteem. Success-fearers tend to be low—or at least unstable—in self-esteem, as well as high in anxiety, particularly in anxiety related to task performance. They can also be considered to be fearful of being different, if this means that they are apprehensive about standing out by succeeding or failing in actual or implied competition with others. The notion of a neurotic fear of success, with a neurotic fear of competition at its core, appears to provide the simplest way to unite these various traits in particular persons when they face contexts in which performance is at issue. We should note here that the set of alternative explanations we have been discussing brings up fundamental issues about the measurement of fear of success and the adequacy of our measuring instruments. These questions will be discussed below in a separate section.

A second family of alternative interpretations that have been offered raises questions about what success-fearers are recoiling from when they recoil from success. These questions are based on the very reasonable assumption that success is a complex notion that can mean many things to many people. What is the active ingredient in success that leads to the effects we have observed? Is it, as we have suggested, a fear of accomplishing one's goal and of doing better than actual or potential competitors? Or is it perhaps a fear of change, or a fear of separation, or a fear of additional responsibility and heightened expectations? We find many of these possibilities intriguing and are of two minds about a strategy for dealing with them.

On the one hand, many of these factors, such as separation, new responsibilities, and change are often contiguous with the attainment of success in people's lives. Success often does mean having to move or having to take on new tasks. These factors are also important in the conflicts we have described as part of the early development of fear of success. In the separation-individuation conflict, the child does indeed fear change; he fears the loss of the support of the parent in a situation in which he feels he may be unable to manage his own survival or well-being. Sibling rivalry and Oedipal rivalry also bring frightening excess baggage to the victor: separation from former supporters and new responsibilities to enact the role and defend the position of victor. The negative components of success described above, then, are clearly implicated in the development of fear of success and are not at all unlikely to play a particularly important role in the later lives of success-fearing persons.

We could, therefore, suggest that since such things as separation, change, new responsibility, and heightened expectations are part and parcel of success, attempting to separate them is not sensible. In this vein, to the critic who says, in effect, "it isn't success these people are fearful of, it's new responsibility," our answer might be that the two are inherently inseparable. Such an answer, however, tends to obscure important opportunities to learn something by attempting to separate these issues in research. For example, asking how success-fearers compare with people who do not fear success in their reactions to separations, changes, and new responsibilities that are not related to success might be highly instructive. How do success-fearing children respond to going away to camp, for example, or to the situation in which the mother returns to full-time employment? What about the occasional success that does not lead to change, separation, or added responsibility—do success-fearers respond with less anxiety to these? An investigation of questions like these could tell us more about the components and boundaries of the phenomenon. It might also help to disentangle the consequences of fear of success acquired primarily in conflicts over separation-individuation issues from fear of success acquired in Oedipal- and sibling-rivalry conflicts.

This family of alternative interpretations recognizes that success often has consequences that are not desirable. It attempts to supplant our ideas about complicated and unconscious conflicts about success with the simpler idea that some persons (presumably the high scorers on our measures) are particularly sensitive to the realistic negative consequences of success. The experiment conducted by Cohen (chapter 3) provides one of several counterexamples for this interpretation, however. Participants in that experiment were told that they had won a preliminary contest involving short-term memory for objects and would now participate in a runoff contest to determine who would be the winner of a prize. The argument that winning the contest would involve the participants in new responsibilities, separation, or change in any realistic sense becomes difficult when we consider that the contest was only an after-school one with no further realistic implications. Thus the simple forms of this set of alternative explanations account for very little of the data. As has been discussed, however, the issues raised by it are interesting and potentially productive.

Since success does often have undesirable byproducts, it is sometimes perfectly reasonable to reject it. This undeniable fact leads us to raise a question that we have frequently been asked by people with whom we have discussed our work: Are all people who shy away from or turn down successes people who have success-fearing personalities? Clearly and emphatically, the answer must be no. Occasionally, we may hear about persons who have refused promotions to positions that carry increased prestige and, in the eyes of others, increased success. Also, not uncommonly we hear of people who choose an apparently lesser romantic partner in lieu of one that might be considered the more desirable or successful choice. Fear of success is not necessarily involved in such choices; in some cases, apparent avoidance of success simply reflects a consciously recognized preference for another alternative. Some persons reject competitive and materialistic goals altogether. This rejection of socially defined success may in some instances be due only to a reasoned preference for an alternative set of values and goals. Since many outcomes that are defined by the culture as successes contain realistically negative as well as positive consequences, some persons can quite rationally evaluate these consequences, consider the negative consequences to be more compelling than the positive ones, and accordingly decide that the culturally defined success should be avoided or foregone. Suppose, for instance, that an important promotion to a high-prestige position also means many changes in personal circumstances, such as moving to another country, severing valued relationships, and taking on unwanted tasks and responsibilities. The person who is offered such a promotion may quite straightforwardly and consciously prefer to stay where he or she is. We must note, however, that many choices are overdetermined, as psychotherapists often point out, and they may be made for unconscious reasons and motivations at the same time that realistic reasons exist for making them. Therefore, distinguishing between steps taken for neurotic reasons and similar steps taken consciously and without neurotic motivation is not always an easy task. In general, we are inclined to suspect the operation of fear of success when people refuse successes that they have worked hard to achieve. We are less inclined to look for fear of success as a motive when the declined success was unsought and unanticipated.

We have not tried to be exhaustive in listing rival explanations for the results of our research.[1] In discussing the two groups of commonly offered explanations above, we have attempted to make clear the issues we think are involved in such explanations and the kinds of responses we have made to them. As is usual in such instances, the alternative explanations have raised interesting issues that have helped us clarify our own thinking.

Some Issues Regarding Measurement

When we discussed possible alternative interpretations of the results of our research, we speculated that our questionnaire measures of fear of success might conceivably be measuring something better called by another name. Thus, we might have chosen to label the high scorers on our scale as people who are anxious, or low in self-esteem, or neurotic; why call our variable fear of success, or by the other name we like, competition anxiety? This kind of question brings us squarely into the center of the conceptual and measurement dilemmas that all investigators of complex personality traits must confront. On what basis do we decide that it is worthwhile to study a particular trait that can be conceived of as a subcategory of another more general characteristic? Once we have decided that the characteristic in question is indeed worthy of significant attention in its own right, how do we go about measuring it? Finally, at what point do we begin to do the difficult task of purifying the measuring instrument that has been devised? We approach these questions with the caution that they are very large, knotty questions for which only partially satisfactory answers have been put forward; they could by themselves take up a volume the size of this one.

Why Study Fear of Success? We have said often in this book that we believe that success-fearing persons are anxious. We have also said that the fear-of-success syndrome is neurotic in the sense that the behaviors and feelings involved are frequently dysfunctional and motivated by out-of-awareness responses learned rather early in life. We could quite reasonably say, then, that all success-fearers are anxious persons, and that all success-fearers are to some degree neurotic. Since fear of success identifies a subcategory of anxious persons and a subcategory of neurotic persons (who, according to one conception, are all coping with anxiety) why not study anxious persons instead of success-fearers?

Anxiety is a highly general concept which has many different subdivisions. Some people are anxious about some issues and some about others; a few persons may experience anxiety in response to a great variety of issues and circumstances. Thus, while it is indeed worthwhile to study general anxiety—and many researchers have done so—it is also important to study the anxiety reactions certain groups of persons have to particular classes of issues and situations. We might then study anxiety that relates specifically to performance and achievement situations. And indeed, anxiety reactions to situations in which performance is the central issue confronting the person have been studied, with interesting results. The approach taken by these investigators, however, has led them to study phenomena that are different than those we have studied in our work on the fear of success.

An excellent illustration of the consequences of these differences in approach may be found in the work of Sarason and his colleagues on test anxiety in elementary school children [97]. These authors constructed a self-report questionnaire that measures the extent to which young children are made anxious by tests and other school tasks in which their performances are evaluated. As we have noted in chapter 5, this instrument turns out to be rather highly correlated with our children's fear-of-success scale. In fact, Sarason and his colleagues take the position in their book [97, pp. 5-27] that many test-anxious children have the following characteristics: unconscious hostility toward parents and parent-surrogates; a defensive tendency toward self-derogation; and unconscious fear of retaliation (hostility, abandonment, and so forth) from parents and parent-surrogates. These characteristics are, of course, centrally involved in our conception of success-fearing persons; we could thus suggest that both these authors and ourselves have identified persons with essentially the same characteristics.

Despite this apparent similarity, the phenomena studied by Sarason et al. are not the same as those we studied. Sarason and his colleagues have not attended to the consequences of success, failure, or competition for the feelings and behaviors of these children; instead, they have focused on such questions as the extent to which test anxiety interferes with intellectual performance, the kinds of tasks that are easier and more difficult for test-anxious children than for others, the kinds of instructions that facilitate or hinder the performance of test-anxious children [98], and the attitudes of the parents of test-anxious children toward their children. The point of this discussion is not that they or we have done the "correct" work, but rather that the name given to a phenomenon and the theoretical perspective within which it is investigated exert considerable influence on the directions taken by the research. All roads, in this case, do not lead to Rome.

We can suggest some criteria, then, for deciding whether to investigate a characteristic that, like fear of success, can apparently be included in a more general characteristic of people. First, we should ask whether the characteristic in question appears to have unique properties. In the case of people who fear success, the anxiety is more or less specific to performance and competition and takes different forms—with different consequences—in particular situations. It is by no means identical with general anxiety. Second, we might ask whether the specific phenomena in question can shed light on the more general ones— whether, for example, studying fear of success can lead us to new insights about anxiety in general. We might also ask whether the phenomena in question are common in the culture, and related to important arenas of activity. Thus the new criteria we suggest involve uniqueness on the one hand, and usefulness on the other, where the usefulness criterion can be met either in practical terms or in terms of shedding light on more general theoretical issues.

Measuring Fear of Success. Fear of success has two characteristics that make it unusually difficult to measure directly. First, it is usually not in conscious awareness, as discussed above. Persons with a success-fearing personality are much more likely to be aware of the defenses they have erected around their anxieties about competition and success than they are to be aware of their motive to avoid succeeding. Furthermore, their strong motive to succeed is likely to be covert as well—that is, to be expressed indirectly in what they do rather than in what they report about themselves. Thus, self-report measures of fear of success must rely on indirection, that is, the derivation from a theoretical framework of a configuration of characteristic defenses, such as tendencies toward self-derogation, recognition of anxiety surrounding evaluation, vigilance against competition, reluctance to assert needs and preferences, and so on.

When a measure is devised containing items that identify such a theoretically derived configuration of characteristic thoughts, feelings, and behaviors, it can come out looking like a sort of hodge-podge. A critic who glances casually at the items can easily point out that they have doubtful face validity as indicators of a tendency to withdraw from success—that is, little or no apparent logical relationship to what they are supposed to measure. The casual critic can also find groups of items that appear to measure low self-esteem, and so forth, and can suggest that the scale really measures one of these characteristics. How, then do we know the scale measures this and not that? We must rely on two basic devices. First, we must test the internal consistency of the scale, which means determining that the items intended to measure the separate characteristics of success-fearing persons are moderately correlated with one another: the items across groups as well as within groups must be reasonably intercorrelated, and the items must be reasonably correlated with total score on the scale. Furthermore, the scale must be designed in such a way that a respondent cannot be characterized as a success-fearer by responding positively only to items that measure one of the component characteristics. All these criteria have been met in the case of all three of our scales. The second basic device that reassures us about what the scale measures tests the predictive validity of the scale, particularly through observations of predicted behavior in circumstances whose characteristics are known or controlled. The group of experiments and field studies reported in part II constitute such validation.

Even after all that, however, the scale is not as good as it could be. All three of our scales are rather long, for example; they could probably be shorter without losing effectiveness. They are also not ideally balanced in terms of positively and negatively scored items. Furthermore, we are certain that the scales do not correctly identify every success-fearing respondent and that at least occasionally they identify people as success-fearers who in reality are not. The fear-of-success scales, then, eventually need technical psychometric work that will further refine them and make them more efficient by removing spurious questions and perhaps adding questions that increase their accuracy, thereby reducing the likelihood of false negatives and false positives (erroneous identification of respondents).

Such psychometric work is difficult and time-consuming and far from straightforward. It is especially difficult in the case of scales that attempt to measure complex characteristics that have several separately identifiable components. The correlational techniques that in other cases have helped researchers to provide convergent and divergent validation through the use of established scales, for example, are less easy to use and interpret in the case of complex characteristics. We believe that our scales can indeed be refined and improved, but we are also convinced that we will have to invent techniques for carrying out the task of refining them.

We could have chosen to do the work of refining our instruments earlier in our research program—before doing some of the experimental validation work reported in part II, for example. No doubt some researchers would have preferred such a strategy. Our decision to assume that the measures were good enough for initial use in research was based on several considerations. Early results on indicators of internal consistency, correlations with other scales, and preliminary experimental validation all encouraged us that we had a workable instrument. Clearly, we believed we were doing more than creating an instrument to identify a category of persons. We were also simultaneously testing some rather elaborate theory pertaining to those persons—theory that had generated the measures in the first place. Therefore, generating evidence relating to the theory before investing large amounts of time and energy in technical work on the scales seemed reasonable to us. If the theory had failed to receive support from our research, the entire project would have been called into question, and the psychometric effort would have been wasted. Generally, then, it is necessary as well as desirable to begin the process with extensive validation research.

We believe that the decision about when to attend to the psychometric refinement of a measuring instrument in personality research must be left largely to the preference and judgment of the investigator, with close attention paid to the purpose of the instrument. If, for example, the scale is being designed for use in clinical diagnosis, the question of avoiding false positives and false negatives is crucial, and the scale must be refined as soon as possible. Likewise if the scale is being used in research of an idiographic nature (in which a very few persons are studied in great detail), the investigator should also be sure that the scale is as error-free as possible. In the kind of research that we have been doing, however, and that most investigators of individual-difference characteristics do, the function of the scale is to assign fairly large numbers of people to categories; a substantial number of persons in each category are studied, and their responses are aggregated. The misassignment of a few persons in such research does not do serious harm; if it did, most personality research would fail, because most scales in common use for research are very far from perfect. The decision depends, then, on the investigator's purposes, and his or her estimate of the risks, costs, and potential payoffs of doing the psychometric work early or late in the process. In our own case, we were reluctant to go through the difficult tasks involved in purifying our measuring instruments until we were certain that the job was worth doing.

The three fear-of-success scales we have been using, which are reproduced in the appendix of this book, are designed to be used not in diagnosis but in research of a nomothetic nature. In our view they do not require further improvement until a piece of research we wish to do calls for a more refined instrument.

Additional Questions for Future Research

Although the research reported herein has provided us with considerable information about the existence and operation of the complex personality syndrome we have called fear of success, we consider investigation of this phenomenon in no way completed. A great many general issues remain for empirical investigation: the etiology of fear of success; the coping mechanisms employed by success-fearers to enable them to succeed despite their fear of success; and the relationship of social structure and fear of success to productivity. Currently our theoretical formulation of fear of success and our preliminary research provide only general and rather abstract ideas about its etiology. Competition has been identified as important in the instigation of fear of success, and problems in the resolution of the Oedipal conflict have been implicated. This information provides only the skeleton for research on the development of fear of success. Because competition is ubiquitous in this culture and all persons are presumed to go through the Oedipal stage of development, these notions alone do not explain why some children develop fear of success and others do not. The observational study described in chapter 10 does provide some preliminary information about interaction patterns among parents and their success-fearing children as the children work on tasks, but it is only a beginning. A fuller understanding of the childhood origins of fear of success requires closer observation of interaction patterns among family members as they occur *in vivo*, and a further specification of the particular attitudes and behaviors of parents and children that contribute to the development of fear of success.

Furthermore, despite their fear of success, many individuals are clearly able to succeed according to the traditional standards of our culture. Many of the studies presented in part II were conducted with students drawn from various prestigious colleges and universities. Our informal experience indicates that success-fearers are often found in graduate and professional schools and among qualified working professionals as well. Obviously, then, they are able somehow to cope with their fear of success and to achieve in spite of it. The research we have presented in this volume has been primarily oriented to investigating the conditions under which success-fearers become anxious and self-sabotage. Future research can fruitfully investigate the coping devices that success-fearers employ to enable them to realize objective successes and the conditions under which they are able to work productively and with minimal interference. In this regard we may speculate that many success fearers achieve in a rather backhanded way.

For instance, their motive to achieve success may encourage them to set high goals and standards for themselves, which at a distance may be highly desirable. As long as they are far from attaining these goals, their motivation to achieve and their motivation to avoid failure enable them to work diligently toward their goals. Along the way, they may accomplish goals they themselves see as only minor subgoals, but that outside observers regard as clear successes. Because they have not reached their own loftier aspirations, however, the success-fearers may be able to avoid considering themselves to be successful at these way stations to the real successes of their dreams and aspirations. Success-fearing persons may also try to choose tasks that others in their occupation are not doing in order to avoid direct competition. Investigation of such coping strategies is not only interesting in its own right, but will shed light on other questions about the fear of success.

Several additional questions that invite investigation have to do with the social contexts in which fear-of-success responses are instigated. We have studied fear of success almost exclusively in schools and universities and concentrated mostly on responses to performance on intellectual tasks such as college courses and reading comprehension tests. We have not studied fear of success among butchers, bakers, waitresses, or automobile salesmen. These groups of people certainly differ from elementary school pupils in the stage of life they are in, and they probably differ from university students in their socioeconomic origins. Conceivably, fear-of-success problems are strongest during periods in which the person is undergoing socialization, as is the case in schools and universities. Another possibility is that fear of success is most common among upwardly mobile members of the middle and professional classes. Investigating these questions is important both from a practical perspective and a theoretical one. The research reported in chapter 4 increases our confidence that fear of success can affect virtually any area of accomplishment the success-fearer considers important: romance, games of skill, child rearing, interpersonal relations, and avocations such as weaving, dancing, or playing the violin. We have read clinical reports and have otherwise heard about instances of success sabotage as varied as, for example, long-term dieters losing many pounds and then at the first sign of attractiveness gaining weight again, aspiring ballet dancers spraining an ankle just before a major performance, adolescents working hard to be popular and then doing things that alienate their friends, and long investments in romantic relationships that go sour just when they are about to succeed. These observations should be backed up by harder empirical evidence.

A last set of questions that deserves research effort has to do with the effects of the social structure within which work takes place on the responses of success fearers to success and failure. The ideas elaborated in chapter 9 provide a starting point for such investigations. Do cooperative work environments, for example, mitigate the tendency for success-fearers to become anxious and to sabotage their performances when they appear to have done their work well?

Understanding the operation of such factors would help us to understand more about the social conditions that are particularly disruptive for success-fearers and the conditions under which they can perform relatively freely. The results of such investigations will also contain implications for the prevention of fear of success in children and for its treatment in children and adults.

Concluding Remarks

We have addressed a wide range of issues in this book. Work on a problem that at first glance seemed to focus only on the relationship between people and the tasks they attempt generated a theory that involved us simultaneously with a great many important psychological phenomena: achievement, self-esteem, anxiety, unconscious conflict, personality development, and interpersonal relations. The notion became increasingly clear as our work proceeded that while fear of success is an intrapsychic problem that is usually manifested in task performance situations, it is most basically an interpersonal problem. Fear of success originates in interpersonal relationships and is stimulated and maintained in what are really interpersonal contexts in which achievement, or success and failure, are important concerns. Thus, while the label "fear of success" implies relations with tasks, the person's relationships with others are really at stake. Through attempts to understand how people's relations with one another affect their responses to tasks, we have gained some insight into their conflicts about work and achievement.

While our work on the success-fearing personality deals in part with matters that are of concern to clinical psychologists and other mental health professionals, the work really bridges two academic subdisciplines in psychology: personality psychology and social psychology. Our approach to the problem has involved us in the ideas and research styles of both groups of investigators, and has, we believe, profited from the conjoining of the two. We have taken the perspective of personality psychology in that we have generated personality scales based upon a coherent theoretical description of the nature and development of a personality characteristic, and then examined behaviors and other characteristics of persons selected by those scales. Thus we have asked the kinds of questions typically asked by personality researchers: What are the enduring characteristics of these persons that distinguish them from others, and how do those characteristics fit together meaningfully? At the same time our work has had a social-psychological emphasis in that we have been concerned with the consequences of certain social forces for people's thoughts, feelings, and actions. We have, then, also asked the kind of question that is typical of the social psychologist's approach to studying human functioning: What are the conditions under which people will have this or that set of feelings and thoughts and do this or that thing, and why do those conditions affect people in that way? One result of taking both points of view is that we have been able to add a new dimension to each. Asking ourselves the social psychologist's question about the conditions under which success-fearing persons behave in one way or in another has helped us demonstrate that success-fearers are very much like other people in some circumstances and that they act very differently in others. Such demonstrations are quite important when they illustrate general principles about how such persons differ from others. Furthermore, this style of asking questions made it more likely that we would uncover differences in the feelings and actions of success-fearers themselves as the conditions under which they performed tasks were changed. When we considered issues that social psychologists typically deal with, on the other hand, such as the social conditions that give rise to various sources of accomplishment motivation, we did so with the personality psychologist's sensitivity to systematic differences in people's responses to social situations. Thus, for example, it is likely that success-fearers respond very differently from other people to the cooperative or competitive features of interpersonal relations. Attending to such characteristic differences helps us, as students of general social forces, to understand better how those forces affect people, and why.

Clinicians and counselors who encounter success-fearing people in their work must deal with particular persons whose problems and personal histories have unique features. Can our investigation of the general nature and general origins of the fear of success be helpful to these practitioners? We believe that it can indeed be useful. We have, in our research, attempted to illuminate the important characteristics that success-fearing persons have in common, and to provide a general blueprint for the ways in which the success-fearing personality can develop. While the characteristics, manifestations, and history of any particular case of fear of success will be different in some ways from the picture provided by our theory and research, the general principles can be used to understand how the pieces of the individual case fit together, and to predict the kinds of reactions and behaviors that are likely to be encountered in any individual case. Such a general theoretical perspective can help the practitioner to plan and guide the interventions he or she makes in a particular case, and to help interpret clients' behaviors that appear ambiguous in purpose and meaning. Does the perspective provided herein differ in significant ways from those generated by clinicians themselves from their observations of their patients? There is one respect at least in which our program of research differs from and supplements research conducted in the consulting room: our research has examined the feelings and behaviors of literally hundreds of persons, often under carefully controlled conditions; it is their frequently-occurring response patterns that are taken as informative. This procedure guards against the possibility of mistaken generalizations from a few cases.

It has been our hope that the social-psychological emphasis of our research and thinking would focus greater-than-usual attention on the importance of the social milieu in the development of the success-fearing personality and in the life of the success-fearing person. The treatment of the individual sufferer is not the only reasonable way of dealing with the problem, or even the most efficient way. Attention must be directed also to the task of preventing the occurrence of the fear of success where possible, and to mitigating its consequences in persons already affected by it.

Note

1. One of our colleagues has offered a more elaborate alternative explanation of our data on success fearers' responses to success and failure (the data presented in chapter 4 showed that success-fearers sabotage their performances in the face of success but improve in the face of failure, while non-success-fearers improve under success but show performance deterioration under failure). He suggested that our scales could really have measured either self-esteem or perception of competence. Thus, people categorized as high in fear of success are really low in self-esteem and believe themselves to be generally incompetent, and those low in fear of success are really high in self-esteem, with a belief that they are competent people who succeed when they try. Then, assuming that people are distracted when their expectations are disconfirmed, he suggested that success feedback is inconsistent with the expectation of low self-esteem persons that they will do poorly. This disconfirmation leads them to feel puzzlement and to be distracted from the task, which, in turn results in worsened performance. Failure feedback, on the other hand, is consistent with their expectation of doing poorly, and there is no performance interference. In similar fashion, people high in self-esteem expect to do well and are therefore neither surprised nor distracted when they succeed; they are, however, puzzled and distracted by failure and are therefore likely to perform less well after receiving information that they are performing poorly. This alternative explanation does provide an interesting and plausible explanation of the data on responses to success and failure and can also explain other data, such as those reported in chapter 2 that show success-fearers sabotage their performances when they are confronted with information that task performance is rapidly improving. The alternative is not serviceable, however, for the task of explaining the data on procrastination and indecisiveness, nor does it do the job of explaining why success-fearers show improved performance on a new task after they have sabotaged a successful performance on an earlier task.

Still another alternative explanation that has been offered for some of our results suggests that it is not the high scorers on our fear-of-success scales who show signs of psychopathology, but the low scorers. This suggestion is based on the assumption that most people are made a bit uncomfortable by competition with others, and the low scorers' apparent complete comfort in competitive circumstances may well be an indicator of a pathological disturbance, such as a psychopathic character disorder. The suggestion is not really a viable alternative explanation of the results of our research, but it does underscore our ignorance about the characteristics of people who score very low on our scales. Could they have some unusual traits that we should attend to? They are, after all, the typical comparison group for the research we have done, and we should attempt to find out whether they are unusual in any way. Recently we have administered the Cohen fear-of-success scale and the entire MMPI (Minnesota Multiphasic Personality Inventory) to a group of 150 college students. Analysis of the clinical profiles of the students in each of the four quartiles of the distribution of fear-of-success scale scores shows that students in the lowest quartile do not differ in any systematic way from those in the next higher quartile. Moreover, the clinical profiles of the students in the lowest quartile show no consistent pattern of pathology. We may conclude that the low-scoring respondents are, in effect, a "normal" group rather than an unusual group.

Appendix:
Fear-of-Success Scales

Appendix:
Fear-of-Success Scales

Pappo's Fear-of-Success Scale

1. It is easy for me to concentrate on my studies.
2. I find it difficult to tell my friends that I do something especially well.
3. Frequently, at crucial points in an intellectual discussion my mind goes blank.
4. Often times, I become self-conscious when someone who "counts" compliments me.
5. Generally, when I complete an important project I am satisfied with the result.
6. As a game (card game, word game, chess, competitive sport, etc.) reaches the winning point I start thinking of other things.
7. The things that I achieve frequently fall short of my fondest hopes.
8. When playing competitive games I make more mistakes near the end than at the beginning.
9. When I write a paper for school I often feel unsure of my ideas until I check them out with teachers or friends.
10. I used to fantasize about doing something that no one else had ever done before.
11. I like it if a teacher I respect tells me my work is good although it makes me somewhat uncomfortable.
12. In areas in which I have talent my products are usually not excellent.
13. When I play competitive games I'm often so concerned with how well I am doing I don't enjoy the game as much as I could.
14. Instead of celebrating, I often feel let down after completing an important task or project.
15. I feel I need someone to push me to do the things I want to do.
16. When I am playing a game and people are watching I am extremely aware of their presence.
17. In my family (cousins included) I tended to be near the top academically.

This appendix contains full copies of the fear-of-success scales developed by Pappo and Cohen for use in research with adult samples and the children's fear-of-success scale developed by ourselves for use in research with children. Pappo's scale originally appeared in "Fear of Success: A Theoretical Analysis and the Construction and Validation of a Measuring Instrument" [87]. © Marice Pappo, 1972. Cohen's scale originally appeared in "Explorations in the Fear of Success" [15]. © Nina E. Cohen, 1974. The authors gratefully acknowledge both Dr. Pappo and Dr. Cohen for permission to reprint these scales in their entirety.

All three scales contained in this appendix have been developed only as research instruments and are not intended for diagnostic purposes. Researchers may request a copy of the scoring system for any of the scales by writing to Dr. Donnah Canavan-Gumpert, Department of Psychology, Boston College, Chestnut Hill, Massachusetts 02167.

18. I tend to misplace things and then when I need them they are difficult to find.
19. It is important to seek the friendship of people with positions of higher status than yours.
20. When I feel confused about material I am learning I work at it myself until it is resolved.
21. If something is easy for me to learn or to do, I have difficulty imagining someone else having trouble with it.
22. I frequently find it difficult to measure up to the standards I set for myself.
23. When a teacher praises my work I wonder whether I can do as well the next time.
24. Often times, I feel as if I do very little studying even though I generally get my work done.
25. I tend to get tired while studying.
26. It is more important to try to win a game than to merely play it.
27. I often get excited when I start a project, but I get bored with it quickly.
28. At times, I believe I have gotten by in school because of good luck and the carelessness of teachers.
29. Sometimes I find myself daydreaming about accomplishing fantastic feats.
30. While developing a new idea I find that my thinking "freezes" at a certain point.
31. If I win a competitive game I feel a little bad for the other player.
32. When I study I am very aware of the passing of time.
33. There are school subjects in which I really excel.
34. I sometimes have difficulty bringing important tasks to a successful conclusion.
35. I like working out tricky puzzles and problems even if I'm not sure I can figure them out.
36. Frequently, I wish I was just a little bit smarter.
37. Persuasive people can influence my ideas.
38. When I get a low grade, I know I could have done better if I had worked harder.
39. It makes me feel good to tell people about the things some of my friends have accomplished.
40. As a competitive game nears the end, I tend to become tired and make more errors.
41. I have had difficulty deciding what work deeply interests me.
42. If someone calls attention to me when I'm doing well, I often feel awkward.
43. When specific work assignments seem to be going extremely well, I get scared that I'll do something to ruin it.
44. I try the hardest when my work is being evaluated.
45. My family saw me as the academically successful one.
46. If I get a low grade on a work assignment, I feel cheated.

47. Once I have completed a task it seems less valuable.
48. I frequently explore academic areas that I know nothing about.
49. I think I often have good ideas, but I frequently forget them.
50. Even though I feel that I have a lot of potential, I sometimes feel like a phony or a fraud.
51. Occasionally, when I am winning a game I get so excited I miss a point.
52. One way to ensure failure is to want something too much.
53. There are times when I don't think I have what it takes to be a success in the area I am interested in.
54. It's very difficult to do anything important really well.
55. Others judge you by the people you associate with.
56. When I hear about the accomplishments of my friends I tend to think about what I, myself, have or have not accomplished.
57. I often don't do as well as I am able because I put off my work until the last minute.
58. Often when I study I keep thinking of other things that I need to do.
59. My parents inaccurately assessed my intelligence.
60. I feel that it is important for people of higher status to like me.
61. While I'm learning something completely new I find praise necessary.
62. If school tasks are easy to finish I feel as though they were meaningless.
63. If I get a high grade on a work assignment I tend to feel that I fooled the teacher.
64. I become more excited while playing a game if people are watching.
65. When friends whose opinions I value compliment my work I feel good but uneasy.
66. At times, my work piles up so much that I have difficulty completing all of it.
67. Often when I win a competitive game, I get the idea that it was because of the other player's carelessness.
68. At times, my grades amaze me because it seems like I rarely prepare adequately.
69. At times I brag about the accomplishments of my friends.
70. It pays to discuss your ideas with a teacher or friend before handing in a finished paper.
71. If I don't think I can learn to do well at something, I prefer not to try.
72. As I near completing a task compliments may make me uneasy.
73. After studying hard for an exam, I often find the test itself tedious.
74. At times, I have accidentally spilled something on the final copy of a school project.
75. My work is characterized by enthusiastic beginnings and indifferent endings.
76. It is easy to become distracted while taking a test.
77. I am doing exactly the work I want to do.
78. There are areas in which I am talented.

79. If it weren't for some remarkably good luck I would probably not have gotten as far as I have.
80. It is important not to get excited about the things one desires.
81. Without someone encouraging me I might not have done some of the important things I've accomplished.
82. I like the idea of having friends who are in positions of power and influence.
83. Although I have much difficulty doing so, I generally finish essential undertakings.

Cohen's Fear-of-Success Scale

1. When I think I've made a particularly "strong" statement to someone I get a bit worried that I might have made them feel bad.
2. I generally feel guilty about my own happiness if a friend tells me that (s)he's depressed.
3. I sometimes get uncomfortable because I've pretended to be more committed to a cause than I really feel.
4. It makes me feel self-conscious to perform a stunt at a party, even if other people are doing the same sort of thing.
5. As a child, I sometimes played sick to get out of something.
6. I must admit that I'm quite nice looking.
7. I've sometimes gone without something rather than to have to ask others for it.
8. I dread the idea of walking into a party by myself when most of the others have been there for some time.
9. Often, when I sit down to solve a problem, my thoughts drift off to a bunch of other things.
10. It's pretty difficult to turn down a gesture of friendship without hurting the other person's feelings.
11. I feel uneasy being the center of attention in a group.
12. I frequently find myself not telling others about my good luck so they won't have to feel envious.
13. I often have trouble saying no to people.
14. I frequently find myself making a date or appointment and then dread having to go through with it.
15. I'm very rarely worried that I'll look clumsy or awkward at a social gathering.
16. I'm reluctant to make a large purchase without consulting someone else first.
17. Before getting down to work on a project, I suddenly find a whole bunch of other things to take care of first.
18. I sometimes find myself apologizing for my behavior even though an apology isn't really called for.

19. I must say that I'm pretty confident when it comes to my sexual ability.
20. I hate having a fuss made over me.
21. I'm quite comfortable in the role of group spokesman.
22. Most people are secretly pleased when someone else gets into trouble.
23. I often brood about something I've said which may have been taken in the wrong way by another person.
24. I tend to believe that people who look out for themselves first are selfish.
25. As a child, when I was called on by a teacher, I often felt my stomach sink, even when I knew the right answer.
26. I sometimes cross the street to avoid meeting someone I know.
27. When someone I know well succeeds at something, I usually feel that I've lost out in comparison.
28. I rarely have trouble concentrating on something for a long period of time.
29. It makes me feel uneasy to have to ask other people for things.
30. When I notice that things have been going particularly well for me, I get the feeling it just can't last.
31. I feel uneasy about breaking a date or an appointment.
32. I'm pretty competent at most things that I try.
33. Often, before I act, I consider how others would regard my action.
34. I'd rather give in on most issues than get into heavy debates with people.
35. I'm not one for organizing group activities, though I usually enjoy them once they're under way.
36. I generally feel uptight about telling a boss or professor that I think I'm entitled to a better deal.
37. When I have to ask others for their help, I often feel that I'm being bothersome.
38. I often compromise in situations in order to avoid conflict.
39. On the whole, I'm quite satisfied with the way I look.
40. I have often "woken-up" during a lecture or meeting and realized that I haven't heard a word of what was said.
41. I sometimes "play down" my competence in front of others so they won't think I'm bragging.
42. Before I make a final decision about something, I like to check with others about their views and ideas.
43. I sometimes have trouble acting like myself when I'm with people I don't know well.
44. I've often felt a little ashamed of the way my house (apartment) looks.
45. When I've made a decision, I usually stick to it.
46. Before going to some type of social gathering, I'm often uptight that I just won't look good enough.
47. Although I usually begin projects with lots of get up and go, I tend to get bored after a while.
48. Secretly, I think I'm pretty special, but I try not to "let on" to others about that.

49. I often feel self-conscious when someone who "counts" compliments me.
50. I used to fantasize about doing something that no one else had ever done before.
51. When I'm involved in a competitive activity (sports, a game, work) I'm often so concerned with how well I'm doing that I don't enjoy the activity as much as I could.
52. When people are watching me while I'm doing something, I have difficulty not being aware that they're watching me.
53. If it's easy for me to learn to do something, I have trouble imagining anyone else having difficulty with it.
54. If someone calls attention to me when I'm doing well, I feel awkward or embarrassed.
55. Even though I feel I have a lot of potential, I sometimes feel like a phony or a fraud.
56. It pays to check out your ideas with other people before making a final decision.
57. It's important not to get too excited about things one really desires.
58. A sure-fire way to end up disappointed is to want something too much.
59. Instead of celebrating, I often feel let down after completing an important task or project.
60. Mostly, I find that I measure up to the standards that I set for myself.
61. When I'm praised for something, I sometimes wonder if I will be able to do as well the next time.
62. When things seem to be going really well for me, I get uneasy that I'll do something to ruin it.
63. In the lower grades in school, if I got a good grade on a work assignment I often felt that I had fooled the teacher.
64. When I have to meet an important deadline, I get so nervous that it's hard to keep my mind on the work I'm doing.

Children's Fear-of-Success Scale

1. I usually feel bad about being happy if a friend is sad.
2. Sometimes when I'm winning a game I get so excited that I make mistakes.
3. I feel shy about performing at a party even if other kids are doing the same thing.
4. Sometimes I'd rather not have something than ask someone for it.
5. I don't like walking into a party by myself if the other kids have all been there for awhile.
6. Often when I start my homework, I start thinking about other things.
7. If someone wants to be your friend, it is hard to say no without hurting their feelings.

8. It makes me feel funny to be the center of attention.
9. I usually don't tell my friends or classmates about my good luck so they won't feel jealous.
10. It is hard to say no to someone when they ask you for something.
11. I often tell kids I'll do something with them and then I don't feel like doing it.
12. If I could buy a special toy or game, I would want to ask a friend if they liked it first.
13. Often, before starting my homework, I suddenly remember some other things I'd like to do.
14. I sometimes say I'm sorry about something I did even though I didn't do anything wrong.
15. I believe I'm very good when it comes to sports.
16. I hate having a fuss made over me.
17. I enjoy being the leader of a group.
18. I've done as well as I have partly because I've had some pretty good luck.
19. Sometimes I worry that something I've said may have hurt someone, though I didn't mean it to.
20. I think that people who look out for themselves first are selfish.
21. When I'm called on by a teacher, my stomach sinks even though I know the right answer.
22. I sometimes pretend not to see someone I know so I won't have to talk to them.
23. When someone I know succeeds at something, I feel I can't do it as well as they did.
24. It is easy for me to keep working at something for a long time.
25. I hate to have to ask other people for things.
26. Sometimes I think I've done O.K. in school because I was lucky or because the teacher didn't pay attention.
27. When a lot of good things happen to me, I start thinking that something bad will happen soon.
28. I feel bad if I tell a friend I will do something with him and then I can't.
29. Often before I do something I think of what other people will think about what I am doing.
30. Most of the time I would rather give in than get into an argument.
31. I don't usually start a group activity, but if someone else does, I enjoy it.
32. Often when I win a game, I think it's because the other person made careless mistakes.
33. When I have to ask someone to help me I feel like I am bothering them.
34. I would rather get less than I want than to argue about it.
35. Often in school I daydream and afterwards find out I haven't heard a word the teacher has been saying.
36. I sometimes say I can't do something as well as I really can, so other kids don't think I am bragging.

37. Before I decide something I like to ask my friends what they think.
38. Sometimes it's hard for me to act like myself when I'm with people I don't know well.
39. I often feel a little ashamed of the way my room at home looks.
40. When I decide to do something, I usually do it.
41. Before going to a party, I often feel I don't look good enough.
42. Even though I am usually excited when I start a project, I usually get bored after a while.
43. I feel uncomfortable when someone special compliments me.
44. I sometimes daydream about doing something no one else has ever done.
45. When I am playing a game I sometimes think so much about whether I am doing well that I don't have much fun.
46. If something is easy for me to learn, I usually think it is easy for everyone else, too.
47. If someone says I am doing something really well, I feel funny.
48. Even though I feel I can do things well, sometimes when I succeed at something I feel that I have fooled other people.
49. It is a good idea to talk to your friends before deciding something.
50. It is not a good idea to get too excited about something you really want.
51. Most of the time I feel I do things as well as I should.
52. When someone says that I have done something well, I wonder whether I will be able to do it as well the next time.
53. A sure way to get disappointed is to want something too much.
54. When things get going really well I'm afraid I'll do something to mess it up.
55. If I get a good grade on a work assignment, I often feel that I have fooled the teacher.
56. When I have to do an important homework assignment in a hurry, I get so scared that I can't keep my mind on it.
57. As I get close to winning a game, I often start thinking about something else.
58. When playing games I could win, I make more mistakes near the end than at the beginning.

References

References

1. Alpert, R., and Haber, R.N. Anxiety in academic achievement situations. *Journal of Abnormal Psychology*, 61 (1960):207-15.

2. Anderson, H.H., and Brandt, H.F. A study of motivation involving self-announced goals of fifth grade children and the concept of level of aspiration. *Journal of Social Psychology*, 10 (1939):209-32.

3. Atkinson, J.W. Studies in Projective Measurement of Achievement Motivation. Unpublished doctoral dissertation, University of Michigan, Ann Arbor, 1950.

4. Atkinson, J.W. (ed.). *Motives in Fantasy, Action, and Society*. New York: Van Nostrand, 1958.

5. Atkinson, J.W. The mainsprings of achievement-oriented activity. In J.W. Atkinson and J. Raynor (eds.), *Motivation and Achievement*. Washington, D.C.: V.H. Winston & Sons, 1974.

6. Atkinson, J.W., and Birch D. *The Dynamics of Action*. New York: Wiley, 1970.

7. Atkinson, J.W., Bongort, K., and Price, L.H. Explorations using computer simulation to comprehend thematic apperceptive measurement of motivation. *Journal of Motivation and Emotion,* 1 (1977):1-28.

8. Atkinson, J.W., and Feather, N.T. (eds.). *A Theory of Achievement Motivation*. New York: Wiley, 1966.

9. Atkinson, J.W., and McClelland, D.C. The projective expression of needs. II. The effect of different intensities of the hunger drive on thematic apperception. *Journal of Experimental Psychology*, 38 (1948):643-58.

10. Atkinson, J.W., and Raynor, J.O. (eds.). *Motivation and Achievement*. Washington, D.C.: V.H. Winston & Co., 1974.

11. Berkowitz, L. Group standards, cohesiveness, and productivity. *Human Relations*, 7 (1954):509-19.

12. Birney, R.C., Burdick, H., and Teevan, R.C. *Fear of Failure*. New York: Van Nostrand-Reinhold, 1969.

13. Bjerstedt, A. Preparation, process, and product in small-group interaction. *Human Relations*, 14 (1961):183-89.

14. Canavan-Gumpert, D. Generating reward and cost orientations through praise and criticism. *Journal of Personality and Social Psychology*, 35 (1977):501-13.

15. Cohen, N.E. Explorations in the fear of success. Unpublished doctoral dissertation, Columbia University, New York, 1974.

16. Collins, B.E., and Guetzkow, H. *A Social Psychology of Group Processes for Decision Making*. New York: Wiley, 1964.

17. Coopersmith, S. *The Antecedents of Self-Esteem*. San Francisco: Freeman, 1967.

18. Cronbach, L.J., and Meehl, P.E. Construct validity in psychological tests. *Psychological Bulletin*, 52 (1955):281-302.

19. DeCharms, R. *Personal Causation: The Internal Affective Determinants of Behavior.* New York: Academic Press, 1968.

20. Deci, E.L. *Intrinsic Motivation.* New York: Plenum, 1975.

21. DeRivera, J. *Field Theory as Human Science: Contributions of Lewin's Berlin Group.* New York: Gardner Press, 1976.

22. Deutsch, H. *The Psychology of Women.* New York: Grune and Stratton, 1944.

23. Deutsch, M. An experimental study of the effects of cooperation and competition upon group process. *Human Relations*, 2 (1949):199-231.

24. Deutsch, M. *The Resolution of Conflict.* New Haven, Conn.: Yale University Press, 1973.

25. Deutsch, M. Equity, equality, and need: What determines which value will be used as the basis of distributive justice? *Journal of Social Issues*, 31 (1975):137-49.

26. Deutsch, M. Theorizing in social psychology. *Personality and Social Psychology Bulletin*, 2 (1976):134-41.

27. Entwhistle, D.R. To dispel fantasies about fantasy-based measures of achievement motivation. *Psychological Bulletin*, 77 (1972):377-91.

28. Feather, N.T. Effects of prior success and failure on expectations of success and subsequent performance. *Journal of Personality and Social Psychology,* 3 (1966):287-98.

29. Fenichel, O. *The Psychoanalytic Theory of Neurosis.* New York: Norton, 1945.

30. Freedman, J.L. *Crowding and Human Behavior.* New York: Viking Press, 1975.

31. Freud, S. Some character-types met with in psychoanalytic work, 1915. In E. Jones (ed.), *Sigmund Freud: Collected Papers*, Vol. IV. New York, Basic Books, 1959.

32. Fromm, E. *Escape from Freedom.* New York: Holt, Rinehart & Winston, 1941.

33. Fromm, E. *The Heart of Man.* New York: Harper & Row, 1964.

34. Fromm, E. *The Anatomy of Human Destructiveness.* New York: Holt, Rinehart & Winston, 1973.

35. Glass, D.C., and Singer, J.E. *Urban Stress.* New York: Academic Press, 1972.

36. Grinker, R., and Spiegel, J. *Men Under Stress.* Philadelphia: Blakiston, 1945.

37. Grossack, M. Some effects of cooperation and competition on small group behavior. *Journal of Abnormal and Social Psychology*, 49 (1954):341-48.

38. Gumpert, P., and Garner, K. Competence and incompetence beliefs: A reconceptualization of task motivation and psychological stress. Mimeo, University of Massachusetts, Boston, 1977.

39. Heckhausen, H. *The Anatomy of Achievement Motivation.* New York: Academic Press, 1967.

40. Hilgard, E.R., Sait, E.M., and Magaret, G.A. Level of aspiration as affected by relative standing in an experimental social group. *Journal of Experimental Psychology*, 27 (1940):411-21.

41. Hoppe, F. Success and failure. In J. DeRivera, *Field Theory as Human Science.* New York: Gardner Press, 1976.

42. Horner, M.S. Sex differences in achievement motivation and performance in competitive and non-competitive situations. Unpublished doctoral dissertation, University of Michigan, Ann Arbor, 1968. An abridged portion ("The measurement and behavioral implications of fear of success in women") in J.W. Atkinson and J.O. Raynor (eds.), *Motivation and Achievement*, Washington, D.C.: V.H. Winston and Sons, 1974.

43. Horner, M.S. Toward an understanding of achievement-related conflicts in women. *Journal of Social Issues*, 28 (1972):157-75.

44. Horner, M.S., Tresemer, D., Berens, A., and Watson, R. Scoring manual for an empirically derived scoring system for motive to avoid success. Paper presented at the annual meeting of the American Psychological Association, Montreal, 1973.

45. Horney, K. Culture and neurosis. *American Sociological Review*, 1 (1936):221-30.

46. Horney, K. *The Neurotic Personality of Our Time.* New York: W.W. Norton, 1937.

47. Horney, K. *Feminine Psychology.* New York: W.W. Norton, 1967.

48. Hornstein, H. Promotive tension: The basis of prosocial behavior from a Lewinian perspective. *Journal of Social Issues,* 28 (1972):191-218.

49. Horsfall, A.B., and Arensberg, C.M. Teamwork and productivity in a shoe factory. *Human Organization*, 8 (1949):13-25.

50. Horwitz, M. The recall of interrupted group tasks: An experimental study of individual motivation in relation to group goals. *Human Relations*, 7 (1953):3-38.

51. Husband, R.W. Cooperative versus solitary problem solution. *Journal of Social Psychology*, 11 (1940):405-09.

52. Jackaway, R., and Teevan, R. Fear of failure and fear of success: Two dimensions of the same motive. *Sex Roles: A Journal of Research*, 2 (1976):283-93.

53. Janis, I.L. *Psychological Stress.* New York: Wiley, 1958.

54. Jucknat, M. Leistung, Anspruchsniveau, und selbstbewusstsein. *Psychologische Forschung*, 22 (1937):89-179. A translation of a 66-page abridged version ("Performance, level of aspiration and self-esteem") is available from University Microfilms, Ann Arbor, Michigan.

55. Kagan, J. Motives and development. *Journal of Personality and Social Psychology,* 22 (1972):51-66.

56. Kelley, H.H., and Thibaut, J.W. Group problem solving. In G. Lindzey

and E. Aronson (eds.), *Handbook of Social Psychology*, 2nd ed., Vol. 4, pp. 1-101. Reading, Mass.: Addison-Wesley, 1969.

57. Kelly, G.A. *The Psychology of Personal Constructs.* New York: W.W. Norton, 1955.

58. Langer, E.J., and Abelson, R.P. The semantics of asking a favor: How to succeed in getting help without really dying. *Journal of Personality and Social Psychology*, 24 (1972):26-32.

59. Lazarus, R.S., and Eriksen, C.W. Effects of failure stress upon skilled performance. *Journal of Experimental Psychology*, 43 (1952):100-05.

60. Levine, A., and Crumrine, J. Women and the fear of success: A problem in replication. *American Journal of Sociology*, 80 (1975):964-74.

61. Lewin, K. *A Dynamic Theory of Personality.* New York: McGraw-Hill, 1936.

62. Lewin, K. Behavior and development as a function of the total situation. In L. Carmichall (ed.), *Manual of Child Psychology*. New York: Wiley, 1946.

63. Lewin, K. *Resolving Social Conflicts.* New York: Harper, 1948.

64. Lewin, K. *Field Theory in Social Science.* New York: Harper, 1951.

65. Lewin, K., Dembo, T., Festinger, L. and Sears, P.S. Level of aspiration. In J. McV. Hunt (ed.), *Personality and The Behavior Disorders.* New York: Ronald Press, 1944.

66. Lewis, H.B., and Franklin, M. An experimental study of the role of the ego in work. II. The significance of task orientation in work. *Journal of Experimental Psychology*, 31 (1944):195-215.

67. Littig, L.W. Motivational correlates of probability preferences. In J.W. Atkinson and N.T. Feather (eds.), *A Theory of Achievement Motivation.* New York: Wiley, 1966.

68. Litwin, G.H. Achievement motivation, expectancy of success and risk-taking behavior. In J.W. Atkinson and N.T. Feather (eds.), *A Theory of Achievement Motivation.* New York: Wiley, 1966.

69. McClelland, D.C. Some social consequences of achievement motivation. In M.R. Jones (ed.), *Nebraska Symposium of Motivation, 1955.* Lincoln: University of Nebraska Press, 1955.

70. McClelland, D.C. *The Achieving Society.* New York: Van Nostrand, 1961.

71. McClelland, D.C., Atkinson, J.W., Clark, R.A., and Lowell, E.L. A Scoring Manual for the Achievement Motive. In J.W. Atkinson (ed.), *Motives in Fantasy, Action, and Society: A Method of Assessment and Study.* New York: Van Nostrand, 1958.

72. McClelland, D.C., and Friedman, G.A. A cross-cultural study of the relationship between child-rearing practices and achievement motivation appearing in folk tales. In G.E. Swanson, T.M. Newcomb, and E.L. Hartley (eds.), *Readings in Social Psychology.* New York: Holt, 1952.

73. Mandler, G., and Cowen, J.E. Test anxiety questionnaires. *Journal of Consulting Psychology*, 22 (1958):228-29.

74. Mandler, G., and Sarason, S.B. A study of anxiety and learning. *Journal of Abnormal and Social Psychology*, 47 (1952):166-73.

75. Maslow, A.H. *Motivation and Personality.* New York: Harper & Row, 1954.

76. Maslow, A.H. *The Farther Reaches of Human Nature.* New York: Viking, 1971.

77. May, R. *The Meaning of Anxiety.* New York: Ronald Press, 1950.

78. May, R. *The Courage to Create.* New York: W.W. Norton, 1975.

79. Mead, G.H. *Mind, Self, and Society.* Chicago: University of Chicago Press, 1934.

80. Menninger, K.A. *Man Against Himself.* New York: Harcourt, Brace, 1938.

81. Miller, N.E. Liberalization of basic S-R concepts: Extensions to conflict behavior, motivation and social learning. In S. Koch (ed.), *Psychology: A Study of a Science*, Vol. 2. New York: McGraw-Hill, 1959.

82. Mizuhara, T., and Tamai, S. Experimental studies of cooperation and competition. *Japanese Journal of Psychology*, 22 (1952):124-27.

83. Murphy, L.B. *The Widening World of Childhood: Paths toward Mastery.* New York: Basic Books, 1962.

84. Murray, H.A. American Icarus. In A. Burton and R.E. Harris (eds.), *Clinical Studies in Personality*, Vol. 2. New York: Harper, 1955.

85. Osler, S.F. Intellectual performance as a function of two types of psychological stress. *Journal of Experimental Psychology*, 47 (1954):115-21.

86. Ovesey, L. Fear of vocational success. *Archives of General Psychology*, 7 (1962):82-92.

87. Pappo, M. Fear of success: A theoretical analysis and the construction and validation of a measuring instrument. Unpublished doctoral dissertation, Columbia University, New York, 1972.

88. Patterson, T.T., and Willett, E.J. An anthropological experiment in a British colliery. *Human Organization*, 10 (1951):19-23.

89. Philp, A.J. Strangers and friends as competitors and cooperators. *Journal of Genetic Psychology*, 57 (1940):249-58.

90. Piaget, J. *The Origins of Intelligence in Children.* New York: Norton, 1952.

91. Rank, O. *The Trauma of Birth.* New York: Harcourt, Brace, 1929.

92. Rank, O. *Will Therapy.* New York: Alfred Knopf, 1936.

93. Raven, B.H. and Eachus, H.T. Cooperation and competition in means-interdependent triads. *Journal of Abnormal and Social Psychology*, 67 (1963):307-16.

94. Reik, T. *Masochism in Modern Man.* New York: Farrar, Strauss, 1941.

95. Rosenberg, M. *Society and the Adolescent Self-Image.* Princeton, N.J.: Princeton University Press, 1965.

244

96. Rotter, J.B. Generalized expectancies for internal versus external control of reinforcement. *Psychology Monographs*, 80 (1966).

97. Sarason, S.B., Davidson, K.S., Lighthall, F.F., Waite, R.R., and Ruebush, D.K. *Anxiety in Elementary School Children.* New York: W.W. Norton, 1953.

98. Sarason, I.G. Experimental approaches to test anxiety: Attention and the uses of information. In C.D. Spielberger (ed.), *Anxiety: Current Trends in Theory and Research*, Vol. II. New York: Academic Press, 1972.

99. Seashore, S.E. *Group Cohesiveness in the Industrial Group.* Ann Arbor: Institute for Social Research, University of Michigan, Ann Arbor, 1954.

100. Sherif, M. *In Common Predicament: Social Psychology of Intergroup Conflict and Cooperation.* Boston: Houghton Mifflin, 1966.

101. Sherif, M., Harvey, O.J., White, B.J., Hood, W.R., and Sherif, C.W. *Intergroup Conflict and Cooperation: The Robbers Cave Experiment.* Norman, Okla.: University Book Exchange, 1961.

102. Shuster, D.B. On the fear of success. *The Psychiatric Quarterly*, 29 (1955):412-20.

103. Siegel, J.P., and Bowen, D. Satisfaction and performance: Causal relationships and moderating effects. *Journal of Vocational Behavior*, 1 (1971):263-69.

104. Smith, M.B. Competence and socialization. In J.A. Clausen, et al. (eds.), *Socialization and Society.* Boston: Little, Brown, 1968.

105. Steiner, I.D. *Group Process and Productivity.* New York: Academic Press, 1972.

106. Sullivan, H.S. *The Interpersonal Theory of Psychiatry.* New York: W.W. Norton, 1953.

107. Sutermeister, R.A. Employee performance and employee need satisfaction—which comes first? *California Management Review*, 13 (1971):43-47.

108. Thomas, E.J. Effects of facilitative role interdependence on group functioning. *Human Relations*, 10 (1957):347-66.

109. Tresemer, D. Fear of success: Popular but unproven. *Psychology Today*, 7 (1974):82ff.

110. Tresemer, D. The cumulative record of research on "Fear of Success." *Sex Roles*, 2(1976):217-36.

111. Tresemer, D. *Fear of Success.* New York: Plenum Press, 1977.

112. Van Zelst, R.H. Sociometrically selected work teams increase production. *Personnel Psychology*, 5 (1952):175-85.

113. Vernon, D.T.A. Information seeking in a natural stress situation. *Journal of Applied Psychology*, 55 (1971):359-63.

114. Wanous, J.P. A causal correlational analysis of the job satisfaction and performance relationship. *Journal of Applied Psychology*, 59 (1974):139-44.

115. Warner, S.J. The problem of the "defeating patient" in psychotherapy. *American Journal of Psychotherapy*, 8 (1954):703-18.

116. Warner, S.J. *Self-Realization and Self-Defeat.* New York: Grove Press, 1966.

117. White, R.W. Motivation reconsidered: The concept of competence. *Psychological Review,* 66 (1959):297-333.

118. Witkin, H.A., Dyk, R.B., Faterson, H.F., Goodenough, D.R., and Karp, S.A. *Psychological Differentiation: Studies of Development.* New York: Wiley, 1962.

119. Workie, A. The effect of cooperation and competition on productivity. Unpublished doctoral dissertation, Columbia University, New York, 1967.

120. Wylie, R.C. *The Self-Concept.* Lincoln, Nebraska: University of Nebraska Press, Revised Edition, 1974.

121. Zeigarnik, B. Über das Behalten von erledigten und unerledigten Handlungen. *Psychologische Forschung,* 9 (1927):1-85. The complete translation ("The Retention of Completed and Uncompleted Activities") is available from University Microfilms, Ann Arbor, Michigan.

122. Zuckerman, M. and Wheeler, L. To dispel fantasies about the fantasy-based measure of fear of success. *Psychological Bulletin,* 82 (1975):932-46.

Indexes

Author Index

Page numbers in italics refer to the bibliography.

249

Subject Index

Accomplishment motivation. *See* Productivity motivation

Achievement motivation, assessment, 117, 120-122, 131; and competition, 121, 124-125; and culture, 118, 125; personality disposition, 118, 120, 125, 131, 137, 138; research, 120, 122-125; theory, 6, 117-120, 136-138, 206

Ambivalence, 12, 13, 16, 18, 21, 22-23, 24, 28, 32, 189-190, 206, 210

American culture, 13, 14, 22, 26, 72, 125, 137, 192-193. *See also* Success, ethos in Western culture

Anxiety, 12, 13, 23, 94, 206, 208, 217; debilitating, 23, 76, 93, 143, 207, 208, 209; facilitating, 23, 76, 207, 208-209; general, 216; success, 13, 23, 24, 25, 48-49, 56, 76, 85, 205-206, 208-209, 217; transmission, 16, 40-41, 73. *See also* Fear of failure; Fear of success; Psychotherapy; Test anxiety

Approach-avoidance, 23-24, 93, 118, 207

Assertiveness, and fear of success, 62, 195, 196, 199, 200, 201; training, 196

Attitudes. *See* Group dynamics

Attributions, causes for outcomes, 16, 21, 25, 26, 70, 93; evaluation and competition, 24-25, 49-51, 189, 208-209; in therapy, 198-199, 200. *See also* Self-derogation; Competence, repudiation of

Behavior therapy. *See* Psychotherapy

Belonging, feelings of. *See* Group dynamics

Body image, 73, 88

Caring. *See* Group structures

Children, 87-92, 176-178, 186-192, 208

Communication. *See* Group dynamics

Competence, development, 39-42; and fear of success, 208; repudiation of, 13, 16, 25, 26, 43, 49, 56, 93, 109-110, 208-209

Competence beliefs, 140-146; antecedents, 145; consequences, 141-143, 144-146; definition, 141; and task motivation, 139, 141-146

Competition, 121, 139, 193; and fear of success, 12-13, 14-16, 17, 19, 21, 23, 24-25, 26-28, 37, 61-73, 147, 176-179, 206, 208, 210, 220. *See also* Group structures

Concentration impairment, 25, 44, 49, 56, 62, 64, 69-70, 84, 88, 208

Conflict. *See* Approach-avoidance; Group dynamics; Oedipal conflict; Separation-individuation conflict; Unconscious

Conscience. *See* Superego

Cooperation, 193. *See also* Group structures

Criticism, 139, 187, 188

Debilitating anxiety scale, 45, 56

Defense mechanisms, 13, 16, 21, 24-26, 40, 41-42, 62, 63, 210, 217

Distractibility, 25, 64

Distributive justice, 149. *See also* Equality; Equity

Dropping out (of college), 108-109

Embedded figures test, 80, 83

Envy, 14, 15, 18, 19, 23

Equality, as a principle of distributive justice, 149, 163

Equity, as a principle of distributive justice, 149

External control. *See* Internal-external control

About the Authors

Donnah Canavan-Gumpert did her undergraduate work in psychology at Emmanuel College in Boston, and her graduate work at Teachers College, Columbia University. After earning the Ph.D. from Teachers College in 1969, she did post-doctoral study and research at the University of California, Los Angeles. She joined the faculty in psychology at Boston College in 1970, and is now associate professor of psychology there. She has been affiliated with the Center for Policy Research in New York since 1970. Dr. Canavan-Gumpert has contributed articles on various topics in personality and social psychology to the *Journal of Conflict Resolution*, the *Journal of Personality,* the *Journal of Experimental Social Psychology*, and the *Journal of Personality and Social Psychology.*

Katherine Garner received the B.A. in psychology at Wellesley College, and was a graduate student in social psychology at Teachers College, Columbia University, where she received the Ph.D. in 1973. She has taught at New York University since 1972, and now holds the position of associate professor of psychology at that institution. Dr. Garner has been affiliated with the Center for Policy Research in New York since 1973. She has contributed articles on various topics in social psychology to the *Journal of Conflict Resolution* and the *Journal of Personality and Social Psychology.*

Peter Gumpert studied psychology as an undergraduate at the University of North Carolina at Chapel Hill, and as a graduate student at Stanford University and at Teachers College, Columbia University, where he earned the Ph.D. in 1967. He served as assistant professor and then associate professor in the doctoral program in social psychology at Teachers College until 1974, and has since taught psychology at Boston University and at the Boston campus of the University of Massachusetts. He has been associated with the Center for Policy Research, New York, since 1969. Dr. Gumpert has contributed articles on various topics in social and personality psychology to such journals as the *Journal of Abnormal and Social Psychology*, the *Journal of Conflict Resolution*, and the *Journal of Personality and Social Psychology.*